A TREASURY OF KAHLIL GIBRAN

Kahlil Gibran was born in 1883 near Mount Lebanon, a region that has produced many prophets. He was a poet, philosopher and artist and his poetry has been translated into more than twenty languages. His drawings and paintings were compared by Auguste Rodin to the work of William Blake. His other books include *The Madman*, *The Forerunner*, *The Prophet* and *The Broken Wings*. Kahlil Gibran died in 1931.

Also by Kahlil Gibran
**available from Mandarin Paperbacks*

The Madman
The Forerunner
*The Prophet
Sand and Foam
Jesus, the Son of Man
The Earth Gods
The Wanderer
The Garden of the Prophet
Prose Poems
Nymphs of the Valley
Spirits Rebellious
A Tear and a Smile
The Broken Wings
The Voice of the Master
A Self-Portrait
Thoughts and Meditations
Spiritual Sayings
Lazarus and His Beloved
(a one-act play)

A Treasury of
Kahlil Gibran

Edited by MARTIN L. WOLF

Translated from the Arabic by Anthony Rizcallah Ferris

Mandarin

A Mandarin Paperback
A TREASURY OF KAHLIL GIBRAN

First published in Great Britain 1974
by William Heinemann Ltd
This edition published 1991
by Mandarin Paperbacks
an imprint of Reed Consumer Books Limited
Michelin House, 81 Fulham Road, London SW3 6RB
and Auckland, Melbourne, Singapore and Toronto

Reprinted 1991, 1992, 1993 (twice)

A CIP catalogue record for this title
is available from the British Library
ISBN 0 7493 0973 3

Printed and bound in Great Britain
by Cox & Wyman Ltd, Reading, Berks

EDITOR'S PREFACE

THE IMMORTAL WRITINGS of Kahlil Gibran, the *Prophet of Lebanon,* possess a rare and distinctive flavor of ancient wisdom and mysticism that is equaled by few—if any—in the history of world literature. Small wonder, then, that the reader never ceases to be amazed at Gibran's recency to this world and age (1883–1931). The delicacy of his mind, the visions of his inner eyes, and the vast but simple insight displayed by his every parable combine to present a momentary incongruity. It is quickly dispelled, however, for one soon realizes that Gibran is of all ages.

The brilliance of Gibran will ever continue to surprise and perplex his millions of followers in dozens of languages. This strange man, born in the shadow of the Holy Cedars of Lebanon, exhibits a weirdly beautiful approach to life and death in all of his writings, never fully revealing the purpose behind his abrupt and intense changes in thought and style . . . from the laciest and tenderest language and meaning to the bitterest and angriest outpourings known to literature. After an attempted analysis that ended in utter despair, a group of scholars at a leading American university could only conclude, *Gibran could write timeless truths in a way that makes the reader feel he is taking a walk in a quiet wood, or bathing in a cool stream; it soothes the spirit. But he could also write with a scorch like fire.* The tremendous "why" could not be found.

Philosopher and artist, his dynamic brush is no less disturbing than his pen. The searching depths of mysticism, the unfettered glory of youth, and the Elysian beauty of death join forces to render his canvases remarkably fascinating and unique. As for his handling of materials and his artistry of representation, all that need be said is that when Auguste Rodin wished to have his own portrait done, he bypassed the multitude of accomplished and aspiring painters of his day and insisted that Gibran execute the project. Hundreds of Gibran's oil paintings are on permanent exhibit in a Lebanese museum erected solely as the repository for these works, and numerous of his paintings and drawings are displayed periodically in the large capitals and art centers of the world.

Gibran has a specific, recognizable message to convey, and the simplicity of his style—whether in delicacy or in bitter invective—brings that message to the inner consciousness of the reader quickly, clearly, and effortlessly. A surprising aspect of many of the writings in this, the largest and most comprehensive volume of Gibran's works ever published, is found in the fact that he was scarcely twenty years old when they were composed and set loose upon the world. In the light of his youth, these works establish unquestioned achievement in literary and philosophic artistry, since they would have been classics coming even at an age of experienced wisdom and mellowness of years. There is broad vision and justifiable anger with respect to religious injustice in *John the Madman* (Book Two); exquisite beauty of thought and language in his series of *Seven Songs* (Books One, Three, Four, Five, Six); enormous maturity of understanding in *The Life of Love* (Book One) and *Madame Rose Hanie* (Book Five); keen invention of plot and element of surprise in *Satan* (Book One), one of the few truly original and different forms of literary development to appear in many years; tear-enriched distress in *The City of the Dead* (Book One) and *Contemplations in Sadness* (Book Six); mystical strength surpassing William Blake in *Ashes of the Ages and Eternal Fire* (Book Four); heartfelt pain and bitterness in *The Crucified* (Book Three).

That Gibran earnestly feels the genuineness of the message he endeavors to carry to the reader is shown in many of his passages, as in the closing words of *A Poet's Voice* (Book One), in which he proclaims: *What I say now with one heart will be said tomorrow with many hearts.* These profound broodings and exaltations in prose and poetry are of particular timeliness in contemplation of the difficulties besetting the world today, and much can be gleaned therefrom in furtherance of tolerance, understanding, and the universal brotherhood of man. His warnings are neither crusades nor preachments, yet every thought is conveyed completely, clearly, dynamically. He muses over the beautiful, not the ugly; over the system, not the crime *(The Criminal,* Book Three). All of his criticisms are imbued with a gentle melancholy, subordinated finally to his magnificent descriptive powers, abounding with fine, metaphorical terseness.

Reference has been made to Gibran's youth at the time of these writings, and this factor cannot be regarded lightly, for it renders all the more remarkable his ripe and mature grasp on a subject that has baffled and intrigued philosophers and other thinkers from the beginning—the destiny of man and the inexplicable *why* of his being. Likewise, his unquestioned mastery of the art of symbolism and simile, sparkling throughout this extensive collection of his writings, is a tribute to his astonishing stature in literary accomplishment, for this is an achievement that few have been able to attain at any age. His sympathetic approach to the prospect of death is also a creature of the mind belonging to the aged, but a knowledge of Gibran's love for tears, as well as his deep, sincere affection for fellow sufferers, can explain his philosophically pleasant contemplations of death. Numerous instances reveal his full understanding of the facts of maturity and stability in connection with marriage, despite his years. In *The Life of Love* (Book One), a poem likening the four seasons of the year to the comparable periods of married life, the aging couple exchanges reminiscences in winter time, the husband sighing affectionately:

> Feed the lamp with oil and let it not dim, and
> Place it by you, so I can read with tears what
> Your life with me has written upon your face.
> Bring Autumn's wine. Let us drink and sing the
> Song of remembrance to Spring's carefree sowing,
> And Summer's watchful tending, and Autumn's
> Reward in harvest.
> Come close to me, oh beloved of my soul; the
> Fire is cooling and fleeing under the ashes.
> Embrace me, for I feel loneliness; the lamp is
> Dim, and the wine which we pressed is closing
> Our eyes. Let us look upon each other before
> They are shut.

Surprisingly, the mysticism that characterizes much of Gibran's writing is found not in his poetry, where it would be granted a great latitude of expression through the very nature of poetic freedom, but in his prose stories exclusively. This feature of his works is not a deterrent to reader interest, for his depth establishes itself at a level of complete lucidity to all who endeavor to find it, and his frequent voyages into the field of mysticism supplement with spiritual argument the precepts of his earthly discourses. His blending of oriental and occidental philosophy is occasionally disconcerting to the Western mind. One invariably has the feeling that the emotions expressed so plainly were too large for words, and were wrenched from him reluctantly through his soul's compulsion. One cannot fail to recognize in him the strong expression of a passionate urge to improve the lot of suffering, exploited humanity, an impulse that fired his mind and heart from childhood. It is a message, moreover, that emanates from painful, soul-searing knowledge of man's inhumanity to man, drawn from a poignant memory of what his eyes had seen and his ears had heard in his close observance of the perpetual human tragedy. He conveys his sense of sorrow for the cruel waste of youth and beauty and talent and sensitivity implicit in the neglect and degradation of the millions throughout the East.

But far more than local evils and the abuse of power by Eastern regimes is woven into the living fabric of Gibran's verbal tapestry. With the moving intensity that characterizes truly significant utterance, his earliest—like his latest—writings project timeless, universal truths. And these are often presented in the captivating literary form of the parable, peculiarly a heritage of the ancient Aramaic tradition.

His sentiments herein give new force to his other great works, for all possess the power and effective ness of his one enormous theme. They stress the generally understood, yet completely ignored fact that but few things in life have real importance. Again and again this Lebanese savant reminds us that if human relationships are wrong, no other factors of life can really matter. For what power, or wealth, or prestige can compensate for the silent agony of the heart's bereavement? In what fashion can existence on earth be fulfilled when love departs or friendship withers? The bonds of a common brotherhood without demarcation, no less than personal and family ties, must be strengthened if, individually and collectively, we are to meet competently the challenge of progress—or even of survival itself.

Gibran drives these teachings forcefully to the heart, and they persist in agitating the heart to complete accord. Like Beethoven's deathless music, of which the composer said, "From the heart it has sprung, and to the heart it shall penetrate," these writings, through their own rich sincerity, reach the deepest recesses of our emotional and spiritual awareness.

Among the outstanding pieces in this volume is the strangely gripping story *The Bride's Bed* (Book Seven), actually an eye-witness account of the incident related. Its theme is not new to the great number of readers and students of Gibran, for the vicious inequality of man and woman had long been the object of his strongest literary attacks.* One of the world's most fervent and outspoken champions of the cause of human rights, Gibran had waged a long and bitter struggle to strengthen the recognition of youth's freedom of action in love, and to abolish from the social structure of the Middle East some of the ancient marriage customs prevailing. Particularly intense was his condemnation of the tradition of prearranged marriages of children by their parents, in complete disregard of the wishes and reactions of those so betrothed. It is a matter of common knowledge that these transactions often took place when the children concerned were scarcely old enough to walk, much less realize the enormous significance of the steps then planned irrevocably for them.

The ill-fated Lyla in this story, with courageous, anguished heroism, broke in unrestrained fury from this custom, bringing upon herself—fully anticipated—consequences so tragic, so far-reaching as to establish beyond question the widespread, deep-rooted nature of this practice in all of its personal, social, political, and ironically enough, even religious ramifications. Examine, for instance, the words of the priest addressed to the throng gathered about the lifeless bodies of the bride and the man she had really loved:

* See also *Madame Rose Hanie* (Book Five).

Cursed are the hands that touch these blood-spattered carcasses that are soaked with sin. And cursed are the eyes that shed tears of sorrow upon these two evil souls. Let the corpse of the son of Sodom and that of the daughter of Gomorrah remain lying in this diseased spot until the beasts devour their flesh and the wind scatters their bones. Go back to your homes and flee from the pollution of these sinners! Disperse now, before the flames of hell sting you, and he who remains here shall be cursed and excommunicated from the church and shall never again enter the temple and join the Christians in offering prayers to God!

It is a story of truth, of bravery, of all humanity's interest, going to the very core of individual liberty. It is recognized conclusively by authorities the world over that Gibran, through the knife-edged attacks of this story and others,* was largely responsible for many of the social, political and religious reforms finally undertaken by the rulers of the East.

Gibran's doctrine is of kindness, of brotherhood, and of charity, and he requires but few words to transmit great thoughts. On charity he discloses:

I sing the praise of my home and long to see again my birthplace; but if it refused shelter and food to

* See also *Khalil the Heretic* (Book Six), *John the Madman* (Book Two), and *The Cry of the Graves* (Book Seven).

the needy wayfarer, I would, in my inner voice, convert my praise into anger, and my longing into forgetfulness.

And again:

Remember, my brother, that the coin which you drop into the withered hand stretching toward you is the only golden chain that binds your rich heart to the loving heart of God.

On brotherhood:

Love is stronger than death, and death is stronger than life; it is sad that men divide amongst themselves.

He adds:

Humanity is the spirit of the Supreme Being on earth, and humanity is standing amidst unseen ruins, hiding its nakedness behind tattered rags, shedding tears upon hollow cheeks, calling for its children in pitiful voice. But the children are busy singing the anthem; they are busy sharpening the swords and cannot hear the cries of their mothers.

Small wonder that the present world gives heed to Gibran in its acute difficulty! His thoughts are ageless, and the real, the essential Gibran will live on and grow through the centuries.

On a level with Gibran's desire to bring to the world his strong but simple philosophy of life and death, was his burning ambition to revolutionize and give impetus to the previously neglected and unrecognized Arabic contribution to world literature. With his close friend and associate, Mikhail Naimy, he was instrumental in maintaining the journalistic endeavor known as *Al-Funoon* (The Arts), conceived and launched by Nasseeb Ariba. However, the years embracing World War I saw both its inception and demise, despite all efforts of its few supporters to see it through. Somewhat earlier, Gibran had enthusiastically created a literary enterprise which he had called *The Seven Arts,* essentially an organ of poetry. Although it, too, was but a short-lived proposition, it nevertheless served as the instrument which carried Gibran's name to various art organizations, among them the important Poetry Society which invited him to read some of his works to its membership body at a special gathering. He emerged from the meeting with uncontrolled bitterness and resentment, for the literati had received him and his carefully prepared work with nothing short of unconcealed mockery.

He neither despaired nor relented, nor acknowledged defeat. On the contrary, he resorted to his pen—his closest friend in moments of travail—and composed his now famous prose-poem *Defeat,** in which

* Hitherto unpublished in any English-language collection of Gibran's writings.

he converted his failure into a sword with which to avenge his assailants:

> Defeat, my Defeat, my shining sword and shield,
> In your eyes I have read
> That to be enthroned is to be enslaved,
> And to be understood is to be leveled down,
> And to be grasped is but to reach one's fulness
> And like a ripe fruit to fall and be consumed.
>
> Defeat, my Defeat, my deathless courage,
> You and I shall laugh together with the storm,
> And together we shall dig graves
> For all that die in us,
> And we shall stand in the sun with a will,
> And we shall be dangerous.

This incident may have provoked (at least in part) the unorthodox writings that followed. In this broad segment of his literary creations he worships the poor, the meek, the downtrodden; he brings down heavens of wrath and invective upon exploiters, unsympathetic rulers, and grasping officials—political, ecclesiastical, and others. He adores simplicity; he deplores the complications growing alongside the "advances" of our civilization. He finds freshness and freedom in the field; * he discovers only stifling nothingness in the city streets. He gives his words and thoughts of beauty to the *fellahin,* to the ignorant, to the sad; he casts his unleashed vituperation

* See *Contemplations in Sadness* (Book Six).

upon those employing improper use of power and position.

The painful death-by-starvation of both *The Seven Arts* and *Al-Funoon,* and the threadbare struggle of the one remaining Arab voice in America, *As-Sayeh* (The Traveler), left burning all the stronger the desire—the desperate need—to establish an Arab-American publication which would close the abysmal gap between East and West through the great medium of literature.

On April 20, 1920, a serious group of ten writers of Arabic descent met at Gibran's studio in New York, and remained in almost endless session fostering the birth of what was to become *Arrabitah* (The Pen Bond). This weary but enthusiastic nucleus included Kahlil Gibran, Nasseeb Ariba, Rasheed Ayoub, William Catzelflis, Mikhail Naimy,* Abdul-Masseeh Haddad, Nadra Haddad, and Elias Atallah. Its purposes, according to the manuscript of the secretary's notes made that night, were: (1) to publish the works of its own members and those of other Arab writers considered worthy, and to encourage the translation of masterpieces of world literature; (2) to foster new talent by offering prizes for the best in poetry and prose. (It might be added parenthetically that the only available "prize" was probably a subscription to the publication.)

* Now the leading literary figure of the East, Mr. Naimy is author of *Kahlil Gibran: A Biography,* the only authoritative biography of Gibran extant (Philosophical Library, publishers, 1950).

As his preliminary contribution, Gibran painted an attractive emblem for *Arrabitah* (Arabic, *Ar-Rabitatul Qalamyiat*) representing a circle having an open book at its center. Across the pages appeared the quotation *How wonderful the treasures beneath God's throne which only poets' tongues can unlock!* —taken from the *Hadith.**

The preamble to the by-laws stated, in part:

. . . Not everything parading as literature is literature; nor is every rimester a poet. The literature we esteem as worthy is that only which draws its nourishment from Life's soil and light and air. . . . And the man of letters is he who is endowed with more than the average mortal's share of sensitiveness and taste, and the power of estimation and penetration together with the talent of expressing clearly and loftily whatever imprints Life's constant waves leave upon his soul. . . .

This new movement, aimed at transporting our literature from stagnation to life, from imitation to creation, is worthy of all encouragement; if left fallow, decay and disintegration will take hold. . . .

Gibran gave untiringly to *Arrabitah* from his two only resources . . . time and effort. He showered the publication with many works which were to become

* *Al-Hadith* is a compendium of the sayings of the prophet Mohammed, as distinguished from *Al-Koran,* believed to be the direct word of God.

internationally known, including his highly controversial *The Tempest* (Book One).

Gibran's feeling for his homeland and his countrymen remained strong despite such of his writings as *Dead are my People* (Book Seven), and despite the public burning of his *Spirits Rebellious* in the market place of Beirut, his subsequent excommunication from the church, and his exile from the country. The two specific works in *Spirits Rebellious* which appear to have precipitated the drastic official measures are *Cry of the Graves* (Book Seven) and *Khalil the Heretic* (Book Six), both of which condemned in previously unheard language the evils of church and state administration prevailing at the turn of the twentieth century.

His exile and excommunication did not accomplish the purpose for which they were obviously intended. His attacks grew stronger, and he brought to the interested attention of the entire civilized world the dishonest, inequitable, and sordid conditions existing in his homeland. He simply stated, upon learning of the ceremonial burning of his writings, that it was proof of the urgent need for a second edition. Years later his exile was remanded, and the church embraced him without conciliation on his part. A mourner who witnessed the Gibran funeral procession in 1931 states that the ecclesiastical pageantry of the event was beyond description. Hundreds of priests and religious leaders, representing every denomination under Eastern and Western skies, were in solemn attendance. Included were Maronites, Catholics, Shiites, Jews, Protestants, Mohammedans, Greek Orthodox, Sunnites, Druzes, and others. And to render complete Gibran's restoration to the fold of religion, he was buried in the grotto of the Monastery of *Mar Sarkis,* his childhood church.

Recent world developments have heightened interest in Arabic literature to a surprising degree, and English-speaking peoples today are making deep, exploratory studies of these venerable writings, as yet unspoiled by Western influence.

The Arabs, despite centuries of internal political turbulence and external interference, have retained and improved their strong esthetic and imaginative spirit. While the Western world has been looking at life and seeking practical solutions to its problems through science, the various peoples of Arabic heritage have preferred to indulge primarily in poetic, meditative, and philosophical thinking. Under a cultural climate determined by the indigenous doctrines of Mohammed and those following him, the Arab writers have captured intact the spirit of their people, portraying the filial piety of the home, and the blind fidelity of all to their rulers, right or wrong. Never having suffered under religious bias (as contrasted with the Catholic and the Jew), nor adhered to scientific theories, Arabic writers have felt a freedom of expression of which the Western literati may well be envious. They set their own unconventional pattern, and no amount of outside pressure or criticism has been able to divert them from it.

In the present pursuit of higher learning in Arabic writings, no author of the East offers greater reward than does Kahlil Gibran, for he stands alone on the summit of all that is fascinating, terrible and beautiful in *Sufi* literature.

MARTIN L. WOLF

New York City, 1951.

CONTENTS

BOOK FOUR

BOOK FIVE

BOOK SIX

CONTENTS

BOOK SEVEN

BOOK EIGHT

BOOK NINE

A TREASURY OF KAHLIL GIBRAN

BOOK 1

A POET'S VOICE

PART ONE

THE POWER of charity sows deep in my heart, and I reap and gather the wheat in bundles and give them to the hungry.

My soul gives life to the grapevine and I press its bunches and give the juice to the thirsty.

Heaven fills my lamp with oil and I place it at my window to direct the stranger through the dark.

I do all these things because I live in them; and if destiny should tie my hands and prevent me from so doing, then death would be my only desire. For I am a poet, and if I cannot give, I shall refuse to receive.

Humanity rages like a tempest, but I sigh in silence for I know the storm must pass away while a sigh goes to God.

Human kinds cling to earthly things, but I seek ever to embrace the torch of love so it will purify me by its fire and sear inhumanity from my heart.

Substantial things deaden a man without suffering; love awakens him with enlivening pains.

BOOK ONE

Humans are divided into different clans and tribes, and belong to countries and towns. But I find myself a stranger to all communities and belong to no settlement. The universe is my country and the human family is my tribe.

Men are weak, and it is sad that they divide amongst themselves. The world is narrow and it is unwise to cleave it into kingdoms, empires, and provinces.

Human kinds unite themselves only to destroy the temples of soul, and they join hands to build edifices for earthly bodies. I stand alone listening to the voice of hope in my deep self saying, "As love enlivens a man's heart with pain, so ignorance teaches him the way to knowledge." Pain and ignorance lead to great joy and knowledge because the Supreme Being has created nothing vain under the sun.

PART TWO

I have a yearning for my beautiful country, and I love its people because of their misery. But if my people rose, stimulated by plunder and motivated by what they call "patriotic spirit" to murder, and invaded my neighbour's country, then upon the committing of any human atrocity I would hate my people and my country.

I sing the praise of my birthplace and long to see the home of my childhood; but if the people in that home refused to shelter and feed the needy wayfarer, I would convert my praise into anger and my longing into forgetfulness. My inner voice would say, "The house that does not comfort the needy is worthy of naught but destruction."

I love my native village with some of my love for my country; and I love my country with part of my love for the earth, all of which is my country; and I love the earth with all of myself because it is the haven of humanity, the manifest spirit of God.

Humanity is the spirit of the Supreme Being on earth, and that humanity is standing amidst ruins, hiding its nakedness behind tattered rags, shedding tears upon hollow cheeks, and calling for its children with pitiful voice. But the children are busy singing their clan's anthem; they are busy sharpening the swords and cannot hear the cry of their mothers.

Humanity appeals to its people but they listen not. Were one to listen, and console a mother by wiping her tears, others would say, "He is weak, affected by sentiment."

Humanity is the spirit of the Supreme Being on earth, and that Supreme Being preaches love and good-will. But the people ridicule such teachings. The Nazarene Jesus listened, and crucifixion was his lot; Socrates heard the voice and followed it, and he too fell victim in body. The followers of The Nazarene and Socrates are the followers of Deity, and since people will not kill them, they deride them, saying, "Ridicule is more bitter than killing."

Jerusalem could not kill The Nazarene, nor

Athens Socrates; they are living yet and shall live eternally. Ridicule cannot triumph over the followers of Deity. They live and grow forever.

PART THREE

Thou art my brother because you are a human, and we both are sons of one Holy Spirit; we are equal and made of the same earth.

You are here as my companion along the path of life, and my aid in understanding the meaning of hidden Truth. You are a human, and, that fact sufficing, I love you as a brother. You may speak of me as you choose, for Tomorrow shall take you away and will use your talk as evidence for his judgment, and you shall receive justice.

You may deprive me of whatever I possess, for my greed instigated the amassing of wealth and you are entitled to my lot if it will satisfy you.

You may do unto me whatever you wish, but you shall not be able to touch my Truth.

You may shed my blood and burn my body, but you cannot kill or hurt my spirit.

You may tie my hands with chains and my feet with shackles, and put me in the dark prison, but you shall not enslave my thinking, for it is free, like the breeze in the spacious sky.

You are my brother and I love you. I love you worshipping in your church, kneeling in your temple, and praying in your mosque. You and I and all are children of one religion, for the varied paths of religion are but the fingers of the loving hand of the Supreme Being, extended to all, offering completeness of spirit to all, anxious to receive all.

I love you for your Truth, derived from your knowledge; that Truth which I cannot see because of my ignorance. But I respect it as a divine thing, for it is the deed of the spirit. Your Truth shall meet my Truth in the coming world and blend together like the fragrance of flowers and become one whole and eternal Truth, perpetuating and living in the eternity of Love and Beauty.

I love you because you are weak before the strong oppressor, and poor before the greedy rich. For these reasons I shed tears and comfort you; and from behind my tears I see you embraced in the arms of Justice, smiling and forgiving your persecutors. You are my brother and I love you.

PART FOUR

You are my brother, but why are you quarreling with me? Why do you invade my country and try to subjugate me for the sake of pleasing those who are seeking glory and authority?

Why do you leave your wife and children and follow Death to the distant land for the sake of those who buy glory with your blood, and high honour with your mother's tears?

Is it an honour for a man to kill his brother man? If you deem it an honour, let it be an act of worship, and erect a temple to Cain who slew his brother Abel.

Is self-preservation the first law of Nature? Why, then, does Greed urge you to self-sacrifice in order only to achieve his aim in hurting your brothers? Beware, my brother, of the leader who says, "Love of existence obliges us to deprive the people of their rights!" I say unto you but this: protecting others' rights is the noblest and most beautiful human act; if my existence requires that I kill others, then death is more honourable to me, and if I cannot find someone to kill me for the protection of my honour, I will not hesitate to take my life by my own hands for the sake of Eternity before Eternity comes.

Selfishness, my brother, is the cause of blind superiority, and superiority creates clanship, and clanship creates authority which leads to discord and subjugation.

The soul believes in the power of knowledge and justice over dark ignorance; it denies the authority that supplies the swords to defend and strengthen ignorance and oppression—that authority which destroyed Babylon and shook the foundation of Jerusalem and left Rome in ruins. It is that which made people call criminals great men; made writers respect their names; made historians relate the stories of their inhumanity in manner of praise.

The only authority I obey is the knowledge of guarding and acquiescing in the Natural Law of Justice.

What justice does authority display when it kills the killer? When it imprisons the robber? When it descends on a neighbouring country and slays its people? What does justice think of the authority under which a killer punishes the one who kills, and a thief sentences the one who steals?

You are my brother, and I love you; and Love is justice with its full intensity and dignity. If justice did not support my love for you, regardless of your tribe and community, I would be a deceiver concealing the ugliness of selfishness behind the outer garment of pure love.

CONCLUSION

My soul is my friend who consoles me in misery and distress of life. He who does not befriend his soul is an enemy of humanity, and he who does not find human guidance within himself will perish desperately. Life emerges from within, and derives not from environs.

I came to say a word and I shall say it now. But if death prevents its uttering, it will be said by Tomorrow, for Tomorrow never leaves a secret in the book of Eternity.

I came to live in the glory of Love and the light of Beauty, which are the reflections of God. I am here living, and the people are unable to exile me from the domain of life for they know I will live in death. If they pluck my eyes I will hearken to the murmurs of Love and the songs of Beauty.

If they close my ears I will enjoy the touch of the breeze mixed with the incense of Love and the fragrance of Beauty.

If they place me in vacuum, I will live together with my soul, the child of Love and Beauty.

I came here to be for all and with all, and what I do today in my solitude will be echoed by Tomorrow to the people.

What I say now with one heart will be said tomorrow by many hearts.

SONG OF THE RAIN

I AM dotted silver threads dropped from heaven
By the gods. Nature then takes me, to adorn
Her fields and valleys.

I am beautiful pearls, plucked from the
Crown of Ishtar by the daughter of Dawn
To embellish the gardens.

When I cry the hills laugh;
When I humble myself the flowers rejoice;
When I bow, all things are elated.

The field and the cloud are lovers
And between them I am a messenger of mercy.
I quench the thirst of the one;
I cure the ailment of the other.

The voice of thunder declares my arrival;
The rainbow announces my departure.
I am like earthly life, which begins at
The feet of the mad elements and ends
Under the upraised wings of death.

I emerge from the heart of the sea and
Soar with the breeze. When I see a field in
Need, I descend and embrace the flowers and
The trees in a million little ways.

I touch gently at the windows with my
Soft fingers, and my announcement is a
Welcome song. All can hear, but only
The sensitive can understand.

The heat in the air gives birth to me,
But in turn I kill it,
As woman overcomes man with
The strength she takes from him.

I am the sigh of the sea;
The laughter of the field;
The tears of heaven.

So with love–
Sighs from the deep sea of affection;
Laughter from the colourful field of the spirit;
Tears from the endless heaven of memories.

THE TEMPEST

PART ONE

YUSIF EL FAKHRI was thirty years of age when he withdrew himself from society and departed to live in an isolated hermitage in the vicinity of Kedeesha Valley in North Lebanon. The people of the nearby villages heard various tales concerning Yusif; some related that his was a wealthy and noble family, and that he loved a woman who betrayed him and caused him to lead a solitary life, while others said that he was a poet who deserted the clamourous city and retired to that place in order to record his thoughts and compose his inspiration; and many were sure that he was a mystic who was contented with the spiritual world, although most people insisted that he was a madman.

As for myself, I could not draw any conclusion regarding the man, for I knew that there must be a deep secret within his heart whose revelation I would not trust to mere speculation. I had long hoped for the opportunity to meet this strange man. I had endeavoured in devious ways to win his friendship in order to study his reality and learn his story by inquiring as to his purpose in life, but my efforts were in vain. When I met him for the first time, he was walking by the forest of the Holy Cedars of Lebanon, and I greeted him with the finest choice of words, but he returned my greeting by merely shaking his head and striding off.

On another occasion I found him standing in the midst of a small vineyard by a monastery, and again I approached and greeted him, saying, "It is said by the villagers that this monastery was built by a Syriac group in the Fourteenth Century; do you know anything of its history?" He replied coldly, "I do not know who built this monastery, nor do I care to know." And he turned his back to me and added, "Why do you not ask your grandparents, who are older than I, and who know more of the history of these valleys than I do?" Realizing at once my utter failure, I left him.

Thus did two years pass, and the bizarre life of this strange man preyed on my mind and disturbed my dreams.

PART TWO

One day in Autumn, as I was roaming the hills and knolls adjacent to the hermitage of Yusif El Fakhri, I was suddenly caught in a strong wind and torrent rain, and the tempest cast me here and there like a boat whose rudder has been broken and whose masts have been torn by a gale in a rough sea. I directed my steps with difficulty toward Yusif's place, saying to myself, "This is an opportunity I have long sought, and the tempest will be my excuse for entering, while my wet clothes will serve as good reason for lingering."

I was in a miserable plight when I reached the hermitage, and as I knocked on the door, the man whom I had been longing to see opened it. He was holding in one hand a dying bird whose head had been injured and whose wings had been broken. I greeted him saying, "I beg your forgiveness for this annoying intrusion. The raging tempest trapped me while I was afar from home." He frowned, saying, "There are many caves in this wilderness in which you might have taken refuge." However, he did not close the door, and the beat of my heart quickened in anticipation, for the realization of my great wish was close at hand. He commenced to touch the bird's head gently and with the utmost care and interest, exhibiting a quality important to my heart. I was surprised over the two opponent characteristics I found in that man—mercy and cruelty at the same time. We became aware of the strained silence. He resented my presence, I desired to remain.

It seemed as if he felt my thought, for he looked up and said, "The tempest is clean, and declines to eat soured meat. Why do you seek to escape from it?" And with a touch of humour, I responded, "The tempest may not desire salted or soured things, but she is inclined to chill and tender all things, and undoubtedly she would enjoy consuming me if she grasped me again." His expression was severe when he retorted, "The tempest would have bestowed upon you a great honour, of which you are not worthy, if she had swallowed you." I agreed, "Yes, Sir, I fled the tempest so I might not be awarded an honour which I do not merit." He turned his face from me in an effort to choke his smile, and then motioned toward a wooden bench by the fireplace and invited me to rest and dry my raiment. I could scarcely control my elation.

I thanked him and sat down while he seated himself opposite, on a bench carved of rock. He commenced to dip his finger tips into an earthenware jar containing a kind of oil, applying it softly to the bird's head and wings. Without looking up he said, "The strong winds have caused this bird to fall upon the rocks between Life and Death." I replied, rendering comparison, "And the strong winds have sent me, adrift, to your door, in time to prevent having my head injured and my wings broken."

He looked at me seriously and said, "It is my wish that man would show the bird's instinct, and it is my wish that the tempest would break the people's wings. For man inclines toward fear and cowardice, and as he feels the awakening of the tempest he crawls into the crevices and the caves of the earth and hides himself."

My purpose was to extract the story of his self-imposed exile, and I provoked, "Yes, the birds possess an honour and courage that man does not possess. . . . Man lives in the shadow of laws and customs which he made and fashioned for himself, but the birds live according to the same free Eternal Law which causes the earth to pursue its mighty path about the sun." His eyes and face brightened, as if he had found in me an understanding disciple, and he exclaimed, "Well done! If you place belief in your own words you should leave civilization and its corrupt laws and traditions, and live like the birds in a place empty of all things except the magnificent law of heaven and earth.

"Believing is a fine thing, but placing those beliefs into execution is a test of strength. Many are those who talk like the roar of the sea, but their lives are shallow and stagnant, like the rotting marshes. Many are those who lift their heads above the mountain tops, but their spirits remain dormant in the obscurity of the caverns." He rose trembling from his seat and placed the bird upon a folded cloth by the window.

He placed a bundle of dry sticks upon the fire, saying, "Remove your sandals and warm your feet, for dampness is dangerous to man's health. Dry well your garments, and be comfortable."

Yusif's continued hospitality kept my hopes high. I approached near to the fire, and the steam sifted from my wet robe. While he stood at the door gazing at the grey skies, my mind searched and scurried for the opening wedge into his background. I asked, innocently, "Has it been long since you came to this place?"

Without looking at me, he answered quietly, "I came to this place when the earth was without form, and void; and darkness was upon the face of the deep. And the Spirit of God moved upon the face of the waters."

I was aghast at these words! Struggling to gather my shocked and scattered wits, I said to myself, "How fantastic this man is! And how difficult is the path that leads to his reality! But I shall attack cautiously and slowly and patiently, until his reticence turns into communication, and his strangeness into understanding."

PART THREE

Night was spreading her black garment upon those valleys, and the tempest was shrieking dizzily and the rain becoming stronger. I began to fancy that the Biblical flood was coming again, to abolish life and wash man's filth from God's earth.

It seemed that the revolution of elements had created in Yusif's heart a tranquility which often comes as a reaction to temperament and converts aloneness into conviviality. He ignited two candles, and then placed before me a jar of wine and a large tray containing bread, cheese, olives, honey, and some dry fruits. Then he sat near me, and after apologizing for the small quantity—but not for the simplicity—of the food, asked me to join him.

We partook of the repast in understanding silence, listening to the wailing of the wind and the crying of the rain, and at the same time I was contemplating his face and trying to dig out his secrets, meditating the possible motive underlying his unusual existence. Having finished, he took a copper kettle from the fire and poured pure, aromatic coffee into two cups; then he opened a small box and offered me a cigarette, addressing me as "Brother." I took one while drinking my coffee, not believing what my eyes were seeing. He looked at me smilingly, and after he had inhaled deeply of his cigarette and sipped some coffee, he said, "Undoubtedly you are thinking upon the existence here of wine and tobacco and coffee, and you may also be wondering over my food and comforts. Your curiosity is justified in all respects, for you are one of the many who believe that in being away from the people, one is absent from life, and must abstain from all its enjoyment." Quickly I agreed, "Yes, it is related by the wise men that he who deserts the world for the purpose of worshipping God alone will leave behind all the enjoyment and plenty of life, contenting himself with the simple products of God alone, and existing on plants and water."

After a pause, heavy with thought, he mused, "I could have worshipped God while living among His creatures, for worship does not require solitude. I did not leave the people in order to see God, for I had always seen Him at the home of my father and mother. I deserted the people because their natures were in conflict with mine, and their dreams did not agree with my dreams. . . . I left man because I found that the wheel of my soul was turning one way and grinding harshly against the wheels of other souls which were turning in the opposite direction. I left civilization because I found it to be an old and corrupt tree, strong and terrible, whose roots are locked into the obscurity of the earth and whose branches are reaching beyond the cloud; but its blossoms are of greed and evil and crime, and its fruit is of woe and misery and fear. Crusaders have undertaken to blend good into it and change its nature, but they could not succeed. They died disappointed, persecuted and torn."

Yusif leaned toward the side of the fireplace as if awaiting the impression of his words upon my heart. I thought it best to remain a listener, and he continued, "No, I did not seek solitude to pray and lead a hermit's life . . . for prayer, which is the song of the heart, will reach the ears of God even when mingled with the shout and cry of thousands of voices. To live the life of a recluse is to torture the body and soul and deaden the inclinations, a kind of existence which is repugnant to me, for God has erected the bodies as temples for the spirits, and it is our mission to deserve and maintain the trust reposed in us by God.

"No, my brother, I did not seek solitude for religious purposes, but solely to avoid the people and their laws, their teachings and their traditions, their ideas and their clamour and their wailing.

"I sought solitude in order to keep from seeing the faces of men who sell themselves and buy with the same price that which is lower than they are, spiritually and materially.

"I sought solitude in order that I might not encounter the women who walk proudly, with one thousands smiles upon their lips, while in the depths of their thousands of hearts there is but one purpose.

"I sought solitude in order to conceal myself from those self-satisfied individuals who see the spectre of knowledge in their dreams and believe that they have attained their goal.

"I fled from society to avoid those who see but the phantom of truth in their awakening, and shout to the world that they have acquired completely the essence of truth.

"I deserted the world and sought solitude because I became tired of rendering courtesy to those multitudes who believe that humility is a sort of weakness, and mercy a kind of cowardice, and snobbery a form of strength.

"I sought solitude because my soul wearied of association with those who believe sincerely that the sun and moon and stars do not rise save from their coffers, and do not set except in their gardens.

"I ran from the office-seekers who shatter the earthly fate of the people while throwing into their eyes the golden dust and filling their ears with sounds of meaningless talk.

"I departed from the ministers who do not live according to their sermons, and who demand of the people that which they do not solicit of themselves.

"I sought solitude because I never obtained kind ness from a human unless I paid the full price with my heart.

"I sought solitude because I loathe that great and terrible institution which the people call civilization—that symmetrical monstrosity erected upon the perpetual misery of human kinds.

"I sought solitude for in it there is a full life for the spirit and for the heart and for the body. I found the endless prairies where the light of the sun rests, and where the flowers breathe their fragrance into space, and where the streams sing their way to the sea. I discovered the mountains where I found the fresh awakening of Spring, and the colourful longing of Summer, and the rich songs of Autumn, and the beautiful mystery of Winter. I came to this far corner of God's domain for I hungered to learn the secrets of the Universe, and approach close to the throne of God."

Yusif breathed deeply, as if he had been relieved of a heavy burden. His eyes shone with strange and magical rays, and upon his radiant face appeared the signs of pride, will, and contentment.

A few minutes passed, and I was gazing placidly

at him, and pondering the unveiling of what had been hidden from me; then I addressed him, saying, "You are undoubtedly correct in most of the things you have said, but through your diagnosis of the social ailment, you prove at the same time that you are a good doctor. I believe that the sick society is in dire need of such a physician, who should cure it or kill it. This distressed world begs your attention. Is it just or merciful to withdraw yourself from the ailing patient and deny him your benefit?"

He stared at me thoughtfully, and then said with futility, "Since the beginning of the world, the doctors have been trying to save the people from their disorders; some used knives, while others used potions, but pestilence spread hopelessly. It is my wish that the patient would content himself with remaining in his filthy bed, meditating his long-continued sores; but instead, he stretches his hands from under the robe and clutches at the neck of each who comes to visit him, choking him to death. What irony it is! The evil patient kills the doctor, and then closes his eyes and says within himself, 'He was a great physician.' No, Brother, no one on earth can benefit humanity. The sower, however wise and expert he may be, cannot cause the field to sprout in Winter."

And I argued, "The people's Winter will pass away, and then comes the beautiful Spring, and the flowers must surely bloom in the fields, and the brooks will again leap in the valleys."

He frowned, and said bitterly, "Alas! Has God

divided man's life—which is the whole creation—into seasons like those of the year? Will any tribe of human beings, living now in God's truth and spirit, desire to re-appear on the face of this earth? Will ever the time come when man settles and abides at the right arm of Life, rejoicing with the brilliant light of day and the peaceful silence of night? Can that dream become reality? Can it materialize after the earth has been covered with human flesh and drenched with man's blood?"

And Yusif stood and raised his hand toward the sky, as if pointing at a different world, and he continued, "This is naught but a vain dream for the world, but I am finding its accomplishment for myself, and what I am discovering here occupies every space in my heart and in the valleys and in the mountains." He now raised his intense voice, "What I really know to be true is the crying of my inner self. I am here living, and in the depths of my existence there is a thirst and hunger, and I find joy in partaking of the bread and wine of Life from the vases which I make and fashion by my own hands. For this reason I abandoned the boards of the people and came to this place, and I shall remain here until the Ending!"

He continued walking back and forth across the room in agitation while I was pondering his sayings and meditating the description of society's gaping wounds. I ventured again a tactful criticism. "I hold the utmost regard for your opinion and intentions, and I envy and respect your solitude and aloneness, but I know that this miserable nation has sustained a great loss in your expatriation, for she is in need of an understanding healer to help her through her difficulties and awaken her spirit."

He shook his head slowly and said, "This nation is like all the nations. And the people are made of the same element and do not vary except in their exterior appearance, which is of no consequence. The misery of our Oriental nations is the misery of the world, and what you call civilization in the West is naught but another spectre of the many phantoms of tragic deception.

"Hypocrisy will always remain, even if her finger tips are coloured and polished; and Deceit will never change even if her touch becomes soft and delicate; and Falsehood will never turn into Truth even if you dress her with silken robes and place her in the palace; and Greed will not become Contentment; nor will Crime become Virtue. And Eternal Slavery to teachings, to customs, and to history will remain Slavery even if she paints her face and disguises her voice. Slavery will remain Slavery in all her horrible form, even if she calls herself Liberty.

"No, my brother, the West is not higher than the East, nor is the West lower than the East, and the difference that stands between the two is not greater than the difference between the tiger and the lion. There is a just and perfect law that I have found behind the exterior of society, which equalizes misery, prosperity, and ignorance; it does not prefer one nation to another, nor does it oppress one tribe in order to enrich another."

I exclaimed, "Then civilization is vanity, and all in it is vanity!" He quickly responded, "Yes, civilization is vanity and all in it is vanity. . . . Inventions and discoveries are but amusement and comfort for the body when it is tired and weary. The conquest of distance and the victory over the seas are but false fruit which do not satisfy the soul, nor nourish the heart, neither lift the spirit, for they are afar from nature. And those structures and theories which man calls knowledge and art are naught except shackles and golden chains which man drags, and he rejoices with their glittering reflections and ringing sounds. They are strong cages whose bars man commenced fabricating ages ago, unaware that he was building from the inside, and that he would soon become his own prisoner to eternity. Yes, vain are the deeds of man, and vain are his purposes, and all is vanity upon the earth." He paused, then slowly added, "And among all vanities of life, there is only one thing that the spirit loves and craves. One thing dazzling and alone."

"What is it?" I inquired with quivering voice. He looked at me for a long minute and then closed his eyes. He placed his hands on his chest, while his face brightened, and with a serene and sincere voice he said, "It is an awakening in the spirit; it is an awakening in the inner depths of the heart; it is an overwhelming and magnificent power that descends suddenly upon man's conscience and opens his eyes, whereupon he sees Life amid a dizzying shower of brilliant music, surrounded by a circle of great light, with man standing as a pillar of beauty between the earth and the firmament. It is a flame that suddenly rages within the spirit and sears and purifies the heart, ascending above the earth and hovering in the spacious sky. It is a kindness that envelops the individual's heart whereby he would bewilder and disapprove all who opposed it, and revolt against those who refuse to understand its great meaning. It is a secret hand which removed the veil from my eyes while I was a member of society amidst my family, my friends and my countrymen.

"Many times I wondered, and spoke to myself, saying, 'What is this Universe, and why am I different from those people who are looking at me, and how do I know them, and where did I meet them, and why am I living among them? Am I a stranger among them, or is it they who are strange to this earth, built by Life who entrusted me with the keys?' "

He suddenly became silent, as if remembering something he had seen long before, refusing to reveal it. Then he stretched his arms forward and whispered, "That is what happened to me four years ago, when I left the world and came to this void place to live in the awakeness of life and enjoy kind thoughts and beautiful silence."

He walked toward the door, looking at the depths of the darkness as if preparing to address the tempest. But he spoke in a vibrating voice, saying, "It is an awakening within the spirit; he who knows it, is unable to reveal it by words; and he who knows it not, will never think upon the compelling and beautiful mystery of existence."

PART FOUR

An hour had passed and Yusif El Fakhri was striding about the room, stopping at random and gazing at the tremendous grey skies. I remained silent, reflecting upon the strange unison of joy and sorrow in his solitary life.

Later in the night he approached me and stared long into my face, as if wanting to commit to memory the picture of the man to whom he had disclosed the piercing secrets of his life. My mind was heavy with turmoil, my eyes with mist. He said quietly, "I am going now to walk through the night with the tempest, to feel the closeness of Nature's expression; it is a practise that I enjoy greatly in Autumn and Winter. Here is the wine, and there is the tobacco; please accept my home as your own for the night."

He wrapped himself in a black robe and added smilingly, "I beg you to fasten the door against the intruding humans when you leave in the morning, for I plan to spend the day in the forest of the Holy Cedars." Then he walked toward the door, carrying a long walking staff and he concluded, "If the tempest surprises you again while you are in this vicinity, do not hesitate to take refuge in this hermitage. . . . I hope you will teach yourself to love, and not to fear, the tempest. . . . Good night, my brother."

He opened the door and walked out with his head high, into the dark. I stood at the door to see which course he had taken, but he had disappeared from view. For a few minutes I heard the fall of his feet upon the broken stones of the valley.

PART FIVE

Morning came, after a night of deep thought, and the tempest had passed away, while the sky was clear and the mountains and the plains were reveling in the sun's warm rays. On my way back to the city I felt that spiritual awakening of which Yusif El Fakhri had spoken, and it was raging throughout every fibre of my being. I felt that my shivering must be visible. And when I calmed, all about me was beauty and perfection.

As soon as I reached the noisome people and heard their voices and saw their deeds, I stopped and said within myself, "Yes, the spiritual awakening is the most essential thing in man's life, and it is the sole purpose of being. Is not civilization, in all its tragic forms, a supreme motive for spiritual awakening? Then how can we deny existing matter, while its very existence is unwavering proof of its conformability into the intended fitness? The present civilization may possess a vanishing purpose, but the eternal law has offered to that purpose a ladder whose steps can lead to a free substance."

I never saw Yusif El Fakhri again, for through my endeavours to attend the ills of civilization, Life had expelled me from North Lebanon in late Autumn of that same year, and I was required to live in exile in a distant country whose tempests are domestic. And leading a hermit's life in that country is a sort of glorious madness, for its society, too, is ailing.

THE LIFE OF LOVE

SPRING

COME, my beloved; let us walk amidst the knolls,
For the snow is water, and Life is alive from its
Slumber and is roaming the hills and valleys.
Let us follow the footprints of Spring into the
Distant fields, and mount the hilltops to draw
Inspiration high above the cool green plains.

Dawn of Spring has unfolded her winter-kept garment
And placed it on the peach and citrus trees; and
They appear as brides in the ceremonial custom of
The Night of Kedre.

The sprigs of grapevine embrace each other like
Sweethearts, and the brooks burst out in dance
Between the rocks, repeating the song of joy;
And the flowers bud suddenly from the heart of
Nature, like foam from the rich heart of the sea.

Come, my beloved; let us drink the last of Winter's
Tears from the cupped lilies, and soothe our spirits

With the shower of notes from the birds, and wander
In exhilaration through the intoxicating breeze.

Let us sit by that rock, where violets hide; let us
Pursue their exchange of the sweetness of kisses.

SUMMER

Let us go into the fields, my beloved, for the
Time of harvest approaches, and the sun's eyes
Are ripening the grain.
Let us tend the fruit of the earth, as the
Spirit nourishes the grains of Joy from the
Seeds of Love, sowed deep in our hearts.
Let us fill our bins with the products of
Nature, as life fills so abundantly the
Domain of our hearts with her endless bounty.
Let us make the flowers our bed, and the
Sky our blanket, and rest our heads together
Upon pillows of soft hay.
Let us relax after the day's toil, and listen
To the provoking murmur of the brook.

AUTUMN

Let us go and gather the grapes of the vineyard
For the winepress, and keep the wine in old
Vases, as the spirit keeps Knowledge of the
Ages in eternal vessels.

Let us return to our dwelling, for the wind has
Caused the yellow leaves to fall and shroud the
Withering flowers that whisper elegy to Summer.

Come home, my eternal sweetheart, for the birds
Have made pilgrimage to warmth and left the chilled
Prairies suffering pangs of solitude. The jasmine
And myrtle have no more tears.

Let us retreat, for the tired brook has
Ceased its song; and the bubblesome springs
Are drained of their copious weeping; and
The cautious old hills have stored away
Their colourful garments.

Come, my beloved; Nature is justly weary
And is bidding her enthusiasm farewell
With quiet and contented melody.

WINTER

Come close to me, oh companion of my full life;
Come close to me and let not Winter's touch
Enter between us. Sit by me before the hearth,
For fire is the only fruit of Winter.

Speak to me of the glory of your heart, for
That is greater than the shrieking elements
Beyond our door.
Bind the door and seal the transoms, for the
Angry countenance of the heaven depresses my
Spirit, and the face of our snow-laden fields
Makes my soul cry.

Feed the lamp with oil and let it not dim, and
Place it by you, so I can read with tears what
Your life with me has written upon your face.

Bring Autumn's wine. Let us drink and sing the
Song of remembrance to Spring's carefree sowing,
And Summer's watchful tending, and Autumn's
Reward in harvest.

Come close to me, oh beloved of my soul; the
Fire is cooling and fleeing under the ashes.
Embrace me, for I fear loneliness; the lamp is
Dim, and the wine which we pressed is closing
Our eyes. Let us look upon each other before
They are shut.
Find me with your arms and embrace me; let
Slumber then embrace our souls as one.
Kiss me, my beloved, for Winter has stolen
All but our moving lips.

You are close by me, My Forever.
How deep and wide will be the ocean of Slumber;
And how recent was the dawn!

THE CITY OF THE DEAD

YESTERDAY I drew myself from the noisome throngs and proceeded into the field until I reached a knoll upon which Nature had spread her comely garments. Now I could breathe.

I looked back, and the city appeared with its magnificent mosques and stately residences veiled by the smoke of the shops.

I commenced analyzing man's mission, but could conclude only that most of his life was identified with struggle and hardship. Then I tried not to ponder over what the sons of Adam had done, and centered my eyes on the field which is the throne of God's glory. In one secluded corner of the field I observed a burying ground surrounded by poplar trees.

There, between the city of the dead and the city of the living, I meditated. I thought of the eternal silence in the first and the endless sorrow in the second.

In the city of the living I found hope and despair, love and hatred, joy and sorrow, wealth and poverty, faith and infidelity.

In the city of the dead there is buried earth in earth that Nature converts, in the night's silence, into vegetation, and then into animal, and then into man. As my mind wandered in this fashion, I saw a procession moving slowly and reverently, accompanied by pieces of music that filled the sky with sad melody. It was an elaborate funeral. The dead was followed by the living who wept and lamented his going. As the cortege reached the place of interment the priests commenced praying and burning incense, and the musicians blowing and plucking their instruments, mourning the departed. Then the leaders came forward one after the other and recited their eulogies with fine choice of words.

At last the multitude departed, leaving the dead resting in a most spacious and beautiful vault, expertly designed in stone and iron, and surrounded by the most expensively-entwined wreaths of flowers.

The farewell-bidders returned to the city and I remained, watching them from a distance and speaking softly to myself while the sun was descending to the horizon and Nature was making her many preparations for slumber.

Then I saw two men labouring under the weight of a wooden casket, and behind them a shabby-appearing woman carrying an infant on her arms. Following last was a dog who, with heartbreaking eyes, stared first at the woman and then at the casket.

It was a poor funeral. This guest of Death left to cold society a miserable wife and an infant to share her sorrows, and a faithful dog whose heart knew of his companion's departure.

As they reached the burial place they deposited the casket into a ditch away from the tended shrubs and marble stones, and retreated after a few simple words to God. The dog made one last turn to look at his friend's grave as the small group disappeared behind the trees.

I looked at the city of the living and said to myself, "That place belongs to the few." Then I looked upon the trim city of the dead and said, "That place, too, belongs to the few. Oh Lord, where is the haven of all people?"

As I said this, I looked toward the clouds, mingled with the sun's longest and most beautiful golden rays. And I heard a voice within me saying, "Over there!"

SONG OF FORTUNE

MAN and I are sweethearts
He craves me and I long for him,
But alas! Between us has appeared
A rival who brings us misery.
She is cruel and demanding,
Possessing empty lure.
Her name is Substance.
She follows wherever we go
And watches like a sentinel, bringing
Restlessness to my lover.

I ask for my beloved in the forest,
Under the trees, by the lakes.
I cannot find him, for Substance
Has spirited him to the clamourous
City and placed him on the throne
Of quaking, metal riches.

I call for him with the voice of
Knowledge and the song of Wisdom.
He does not hearken, for Substance
Has enticed him into the dungeon
Of selfishness, where avarice dwells.

I seek him in the field of Contentment,
But I am alone, for my rival has
Imprisoned him in the cave of gluttony
And greed, and locked him there
With painful chains of gold.

I call to him at dawn, when Nature smiles,
But he does not hear, for excess has
Laden his drugged eyes with sick slumber.

I beguile him at eventide, when Silence rules
And the flowers sleep. But he responds not,
For his fear over what the morrow will
Bring, shadows his thoughts.

He yearns to love me;
He asks for me in his own acts. But he
Will find me not except in God's acts.
He seeks me in the edifices of his glory
Which he has built upon the bones of others;
He whispers to me from among
His heaps of gold and silver;
But he will find me only by coming to
The house of Simplicity which God has built
At the brink of the stream of affection.

He desires to kiss me before his coffers,
But his lips will never touch mine except
In the richness of the pure breeze.

He asks me to share with him his
Fabulous wealth, but I will not forsake God's
Fortune; I will not cast off my cloak of beauty.

He seeks deceit for medium; I seek only
The medium of his heart.
He bruises his heart in his narrow cell;
I would enrich his heart with my love.

My beloved has learned how to shriek and
Cry for my enemy, Substance; I would
Teach him how to shed tears of affection
And mercy from the eyes of his soul
For all things,
And utter sighs of contentment through
Those tears.

Man is my sweetheart;
I want to belong to him.

SATAN

THE PEOPLE looked upon Father Samaan as their guide in the field of spiritual and theological matters, for he was an authority and a source of deep information on venial and mortal sins, well versed in the secrets of Paradise, Hell, and Purgatory.

Father Samaan's mission in North Lebanon was to travel from one village to another, preaching and curing the people from the spiritual disease of sin, and saving them from the horrible trap of Satan. The Reverend Father waged constant war with Satan. The fellaḥin honoured and respected this clergyman, and were always anxious to buy his advice or prayers with pieces of gold and silver; and at every harvest they would present him with the finest fruits of their fields.

One evening in Autumn, as Father Samaan walked his way toward a solitary village, crossing those valleys and hills, he heard a painful cry emerging from a ditch at the side of the road. He stopped and looked in the direction of the voice, and saw an unclothed man lying on the ground. Streams of blood oozed from deep wounds in his head and chest. He was moaning pitifully for aid, saying, "Save me, help me. Have mercy on me, I am dying." Father Samaan looked with perplexity at the sufferer, and said within himself, "This man must be a thief. . . . He probably tried to rob the wayfarers and failed. Some one has wounded him, and I fear that should he die I may be accused of having taken his life."

Having thus pondered the situation, he resumed his journey, whereupon the dying man stopped him, calling out, "Do not leave me! I am dying!" Then the Father meditated again, and his face became pale as he realized he was refusing to help. His lips quivered, but he spoke to himself, saying, "He must surely be one of the madmen wandering in the wilderness. The sight of his wounds brings fear into my heart; what shall I do? Surely a spiritual doctor is not capable of treating flesh-wounded bodies." Father Samaan walked ahead a few paces when the near-corpse uttered a painful plaint that melted the heart of the rock and he gasped, "Come close to me! Come, for we have been friends a long time. . . . You are Father Samaan, the Good Shepherd, and I am not a thief nor a madman. . . . Come close, and do not let me die in this deserted place. Come, and I will tell you who I am."

Father Samaan came close to the man, knelt, and stared at him; but he saw a strange face with contrasting features; he saw intelligence with slyness, ugliness with beauty, and wickedness with softness. He withdrew to his feet sharply, and exclaimed, "Who are you?"

With a fainting voice, the dying man said, "Fear me not, Father, for we have been strong friends for long. Help me to stand, and take me to the nearby streamlet and cleanse my wounds with your linens." And the Father inquired, "Tell me who you are, for I do not know you, nor even remember having seen you."

And the man replied with an agonizing voice, "You know my identity! You have seen me one thousand times and you speak of me each day. . . . I am dearer to you than your own life." And the Father reprimanded, "You are a lying imposter! A dying man should tell the truth. . . . I have never seen your evil face in my entire life. Tell me who you are, or I will suffer you to die, soaked in your own escaping life." And the wounded man moved slowly and looked into the clergyman's eyes, and upon his lips appeared a mystic smile; and in a quiet, deep and smooth voice he said, "I am Satan."

Upon hearing the fearful word, Father Samaan uttered a terrible cry that shook the far corners of the valley; then he stared, and realized that the dying man's body, with its grotesque distortions, coincided with the likeness of Satan in a religious picture hanging on the wall of the village church. He trembled and cried out, saying, "God has shown me your hellish image and justly caused me to hate you;

cursed be you forevermore! The mangled lamb must be destroyed by the shepherd lest he will infect the other lambs!"

Satan answered, "Be not in haste, Father, and lose not this fleeting time in empty talk. . . . Come and close my wounds quickly, before Life departs from my body." And the clergyman retorted, "The hands which offer a daily sacrifice to God shall not touch a body made of the secretion of Hell. . . . You must die accursed by the tongues of the Ages, and the lips of Humanity, for you are the enemy of Humanity, and it is your avowed purpose to destroy all virtue."

Satan moved in anguish, raising himself upon one elbow, and responded, "You know not what you are saying, nor understand the crime you are committing upon yourself. Give heed, for I will relate my story. Today I walked alone in this solitary valley. When I reached this place, a group of angels descended to attack, and struck me severely; had it not been for one of them, who carried a blazing sword with two sharp edges, I would have driven them off, but I had no power against the brilliant sword." And Satan ceased talking for a moment, as he pressed a shaking hand upon a deep wound in his side. Then he continued, "The armed angel–I believe he was Michael –was an expert gladiator. Had I not thrown myself to the friendly ground and feigned to have been slain, he would have torn me into brutal death."

With voice of triumph, and casting his eyes heavenward, the Father offered, "Blessed be Michael's name, who has saved Humanity from this vicious enemy."

And Satan protested, "My disdain for Humanity is not greater than your hatred for yourself. . . . You are blessing Michael who never has come to your rescue. . . . You are cursing me in the hour of my defeat, even though I was, and still am, the source of your tranquility and happiness. . . . You deny me your blessing, and extend not your kindness, but you live and prosper in the shadow of my being. . . . You have adopted for my existence an excuse and weapon for your career, and you employ my name in justification for your deeds. Has not my past caused you to be in need of my present and future? Have you reached your goal in amassing the required wealth? Have you found it impossible to extract more gold and silver from your followers, using my kingdom as a threat?

"Do you not realize that you will starve to death if I were to die? What would you do tomorrow if you allowed me to die today? What vocation would you pursue if my name disappeared? For decades you have been roaming these villages and warning the people against falling into my hands. They have bought your advice with their poor denars and with the products of their land. What would they buy from you tomorrow, if they discovered that their wicked enemy no longer existed? Your occupation would die with me, for the people would be safe from sin. As a clergyman, do you not realize that Satan's existence alone has created his enemy, the church? That ancient conflict is the secret hand which removes the gold and silver from the faithful's pocket and deposits it forever into the pouch of the preacher and missionary. How can you permit me to die here, when you know it will surely cause you to lose your prestige, your church, your home, and your livelihood?"

Satan became silent for a moment and his humility was now converted into a confident independence, and he continued, "Father, you are proud, but ignorant. I will disclose to you the history of belief, and in it you will find the truth which joins both of our beings, and ties my existence with your very conscience.

"In the first hour of the beginning of time, man stood before the face of the sun and stretched forth his arms and cried for the first time, saying, 'Behind the sky there is a great and loving and benevolent God.' Then man turned his back to the great circle of light and saw his shadow upon the earth, and he hailed, 'In the depths of the earth there is a dark devil who loves wickedness.'

"And the man walked toward his cave, whispering to himself, 'I am between two compelling forces, one in whom I must take refuge, and the other against whom I must struggle.' And the ages marched in procession while man existed between two powers, one that he blessed because it exalted him, and one that he cursed because it frightened him. But he never perceived the meaning of a blessing or of a curse; he was between the two, like a tree between Summer, when it blooms, and Winter, when it shivers.

"When man saw the dawn of civilization, which is human understanding, the family as a unit came into being. Then came the tribes, whereupon labour was divided according to ability and inclination; one clan cultivated the land, another built shelters, others wove raiment or hunted food. Subsequently divination made its appearance upon the earth, and this was the first career adopted by man which possessed no essential urge or necessity."

Satan ceased talking for a moment. Then he laughed and his mirth shook the empty valley, but his laughter reminded him of his wounds, and he placed his hand on his side, suffering with pain. He steadied himself and continued, "Divination appeared and grew on earth in strange fashion.

"There was a man in the first tribe called La Wiss. I know not the origin of his name. He was an intelligent creature, but extremely indolent and he detested work in the cultivation of land, construction of shelters, grazing of cattle or any pursuit requiring body movement or exertion. And since food, during that era, could not be obtained except by arduous toil, La Wiss slept many nights with an empty stomach.

"One Summer night, as the members of that clan

were gathered around the hut of their Chief, talking of the outcome of their day and waiting for their slumber time, a man suddenly leaped to his feet, pointed toward the moon, and cried out, saying, 'Look at the Night God! His face is dark, and his beauty has vanished, and he has turned into a black stone hanging in the dome of the sky!' The multitude gazed at the moon, shouted in awe, and shook with fear, as if the hands of darkness had clutched their hearts, for they saw the Night God slowly turning into a dark ball which changed the bright countenance of the earth and caused the hills and valleys before their eyes to disappear behind a black veil.

"At that moment, La Wiss, who had seen an eclipse before, and understood its simple cause, stepped forward to make much of this opportunity. He stood in the midst of the throng, lifted his hands to the sky, and in a strong voice he addressed them, saying, 'Kneel and pray, for the Evil God of Obscurity is locked in struggle with the Illuminating Night God; if the Evil God conquers him, we will all perish, but if the Night God triumphs over him, we will remain alive. . . . Pray now and worship. . . . Cover your faces with earth. . . . Close your eyes, and lift not your heads toward the sky, for he who witnesses the two gods wrestling will lose his sight and mind, and will remain blind and insane all his life! Bend your heads low, and with all your hearts urge the Night God against his enemy, who is our mortal enemy!'

"Thus did La Wiss continue talking, using many cryptic words of his own fabrication which they had never heard. After this crafty deception, as the moon returned to its previous glory, La Wiss raised his voice louder than before and said impressively, 'Rise now, and look at the Night God who has triumphed over his evil enemy. He is resuming his journey among the stars. Let it be known that through your prayers you have helped him to overcome the Devil of Darkness. He is well pleased now, and brighter than ever.'

"The multitude rose and gazed at the moon that was shining in full beam. Their fear became tranquility, and their confusion was now joy. They commenced dancing and singing and striking with their thick sticks upon sheets of iron, filling the valleys with their clamour and shouting.

"That night, the Chief of the tribe called La Wiss and spoke to him, saying, 'You have done something that no man has ever done. . . . You have demonstrated knowledge of a hidden secret that no other among us understands. Reflecting the will of my people, you are to be the highest ranking member, after me, in the tribe. I am the strongest man, and you are the wisest and most learned person. . . . You are the medium between our people and the gods, whose desires and deeds you are to interpret, and you will teach us those things necessary to gain their blessings and love.'

"And La Wiss slyly assured, 'Everything the Human God reveals to me in my divine dreams will be conveyed to you in awakeness, and you may be confident that I will act directly between you and him.' The chief was assured, and gave La Wiss two horses, seven calves, seventy sheep and seventy lambs; and he spoke to him, saying, 'The men of the tribe shall build for you a strong house, and we will give you at the end of each harvest season a part of the crop of the land so you may live as an honourable and respected Master.'

"La Wiss rose and started to leave, but the Chief stopped him, saying, 'Who and what is the one whom you call the Human God? Who is this daring God who wrestles with the glorious Night God? We have never pondered him before.' La Wiss rubbed his forehead and answered him, saying, 'My Honourable Master, in the olden time, before the creation of man, all the Gods were living peacefully together in an upper world behind the vastness of the stars. The God of Gods was their father, and knew what they did not know, and did what they were unable to do. He kept for himself the divine secrets that existed beyond the eternal laws. During the seventh epoch of the twelfth age, the spirit of Bahtaar, who hated the great God, revolted and stood before his father, and said, 'Why do you keep for yourself the power of great authority upon all creatures, hiding away from us the secrets and laws of the Universe? Are we not your children who believe in you and share with you the great understanding and the perpetual being?'

"The God of Gods became enraged and said, 'I shall preserve for myself the primary power and the great authority and the essential secrets, for I am the beginning and the end.'

"And Bahtaar answered him saying, 'Unless you share with me your might and power, I and my children and my children's children will revolt against you!' At that moment, the God of Gods stood upon his throne in the deep heavens, and drew forth a sword, and grasped the Sun as a shield; and with a voice that shook all corners of eternity he shouted out, saying, 'Descend, you evil rebel, to the dismal lower world where darkness and misery exist! There you shall remain in exile, wandering until the Sun turns into ashes and the stars into dispersed particles!' In that hour, Bahtaar descended from the upper world into the lower world, where all the evil spirits dwelt. Thereupon, he swore by the secret of Life that he would fight his father and brothers by trapping every soul who loved them.'

"As the Chief listened, his forehead wrinkled and his face turned pale. He ventured, 'Then the name of the Evil God is Bahtaar?' and La Wiss responded, 'His name was Bahtaar when he was in upper world, but when he entered into the lower world, he adopted successively the names Baalzaboul, Satanail,

Balial, Zamiel, Ahriman, Mara, Abdon, Devil, and finally Satan, which is the most famous.'

"The Chief repeated the word 'Satan' many times with a quivering voice that sounded like the rustling of the dry branches at the passing of the wind; then he asked, 'Why does Satan hate man as much as he hates the gods?'

"And La Wiss responded quickly, 'He hates man because man is a descendant of Satan's brothers and sisters.' The Chief exclaimed, 'Then Satan is the cousin of man!' In a voice mingled with confusion and annoyance, he retorted, 'Yes, Master, but he is their great enemy who fills their days with misery and their nights with horrible dreams. He is the power who directs the tempest toward their hovels, and brings famine upon their plantation, and disease upon them and their animals. He is an evil and powerful god; he is wicked, and he rejoices when we are in sorrow, and he mourns when we are joyous. We must, through my knowledge, examine him thoroughly, in order to avoid his evil; we must study his character, so we will not step upon his trap-laden path.'

"The Chief leaned his head upon his thick stick and whispered, saying, 'I have learned now the inner secret of that strange power who directs the tempest toward our homes and brings the pestilence upon us and our cattle. The people shall learn all that I have comprehended now, and La Wiss will be blessed, honoured and glorified for revealing to them the mystery of their powerful enemy, and directing them away from the road of evil.'

"And La Wiss left the Chief of the tribe and went to his retiring place, happy over his ingenuity, and intoxicated with the wine of his pleasure and fancy. For the first time, the Chief and all the tribe, except La Wiss, spent the night slumbering in beds surrounded by horrible ghosts, fearful spectres, and disturbing dreams."

Satan ceased talking for a moment, while Father Samaan stared at him as one bewildered, and upon the Father's lips appeared the sickly laughter of Death. Then Satan continued, "Thus divination came to this earth, and thus was my existence the cause for its appearance. La Wiss was the first who adopted my cruelty as a vocation. After the death of La Wiss, this occupation circulated through his children and prospered until it became a perfect and divine profession, pursued by those whose minds are ripe with knowledge, and whose souls are noble, and whose hearts are pure, and whose fancy is vast.

"In Babylon, the people bowed seven times in worshipping before a priest who fought me with his chantings. . . . In Nineveh, they looked upon a man, who claimed to have known my inner secrets, as a golden link between God and man. . . . In Tibet, they called the person who wrestled with me The Son of the Sun and Moon. . . . In Byblus, Ephesus and Antioch, they offered their children's lives in sacrifice to my opponents. . . . In Jerusalem and Rome, they placed their lives in the hands of those who claimed they hated me and fought me with all their might.

"In every city under the sun my name was the axis of the educational circle of religion, arts, and philosophy. Had it not been for me, no temples would have been built, no towers or palaces would have been erected. I am the courage that creates resolution in man. . . . I am the source that provokes originality of thought. . . . I am the hand that moves man's hands. . . . I am Satan everlasting. I am Satan whom the people fight in order to keep themselves alive. If they cease struggling against me, slothfulness will deaden their minds and hearts and souls, in accordance with the weird penalties of their tremendous myth.

"I am the enraged and mute tempest who agitates the minds of man and the hearts of women. And in fear of me, they will travel to places of worship to condemn me, or to places of vice to make me happy by surrendering to my will. The monk who prays in the silence of the night to keep me away from his bed is like the prostitute who invites me to her chamber. I am Satan everlasting and eternal.

"I am the builder of convents and monasteries upon the foundation of fear. I build wine shops and wicked houses upon the foundations of lust and self-gratification. If I cease to exist, fear and enjoyment will be abolished from the world, and through their disappearance, desires and hopes will cease to exist in the human heart. Life will become empty and cold, like a harp with broken strings. I am Satan everlasting.

"I am the inspiration for Falsehood, Slander, Treachery, Deceit and Mockery, and if these elements were to be removed from this world, human society would become like a deserted field in which naught would thrive but thorns of virtue. I am Satan everlasting.

"I am the father and mother of sin, and if sin were to vanish, the fighters of sin would vanish with it, along with their families and structures.

"I am the heart of all evil. Would you wish for human motion to stop through cessation of my heartbeats? Would you accept the result after destroying the cause? I am the cause! Would you allow me to die in this deserted wilderness? Do you desire to sever the bond that exists between you and me? Answer me, clergyman!"

And Satan stretched his arms and bent his head forward and gasped deeply; his face turned to grey and he resembled one of those Egyptian statues laid waste by the Ages at the side of the Nile. Then he fixed his glittering eyes upon Father Samaan's face, and said, in a faltering voice, "I am tired and weak. I did wrong by using my waning strength to speak on things you already knew. Now you may do as you please. . . . You may carry me to your home and treat my wounds, or leave me in this place to die."

Father Samaan quivered and rubbed his hands nervously, and with apology in his voice he said, "I know now what I had not known an hour ago. Forgive my ignorance. I know that your existence in this world creates temptation, and temptation is a measurement by which God adjudges the value of human souls. It is a scale which Almighty God uses to weigh the spirits. I am certain that if you die, temptation will die, and with its passing, death will destroy the ideal power which elevates and alerts man.

"You must live, for if you die and the people know it, their fear of hell will vanish and they will cease worshipping, for naught would be sin. You must live, for in your life is the salvation of humanity from vice and sin.

"As to myself, I shall sacrifice my hatred for you on the altar of my love for man."

Satan uttered a laugh that rocked the ground, and he said, "What an intelligent person you are, Father! And what wonderful knowledge you possess in theological facts! You have found, through the power of your knowledge, a purpose for my existence which I had never understood, and now we realize our need for each other.

"Come close to me, my brother; darkness is submerging the plains, and half of my blood has escaped upon the sand of this valley, and naught remains of me but the remnants of a broken body which Death shall soon buy unless you render aid." Father Samaan rolled the sleeves of his robe and approached, and lifted Satan to his back and walked toward his home.

In the midst of those valleys, engulfed with silence and embellished with the veil of darkness, Father Samaan walked toward the village with his back bent under his heavy burden. His black raiment and long beard were spattered with blood streaming from above him, but he struggled forward, his lips moving in fervent prayer for the life of the dying Satan.

BOOK 2

THE CREATION

THE GOD separated a spirit from Himself and fashioned it into beauty. He showered upon her all the blessings of gracefulness and kindness. He gave her the cup of happiness and said, "Drink not from this cup unless you forget the past and the future, for happiness is naught but the moment." And He also gave her a cup of sorrow and said, "Drink from this cup and you will understand the meaning of the fleeting instants of the joy of life, for sorrow ever abounds."

And the God bestowed upon her a love that would desert her forever upon her first sigh of earthly satisfaction, and a sweetness that would vanish with her first awareness of flattery.

And He gave her wisdom from heaven to lead her to the all-righteous path, and placed in the depth of her heart an eye that sees the unseen, and created in her an affection and goodness toward all things. He dressed her with raiment of hopes spun by the angels of heaven from the sinews of the rainbow. And He cloaked her in the shadow of confusion, which is the dawn of life and light.

Then the God took consuming fire from the furnace of anger, and searing wind from the desert of ignorance, and sharp-cutting sands from the shore of selfishness, and coarse earth from under the feet of ages, and combined them all and fashioned Man. He gave to Man a blind power that rages and drives him into a madness which extinguishes only before gratification of desire, and placed life in him which is the spectre of death.

And the God laughed and cried. He felt an overwhelming love and pity for Man, and sheltered him beneath His guidance.

SLAVERY

THE PEOPLE are the slaves of Life, and it is slavery which fills their days with misery and distress, and floods their nights with tears and anguish.

Seven thousand years have passed since the day of my first birth, and since that day I have been witnessing the slaves of Life, dragging their heavy shackles.

I have roamed the East and West of the earth and wandered in the Light and in the Shadow of Life. I have seen the processions of civilization moving from light into darkness, and each was dragged down to hell by humiliated souls bent under the yoke of slavery. The strong is fettered and subdued, and the faithful is on his knees worshipping before the idols. I have followed man from Babylon to Cairo, and from Ain Dour to Baghdad, and observed the marks of his chains upon the sand. I heard the sad echoes of the fickle ages repeated by the eternal prairies and valleys.

I visited the temples and altars and entered the

palaces, and sat before the thrones. And I saw the apprentice slaving for the artisan, and the artisan slaving for the employer, and the employer slaving for the soldier, and the soldier slaving for the governor, and the governor slaving for the king, and the king slaving for the priest, and the priest slaving for the idol. . . . And the idol is naught but earth fashioned by Satan and erected upon a knoll of skulls.

I entered the mansions of the rich and visited the huts of the poor. I found the infant nursing the milk of slavery from his mother's bosom, and the children learning submission with the alphabet.

The maidens wear garments of restriction and passivity, and the wives retire with tears upon beds of obedience and legal compliance.

I accompanied the ages from the banks of the Kange to the shores of Euphrates; from the mouth of the Nile to the plains of Assyria; from the arenas of Athens to the churches of Rome; from the slums of Constantinople to the palaces of Alexandria. . . . Yet I saw slavery moving over all, in a glorious and majestic procession of ignorance. I saw the people sacrificing the youths and maidens at the feet of the idol, calling her the God; pouring wine and perfume upon her feet, and calling her the Queen; burning incense before her image, and calling her the Prophet; kneeling and worshipping before her, and calling her the Law; fighting and dying for her, and calling her Patriotism; submitting to her will, and calling her the Shadow of God on earth; destroying and demolishing homes and institutions for her sake, and calling her Fraternity; struggling and stealing and working for her, and calling her Fortune and Happiness; killing for her, and calling her Equality.

She possesses various names, but one reality. She has many appearances, but is made of one element. In truth, she is an everlasting ailment bequeathed by each generation unto its successor.

I found the blind slavery, which ties the people's present with their parents' past, and urges them to yield to their traditions and customs, placing ancient spirits in the new bodies.

I found the mute slavery, which binds the life of a man to a wife whom he abhors, and places the woman's body in the bed of a hated husband, deadening both lives spiritually.

I found the deaf slavery, which stifles the soul and the heart, rendering man but an empty echo of a voice, and a pitiful shadow of a body.

I found the lame slavery, which places man's neck under the domination of the tyrant and submits strong bodies and weak minds to the sons of Greed for use as instruments to their power.

I found the ugly slavery, which descends with the infants' spirits from the spacious firmament into the home of Misery, where Need lives by Ignorance, and Humiliation resides beside Despair. And the children grow as miserables, and live as criminals, and die as despised and rejected non-existents.

I found the subtle slavery, which entitles things with other than their names—calling slyness an intelligence, and emptiness a knowledge, and weakness a tenderness, and cowardice a strong refusal.

I found the twisted slavery, which causes the tongues of the weak to move with fear, and speak outside of their feelings, and they feign to be meditating their plight, but they become as empty sacks, which even a child can fold or hang.

I found the bent slavery, which prevails upon one nation to comply with the laws and rules of another nation, and the bending is greater with each day.

I found the perpetual slavery, which crowns the sons of monarchs as kings, and offers no regard to merit.

I found the black slavery, which brands with shame and disgrace forever the innocent sons of the criminals.

Contemplating slavery, it is found to possess the vicious powers of continuation and contagion.

When I grew tired of following the dissolute ages, and wearied of beholding the processions of stoned people, I walked lonely in the Valley of the Shadow of Life, where the past attempts to conceal itself in guilt, and the soul of the future folds and rests itself too long. There, at the edge of Blood and Tears

River, which crawled like a poisonous viper and twisted like a criminal's dreams, I listened to the frightened whisper of the ghosts of slaves, and gazed at nothingness.

When midnight came and the spirits emerged from hidden places, I saw a cadaverous, dying spectre fall to her knees, gazing at the moon. I approached her, asking, "What is your name?"

"My name is Liberty," replied this ghastly shadow of a corpse.

And I inquired, "Where are your children?"

And Liberty, tearful and weak, gasped, "One died crucified, another died mad, and the third one is not yet born."

She limped away and spoke further, but the mist in my eyes and cries of my heart prevented sight or hearing.

JOHN THE MADMAN

In summer John walked every morning into the field, driving his oxen and carrying his plough over his shoulder, hearkening to the soothing songs of the birds and the rustling of the leaves and the grass.

At noon he sat beside a brook in the colourful prairies for repast, leaving a few morsels upon the green grass for the birds of the sky.

At eventide he returned to his wretched hovel that stood apart from those hamlets and villages in North Lebanon. After the evening meal he sat and listened attentively to his parents, who related tales of the past ages until sleep allured and captured his eyes.

In winter he spent his days by the fireside, pondering the wailing of the winds and lamentation of the elements, meditating upon the phenomena of the seasons, and looking through the window toward the snow-laden valleys and leafless trees, symbolizing a multitude of suffering people left helpless in the jaws of biting frost and strong wind.

During the long winter nights he sat up until his parents retired, whereupon he opened a rough wooden closet, brought out his New Testament, and read it secretly under the dim light of a flickering lamp. The priests objected to the reading of the Good Book, and John exercised great caution during these fascinating moments of study. The fathers warned the simple-hearted people against its use, and threatened them with excommunication from the church if discovered possessing it.

Thus John spent his youth between the beautiful earth of God and the New Testament, full of light and truth. John was a youth of silence and contemplation; he listened to his parents' conversations and never spoke a word nor asked a question. When sitting with his contemporaries, he gazed steadily at the horizon, and his thoughts were as distant as his eyes. After each visit to the church he returned home with a depressed spirit, for the teachings of the priests were different from the precepts he found in the Gospel, and the life of the faithful was not the beautiful life of which Christ spoke.

Spring came and the snow melted in the fields and valleys. The snow upon the mountain tops was thawing gradually and forming many streamlets in the winding paths leading into the valleys, combining into a torrent whose roaring bespoke the awakening of Nature. The almond and apple trees were in full bloom; the willow and poplar trees were sprouting with buds, and Nature had spread her happy and colourful garments over the countryside.

John, tired of spending his days by the fireside, and knowing that his oxen were longing for the pastures, released his animals from the sheds and led them to the fields, concealing his New Testament under his cloak for fear of detection. He reached a beautiful arbor adjacent to some fields belonging to the St. Elija Monastery * which stood majestically upon a nearby hill. As the oxen commenced grazing, John leaned upon a rock and began to read his New Testament and meditate the sadness of the children of God on earth, and the beauty of the Kingdom of Heaven.

It was the last day of Lent, and the villagers who abstained from eating meat were impatiently awaiting the coming of Easter. John, like the rest of the poor fellahin, never distinguished Lent from any other day of the year, for his whole life was an extended Lent, and his food never exceeded the simple bread, kneaded with the pain of his heart, or the fruits, purchased with the blood of his body. The only nourishment craved by John during Lent was that spiritual food—the heavenly bread that brought into his heart sad thoughts of the tragedy of the Son of Man and the end of His life on earth.

The birds were singing and hovering about him, and large flocks of doves circled in the sky, while the

* A rich abbey in North Lebanon with vast lands, occupied by scores of monks called Alepoans. (*Editor's note.*)

flowers swayed with the breeze as if exhilarated by the brilliant sunshine.

John busied himself absorbing the Book, and between these intense, light-giving sessions, he watched the domes of the churches in the nearby villages and listened to the rhythmic toll of the bells. Occasionally he would close his eyes and fly on the wings of dreams to Old Jerusalem, following Christ's steps and asking the people of the city about the Nazarene, whereupon he would receive the answer, "Here He cured the paralyzed and restored to the blind their sight; and there they braided for Him a wreath of thorns and placed it upon His head; from that portico He spoke to the multitude with beautiful parables; in that palace they tied Him to the marble columns and scourged Him; on this road He forgave the adulteress her sins, and upon that spot He fell under the weight of His Cross."

One hour passed, and John was suffering physically with God and glorifying with Him in spirit. Noon quickly came, and the oxen were beyond the reach of John's sight. He looked in every direction but could not see them, and as he reached the trail that led to the adjacent fields, he saw a man at a distance, standing amidst the orchards. As he approached and saw that the man was one of the Monastery's monks, he greeted him, bowed reverently, and asked him if he had seen the oxen. The monk appeared to be restraining anger, and he said, "Yes, I saw them.

Follow me and I will show them to you." As they reached the Monastery, John found his oxen tied with ropes in a shed. One of the monks was acting as a watchman over them, and each time an animal moved, he struck the ox across the back with a heavy club. John made a frantic attempt to unbind the helpless animals, but the monk took hold of his cloak and withheld him. At the same time he turned toward the Monastery and shouted, saying, "Here is the criminal shepherd! I have found him!" The priests and monks, preceded by the head priest, hurried to the scene and encircled John, who was bewildered, and felt like a captive. "I have done nothing to merit the treatment of a criminal," said John to the head priest. And the leader replied angrily, "Your oxen have ruined our plantation and destroyed our vineyards. Since you are responsible for the damage we will not give up your oxen until you adjust our loss."

John protested, "I am poor and have no money. Please release my oxen and I pledge my honour that I will never again bring them to these lands." The head priest took a step forward, raised his hand toward heaven, and said, "God has appointed us to be the protectors over this vast land of St. Elija, and it is our sacred duty to guard it with all of our might, for this land is holy, and, like fire, it will burn any who trespass upon it. If you refuse to account for your crime against God, the grass that your oxen have eaten will surely turn into poison and destroy them!"

The head priest started to depart, but John touched his robe and humbly begged, "I appeal to you in the name of Jesus and all the saints, to let me and my animals free. Be kind to me, for I am poor, and the coffers of the Monastery are bursting with silver and gold. Have mercy upon my poor and aged parents, whose lives depend on me. God will forgive me if I have harmed you." The head priest looked at him with severity, and said, "Poor or rich, the Monastery cannot forgive you your debts; three denars will free your oxen." John pleaded, "I do not possess a single coin; have mercy on a poor grazier, Father." And the head priest retorted, "Then you must sell a part of your possessions and bring three denars, for it is better to enter the Kingdom of Heaven without property than to bring the wrath of St. Elija upon you and descend to hell." The other monks nodded their accord.

After a short silence, John's face brightened and his eyes shone as if fear and servility had deserted his heart. With his head high, he looked at the head priest and addressed him boldly, saying, "Do the weak poor have to sell their pitiful belongings, the source of their life's bread, in order to add more gold to the Monastery's wealth? Is it just that the poor should be oppressed and made poorer in order that St. Elija may forgive the oxen their innocent wrongs?" The head priest raised his eyes to heaven and intoned, "It is written in the Book of God that he who has plenty shall be given more, and he who has not shall be taken from."

When John heard these words he became furious, and like a soldier who draws his sword in the face of the enemy, he drew the New Testament from his pocket and shouted out, "This is how you twist the teachings of Christ, you hypocrite! And thus do you pervert the most sacred heritage of life in order to spread your evils. . . . Woe to you when the Son of Man comes again and destroys your Monastery and throws its debris in the valley, and burns your shrine and altars into ashes. . . . Woe to you when the wrath of the Nazarene descends upon you and throws you into the depths of the abyss. . . . Woe to you, worshippers of the idols of greed, who hide the ugliness of hatred under your black garments. . . . Woe to you, foes of Jesus, who move your lips with prayers while your hearts are laden with lusts. . . . Woe to you who kneel before the altar in body while your spirits are revolting against God! You are polluted with your own sin of punishing me for approaching your land, paid for by me and my ancestors. You ridiculed me when I asked for mercy in the name of Christ. Take this Book and show your smiling monks where the Son of God ever refused to forgive. . . . Read this heavenly tragedy and tell them where He spoke not of mercy and of kindness, be it in the Sermon of the Mount, or in the temple. Did He not forgive the adulteress her sins? Did He not part his hands upon the Cross to embrace humanity? Look upon our wretched homes, where the sick suffer upon their hard beds. . . . Look behind the prison bars, where the innocent man is victim of oppression and injustice. . . . Look upon the beggars, stretching forth their hands for alms, humiliated in heart and broken in body. . . . Think upon your slaving followers, who are suffering the pangs of hunger while you are living a life of luxury and indifference, and enjoying the fruits of the fields and the wine of the vineyards. You have never visited a sufferer nor consoled the down-hearted nor fed the hungry; neither have you sheltered the wayfarer nor offered sympathy to the lame. Yet you are not satisfied with what you have pilfered from our fathers, but still stretch your hands like vipers' heads, grasping by threats of hell what little a widow has saved through body-breaking toil, or a miserable fellah has stored away to keep his children alive!"

John took a deep breath, then calmed his voice and quietly added, "You are numerous, and I am alone—you may do unto me what you wish; the wolves prey upon the lamb in the darkness of the night, but the blood stains remain upon the stones in the valley until the dawn comes, and the sun reveals the crime to all."

There was a magic power in John's talk that arrested their attention and injected a defensive anger into the monks' hearts. They were shaking with fury and waiting only for their superior's order to fall upon John and bring him to submission. The brief silence was like the heavy quiet of the tempest, after laying waste the gardens. The head priest then commanded the monks, saying, "Bind this criminal and take the Book from him and drag him into a dark cell, for he who blasphemes the holy representatives of God will never be forgiven on this earth, neither in Eternity." The Monks leaped upon John and led him manacled into a narrow prison and barred him there.

The courage shown by John could not be perceived or understood by one who partakes of the submission or the deceit or the tyranny of this enslaved country, called by the Orientals "The Bride of Syria," and "The Pearl of the Sultan's Crown." And in his cell, John thought of the needless misery brought upon his countrymen by the grip of the things he had just learned. He smiled with a sad sympathy and his smile was mingled with suffering and bitterness; the kind that cuts its way through the depths of the heart; the kind that sets the soul to a choking futility; the kind which, if left unsupported, ascends to the eyes and falls down helplessly.

John then stood proudly, and looked through the window-slit facing the sunlit valley. He felt as if a spiritual joy were embracing his soul and a sweet tranquility possessing his heart. They had imprisoned his body, but his spirit was sailing freely with the breeze amidst the knolls and prairies. His love for Jesus never changed, and the torturing lands could not remove his heart's ease, for persecution cannot harm him who stands by Truth. Did not Socrates fall proudly a victim in body? Was not Paul stoned for the sake of the Truth? It is our inner self that hurts us when we disobey and kills us when we betray.

John's parents were informed of his imprisonment and the confiscation of the oxen. His old mother came to the Monastery leaning heavily over her walking stick and she prostrated herself before the head priest, kissing his feet and begging him for mercy upon her only son. The head priest raised his head reverently toward heaven and said, "We will forgive your son for his madness, but St. Elija will not forgive any who trespass upon his land." After gazing at him with tearful eyes, the old lady took a silver locket from her neck and handed it to the head priest, saying, "This is my most precious possession, given to me as a wedding gift by my mother. . . . Will you accept it as atonement for my son's sin?"

The head priest took the locket and placed it in his pocket, whereupon he looked at John's ancient mother who was kissing his hands and expressing to him her thanks and gratitude, and he said, "Woe to this sinful age! You twist the saying of the Good Book and cause the children to eat the sour, and the parents' teeth sit on edge; go now, good woman, and pray to God for your mad son and ask Him to restore his mind."

John left the prison, and walked quietly by the side of his mother, driving the oxen before him. When they reached their wretched hovel, he led the animals into their mangers and sat silently by the window, meditating the sunset. In a few moments he heard his father whispering to his mother, saying, "Sara, many times have I told you that John was mad, and you disbelieved. Now you will agree, after what you have seen, for the head priest has spoken to you today the very words I spoke to you in past years." John continued looking toward the distant horizon, watching the sun descend.

Easter arrived, and at that time the construction of a new church in the town of Bsherri had just been completed. This magnificent place of worship was like a prince's palace standing amidst the huts of poor subjects. The people were scurrying through the many preparations to receive a prelate who was assigned to officiate at the religious ceremonies inaugurating the new temple. The multitudes stood in rows over the roads waiting for His Grace's arrival. The chanting of the priests in unison with cymbal sounds and the hymns of the throngs filled the sky.

The prelate finally arrived, riding a magnificent horse harnessed with a gold-studded saddle, and as he dismounted, the priests and political leaders met him with the most beautiful of welcoming speeches.

He was escorted to the new altar, where he clothed himself in ecclesiastical raiment, decorated with gold threads and encrusted with sparkling gems; he wore the golden crown, and walked in a procession around the altar, carrying his jewelled staff. He was followed by the priests and the carriers of tapers and incense burners.

At that hour, John stood amongst the fellahin at the portico, contemplating the scene with bitter sighs and sorrowful eyes, for it pained him to observe the expensive robes, and precious crown, and staff, and vases and other objects of needless extravagance, while the poor fellahin who came from the surrounding villages to celebrate the occasion were suffering the gnawing pangs of poverty. Their tattered swaddles and sorrowful faces bespoke their miserable plight.

The rich dignitaries, decorated with badges and ribbons, stood aloof praying loudly, while the suffering villagers, in the rear of the scene, beat their bosoms in sincere prayer that came from the depths of their broken hearts.

The authority of those dignitaries and leaders was like the ever-green leaves of the poplar trees, and the life of those fellahin was like a boat whose pilot had met his destiny and whose rudder had been lost and whose sails had been torn by the strong wind and left at the mercy of the furious depths and the raging tempest.

Tyranny and blind submission . . . which one of

these gave birth to the other? Is tyranny a strong tree that grows not in the low earth, or is it submission, which is like a deserted field where naught but thorns can grow? Such thoughts and contemplations preyed on John's mind while the ceremonies were taking place; he braced his arms about his chest for fear his bosom would burst with agony over the people's plight in this tragedy of opposites.

He gazed upon the withering creatures of severe humanity, whose hearts were dry and whose seeds were now seeking shelter in the bosom of the earth, as destitute pilgrims seek rebirth in a new realm.

When the pageantry came to an end and the multitude was preparing to disperse, John felt that a compelling power was urging him to speak in behalf of the oppressed poor. He proceeded to an extreme end of the square, raised his hands toward the sky, and as the throngs gathered about, he opened his lips and said, "O Jesus, Who art sitting in the heart of the circle of light, give heed! Look upon this earth from behind the blue dome and see how the thorns have choked the flowers which Thy truth hast planted.

"Oh Good Shepherd, the wolves have preyed upon the weak lamb which Thou hast carried in Thy arms. Thy pure blood has been drawn into the depths of the earth which Thy feet have made sacred. This good earth has been made by Thine enemies into an arena where the strong crushes the weak. The cry of the miserable and the lamentation of the helpless can no longer be heard by those sitting upon the thrones, preaching Thy word. The lambs which Thou hast sent to this earth are now wolves who eat the one which Thou hast carried and blessed.

"The word of light which sprang forth from Thy heart has vanished from the scripture and is replaced with an empty and terrible uproar that frightens the spirit.

"Oh Jesus, they have built these churches for the sake of their own glory, and embellished them with silk and melted gold. . . . They left the bodies of Thy chosen poor wrapped in tattered raiment in the cold night. . . . They filled the sky with the smoke of burning candles and incense and left the bodies of Thy faithful worshippers empty of bread. . . . They raised their voices with hymns of praise, but deafened themselves to the cry and moan of the widows and orphans.

"Come again, Oh Living Jesus, and drive the vendors of Thy faith from Thy sacred temple, for they have turned it into a dark cave where vipers of hypocrisy and falsehood crawl and abound."

John's words, strong and sincere, brought murmurs of approval, and the approach of the dignitaries quelled him not. With added courage, strengthened by memories of his earlier experience, he continued, "Come, Oh Jesus, and render accounts with those Caesars who usurped from the weak what is the weak's and from God what is God's. The grapevine which Thou hast planted with Thy right hand has been eaten by worms of greed and its bunches have been trampled down. Thy sons of peace are dividing amongst themselves and fighting one with another, leaving poor souls as victims in the wintry field. Before Thy altar, they raise their voices with prayers, saying, 'Glory to God in the highest, and on earth peace, good will toward men.' Will our Father in heaven be glorified when His name is uttered by empty hearts and sinful lips and false tongues? Will peace be on earth while the sons of misery are slaving in the fields to feed the strong and fill the stomachs of the tyrants? Will ever peace come and save them from the clutches of destitution?

"What is peace? Is it in the eyes of those infants, nursing upon the dry breasts of their hungry mothers in cold huts? Or is it in the wretched hovels of the hungry who sleep upon hard beds and crave for one bite of the food which the priests and monks feed to their fat pigs?

"What is joy, Oh Beautiful Jesus? Is it manifest when the Emir buys the strong arms of men and the honour of women for threats of death or for a few pieces of silver? Or is it found in submission, and slaving of body and spirit to those who dazzle our eyes with their glittering badges and golden diadems? Upon each complaint to Thy peace makers, they reward us with their soldiers, armed with swords and spears to step upon our women and children and steal our blood.

"Oh Jesus, full of love and mercy, stretch forth

Thy strong arms and protect us from those thieves or send welcome Death to deliver us and lead us to the graves where we can rest peacefully under the watchful care of Thy Cross; there we shall wait for Thy return. Oh Mighty Jesus, this life is naught but a dark cell of enslavement. . . . It is a playing ground of horrible ghosts, and it is a pit alive with spectres of death. Our days are but sharp words concealed under the ragged quilts of our beds in the fearful darkness of the night. At dawn, these weapons rise above our heads as demons, pointing out to us our whip-driven slavery in the fields.

"Oh Jesus, have mercy upon the oppressed poor who came today to commemorate Thy Resurrection. . . . Pity them, for they are miserable and weak."

John's talk appealed to one group and displeased another. "He is telling the truth, and speaking in our behalf before heaven," one remarked. And another one said, "He is bewitched, for he speaks in the name of an evil spirit." And a third commented, "We have never heard such infamous talk, not even from our fathers! We must bring it to an end!" And a fourth one said, whispering into the next man's ears, "I felt a new spirit in me when I heard him talking." The next man added, "But the priests know our needs more so than he does; it is a sin to doubt them." As the voices grew from every direction like the roar of the sea, one of the priests approached, placed John in restraint and turned him immediately to the law, whereupon he was taken to the Governor's palace for trial.

Upon his interrogation, John uttered not a single word, for he knew that the Nazarene resorted to silence before His persecutors. The governor ordered John to be placed in a prison, where he slept peacefully and heart-cleansed that night, leaning his head on the rock wall of the dungeon.

The next day John's father came and testified before the Governor that his son was mad, and added, sadly, "Many times have I heard him talking to himself and speaking of many strange things that none could see or understand. Many times did he sit talking in the silence of the night, using vague words. I heard him calling the ghosts with a voice like that of a sorcerer. You may ask the neighbors who talked to him and found beyond doubt that he was insane. He never answered when one spoke to him, and when he spoke, he uttered cryptic words and phrases unknown to the listener and out of the subject. His mother knows him well. Many times she saw him gazing at the distant horizon with glazed eyes and speaking with passion, like a small child, about the brooks and the flowers and the stars. Ask the monks whose teachings he ridiculed and criticized during their sacred Lent. He is insane, Your Excellency, but he is very kind to me and to his mother; he does much to help us in our old age, and he works with diligence to keep us fed and warm and alive. Pity him, and have mercy on us."

The Governor released John, and the news of his madness spread throughout the village. And when the people spoke of John they mentioned his name with humour and ridicule, and the maidens looked upon him with sorrowful eyes and said, "Heaven has its strange purpose in man. . . . God united beauty and insanity in this youth, and joined the kind brightness of his eyes with the darkness of his unseen self."

In the midst of God's fields and prairies, and by the side of the knolls, carpeted with green grass and beautiful flowers, the ghost of John, alone and restless, watches the oxen grazing peacefully, undisturbed by man's hardships. With tearful eyes he looks toward the scattered villages on both sides of the valley and repeats with deep sighs, "You are numerous and I am alone; the wolves prey upon the lambs in the darkness of the night, but the blood stains remain upon the stones in the valley until the dawn comes, and the sun reveals the crime to all."

WE AND YOU

We are the sons of Sorrow, and you are the
Sons of Joy. We are the sons of Sorrow,
And Sorrow is the shadow of a God who
Lives not in the domain of evil hearts.

We are sorrowful spirits, and Sorrow is
Too great to exist in small hearts.
When you laugh, we cry and lament; and he
Who is seared and cleansed once with his
Own tears will remain pure forevermore.

You understand us not, but we offer our
Sympathy to you. You are racing with the
Current of the River of Life, and you
Do not look upon us; but we are sitting by
The coast, watching you and hearing your
Strange voices.

You do not comprehend our cry, for the
Clamour of the days is crowding your ears,
Blocked with the hard substance of your
Years of indifference to truth; but we hear
Your songs, for the whispering of the night

Has opened our inner hearts. We see you
Standing under the pointing finger of light,
But you cannot see us, for we are tarrying
In the enlightening darkness.

We are the sons of Sorrow; we are the poets
And the prophets and the musicians. We weave
Raiment for the goddess from the threads of
Our hearts, and we fill the hands of the
Angels with the seeds of our inner selves.

You are the sons of the pursuit of earthly
Gaiety. You place your hearts in the hands
Of Emptiness, for the hand's touch to
Emptiness is smooth and inviting.

You reside in the house of Ignorance, for
In his house there is no mirror in which to
View your souls.

We sigh, and from our sighs arise the
Whispering of flowers and the rustling of
Leaves and the murmur of rivulets.

When you ridicule us your taunts mingle
With the crushing of the skulls and the
Rattling of shackles and the wailing of the
Abyss. When we cry, our tears fall into the
Heart of Life, as dew drops fall from the
Eyes of Night into the heart of Dawn; and
When you laugh, your mocking laughter pours
Down like the viper's venom into a wound.

We cry, and sympathize with the miserable
Wanderer and distressed widow; but you rejoice
And smile at the sight of resplendent gold.

We cry, for we listen to the moaning of the
Poor and the grieving of the oppressed weak;
But you laugh, for you hear naught but the
Happy sound of the wine goblets.

We cry, for our spirits are at the moment
Separated from God; but you laugh, for your
Bodies cling with unconcern to the earth.

We are the sons of Sorrow, and you are the
Sons of Joy. . . . Let us measure the outcome of
Our sorrow against the deeds of your joy
Before the face of the Sun. . . .

You have built the Pyramids upon the hearts
Of slaves, but the Pyramids stand now upon
The sand, commemorating to the Ages our
Immortality and your evanescence.

You have built Babylon upon the bones of the
Weak, and erected the palaces of Nineveh upon
The graves of the miserable. Babylon is now but
The footprint of the camel upon the moving sand
Of the desert, and its history is repeated
To the nations who bless us and curse you.

We have carved Ishtar from solid marble,
And made it to quiver in its solidity and
Speak through its muteness.

We have composed and played the soothing
Song of Nahawand upon the strings, and caused
The Beloved's spirit to come hovering in the
Firmament near to us; we have praised the
Supreme Being with words and deeds; the words
Became as the words of God, and the deeds
Became overwhelming love of the angels.

You are following Amusement, whose sharp claws
Have torn thousands of martyrs in the arenas
Of Rome and Antioch. . . . But we are following
Silence, whose careful fingers have woven the
Iliad and the Book of Job and the Lamentations
Of Jeremiah.

You lie down with Lust, whose tempest has
Swept one thousand processions of the soul of
Woman away and into the pit of shame and
Horror. . . . But we embrace Solitude, in whose
Shadow the beauties of Hamlet and Dante arose.

You curry for the favor of Greed, and the sharp
Swords of Greed have shed one thousand rivers
Of blood. . . . But we seek company with Truth,
And the hands of Truth have brought down
Knowledge from the Great Heart of the Circle
Of Light.

We are the sons of Sorrow, and you are the
Sons of Joy; and between our sorrow and your
Joy there is a rough and narrow path which

Your spirited horses cannot travel, and upon
Which your magnificent carriages cannot pass.

We pity your smallness as you hate our
Greatness; and between our pity and your
Hatred, Time halts bewildered. We come to
You as friends, but you attack us as enemies;
And between our friendship and your enmity,
There is a deep ravine flowing with tears
And blood.

We build palaces for you, and you dig graves
For us; and between the beauty of the palace
And the obscurity of the grave, Humanity
Walks as a sentry with iron weapons.

We spread your path with roses, and you cover
Our beds with thorns; and between the roses
And the thorns, Truth slumbers fitfully.

Since the beginning of the world you have
Fought against our gentle power with your
Coarse weakness; and when you triumph over
Us for an hour, you croak and clamour merrily
Like the frogs of the water. And when we
Conquer you and subdue you for an Age, we
Remain as silent giants.

You crucified Jesus and stood below Him,
Blaspheming and mocking at Him; but at last
He came down and overcame the generations,

And walked among you as a hero, filling the
Universe with His glory and His beauty.

You poisoned Socrates and stoned Paul and
Destroyed Ali Talib and assassinated
Madhat Pasha, and yet those immortals are
With us forever before the face of Eternity.

But you live in the memory of man like
Corpses upon the face of the earth; and you
Cannot find a friend who will bury you in
The obscurity of non-existence and oblivion,
Which you sought on earth.

We are the sons of Sorrow, and sorrow is a
Rich cloud, showering the multitudes with
Knowledge and Truth. You are the sons of
Joy, and as high as your joy may reach,
By the Law of God it must be destroyed
Before the winds of heaven and dispersed
Into nothingness, for it is naught but a
Thin and wavering pillar of smoke.

THE HOUSE OF FORTUNE

My wearied heart bade me farewell and left for the House of Fortune. As he reached that holy city which the soul had blessed and worshipped, he commenced wondering, for he could not find what he had always imagined would be there. The city was empty of power, money, and authority.

And my heart spoke to the daughter of Love saying, "Oh Love, where can I find Contentment? I heard that she had come here to join you."

And the daughter of Love responded, "Contentment has already gone to preach her gospel in the city, where greed and corruption are paramount; we are not in need of her."

Fortune craves not Contentment, for it is an earthly hope, and its desires are embraced by union with objects, while Contentment is naught but heartfelt.

The eternal soul is never contented; it ever seeks exaltation. Then my heart looked upon Life of Beauty and said, "Thou art all knowledge; enlighten me as to the mystery of Woman." And he answered, "Oh human heart, woman is your own reflection, and whatever you are, she is; wherever you live, she lives; she is like religion if not interpreted by the ignorant, and like a moon, if not veiled with clouds, and like a breeze, if not poisoned with impurities."

And my heart walked toward Knowledge, the daughter of Love and Beauty, and said, "Bestow upon me wisdom, that I might share it with the people." And she responded, "Say not wisdom, but rather fortune, for real fortune comes not from outside, but begins in the Holy of Holies of life. Share of thyself with the people."

TWO INFANTS

A PRINCE stood on the balcony of his palace addressing a great multitude summoned for the occasion and said, "Let me offer you and this whole fortunate country my congratulations upon the birth of a new prince who will carry the name of my noble family, and of whom you will be justly proud. He is the new bearer of a great and illustrious ancestry, and upon him depends the brilliant future of this realm. Sing and be merry!" The voices of the throngs, full of joy and thankfulness, flooded the sky with exhilarating song, welcoming the new tyrant who would affix the yoke of oppression to their necks by ruling the weak with bitter authority, and exploiting their bodies and killing their souls. For that destiny, the people were singing and drinking ecstatically to the health of the new Emir.

Another child entered life and that kingdom at the same time. While the crowds were glorifying the strong and belittling themselves by singing praise to a potential despot, and while the angels of heaven were weeping over the people's weakness and servitude, a sick woman was thinking. She lived in an old, deserted hovel and, lying in her hard bed beside her newly-born infant wrapped with ragged swaddles, was starving to death. She was a penurious and miserable young wife neglected by humanity; her husband had fallen into the trap of death set by the prince's oppression, leaving a solitary woman to whom God had sent, that night, a tiny companion to prevent her from working and sustaining life.

As the mass dispersed and silence was restored to the vicinity, the wretched woman placed the infant on her lap and looked into his face and wept as if she were to baptize him with tears. And with a hunger-weakened voice she spoke to the child saying, "Why have you left the spiritual world and come to share with me the bitterness of earthly life? Why have you deserted the angels and the spacious firmament and come to this miserable land of humans, filled with agony, oppression, and heartlessness? I have nothing to give you except tears; will you be nourished on tears instead of milk? I have no silk clothes to put on you; will my naked, shivering arms give you warmth? The little animals graze in the pasture and return safely to their shed; and the small birds pick the seeds and sleep placidly between the branches. But you, my beloved, have naught save a loving but destitute mother."

Then she took the infant to her withered breast and clasped her arms around him as if wanting to join the two bodies in one, as before. She lifted her burning eyes slowly toward heaven and cried, "God! Have mercy on my unfortunate countrymen!"

At that moment the clouds floated from the face of the moon, whose beams penetrated the transom of that poor home and fell upon two corpses.

THE DAY OF MY BIRTH

It was on this day of the year that my
Mother brought me into the world; on
This day, a quarter-century past, the
Great silence placed me between the arms
Of Existence, replete with lamentation
And tears and conflicts.

Twenty-five times have I encircled the
Blazing sun, and many times more has the
Moon encircled my smallness; yet, I have
Not learned the secrets of light, neither
Do I comprehend the mystery of darkness.

I have journeyed these twenty-five years
With the earth and the sun and the planets
Through the Supreme Infinite; yet, my soul
Yearns for understanding of the Eternal Law
As the hollow grotto reverberates with the
Echo of the waves of the sea, but never fills.

Life exists through the existence of the
Heavenly system, but is not aware of the
Unbounded might of the firmament; and the

Soul sings the praise of the ebb and flow
Of a heavenly melody, but does not perceive
Its meaning.

Twenty-five years past, the hand of Time
Recorded my being, and I am a living page
In the book of the universe; yet, I am now
But naught; but a vague word with meaning
Of complication symbolizing now nothing,
And then many things.

Meditations and memories, on this day of
Each year, congest my soul and halt the
Procession of life, revealing to me the
Phantoms of wasted nights, and sweeping
Them away as the great wind disperses the
Thin cloud from the horizon. And they
Vanish in the obscured corner of my hut
As the murmur of the narrow stream must
Vanish in the distant, broadened valley.

On this day of each year, the spirits
Which have fashioned my soul visit with
Me from all of Eternity and gather about
Me, chanting the sorrowful hymns of memories
Then they retreat swiftly and disappear
Behind the visible objects like a flock of
Birds descending upon a deserted threshing
Floor whereupon they find no seeds; they
Hover in disappointment and depart quickly
For a more rewarding place.

THE DAY OF MY BIRTH

On this day I meditate upon the past,
Whose purpose puzzles me in mind and
Confuses me in heart, and I look
Upon it as I look into a hazy mirror
In which I see naught but death-like
Countenances upon the past years.
As I gaze again, I see my own self
Staring upon my sorrowful self, and
I question Sorrow but find him mute.
Sorrow, if able to speak, would
Prove sweeter than the joy of song.

During my twenty-five years of life
I have loved many things, and often
I loved that which the people hated,
And loathed that which the people
Loved.

And that which I loved when I was a
Child, I still love, and shall continue
To love forevermore. The power to
Love is God's greatest gift to man,
For it never will be taken from the
Blessed one who loves.

I love death, and entitle it with
Sweet names, and praise it with
Loving words, secretly and to the
Throngs of taunting listeners.

Although I have not renounced my great
Allegiance to death, I became deeply

Enamoured with life also, for life and
Death are equal to me in charm and
Sweetness and attraction, and they
Have joined hands in fostering in me
My longings and affections, and in
Sharing with me my love and suffering.

I love freedom, and my love for true
Freedom grew with my growing knowledge
Of the people's surrender to slavery
And oppression and tyranny, and of
Their submission to the horrible idols
Erected by the past ages and polished
By the parched lips of the slaves.

But I love those slaves with my love
For freedom, for they blindly kissed
The jaws of ferocious beasts in calm
And blissful unawareness, feeling not
The venom of the smiling vipers, and
Unknowingly digging their graves with
Their own fingers.

My love for freedom is my greatest love,
For I have found it to be a lovely
Maiden, frailed by aloneness and
Withered by solitude until she became
As a spectre wandering in the midst
Of the dwellings unrecognized and
Unwelcome, and stopping by the waysides
And calling to the wayfarers who did
Not offer heed.

During this score and five years I have
Loved happiness as all men love happiness.
I was in constant search of her but did
Not find her in man's pathway; nor did
I observe the imprints of her footsteps
Upon the sand before man's palaces;
Neither did I hear the echo of her voice
From the windows of man's temples.

I sought happiness in my solitude, and
As I drew close to her I heard my soul
Whisper into my heart, saying, "The
Happiness you seek is a virgin, born
And reared in the depths of each heart,
And she emerges not from her birthplace."
And when I opened my heart to find her,
I discovered in its domain only her
Mirror and her cradle and her raiment,
And happiness was not there.

I love mankind and I love equally all
Three human kinds . . . the one who
Blasphemes life, the one who blesses
It, and the one who meditates upon it.
I love the first for his misery and
The second for his generosity and the
Third for his perception and peace.

Thus, with love, did five and twenty
Years race into nothingness, and thus
Swiftly sped the days and the nights,

Falling from the roadway of my life
And fluttering away like the drying
Leaves of the trees before the winds of
Autumn.

Today I stopped on my road, like the
Weary traveler who has not reached his
Destination but seeks to ascertain his
Position. I look in every direction, but
Cannot find trace of any part of my past
At which I might point and say, "This is
Mine!"

Nor can I reap harvest from the seasons
Of my years, for my bins boast only
These parchments upon which the black
Ink is traced, and these paintings,
Upon which appear simple lines and colours.

With these papers and pictures I have
Succeeded only in shrouding and burying
My love and my thoughts and my dreams,
Even as the sower buries the seeds in
The heart of the earth.

But when the sower sows the seeds in
The heart of the earth he returns home
At eventide, hoping and waiting for
The day of harvest; but I have sown
The inner seeds of my heart in despair,
And hoping and waiting are in vain.

And now, since I have made my five and
Twenty journeys about the sun, I look
Upon the past from behind a deep veil
Of sighs and sorrows, and the silent
Future enlightens itself to me only
Through the sad lamp of the past.

I stare at the universe through the
Transom of my hut and behold the faces
Of men, and hear their voices rise into
Space and hear their footsteps falling
Into the stones; and I perceive the
Revelations of their spirits and the
Vibrations of their desires and the
Throbbings of their hearts.

And I see the children, running and
Laughing and playing and crying; and
I observe the youth walking with their
Heads lifted upward as if reading and
Singing the Kaseeda of youth between
The margins of their eyes, lined with
The radiant rays of the sun.

And I behold the maidens, who are walking
Gracefully and swaying like tender
Branches, and smiling like flowers, and
Gazing upon the youths from behind the
Quivering eyes of love.

And I see the aged walking slowly with
Bent backs, leaning upon their walking

Staffs, staring at the earth as though
Seeking there a treasure lost in youth.

I observe these images and phantoms
Moving and crawling in the paths and
Roadways of the city.

Then I look beyond the city and meditate
Upon the wilderness and its revered
Beauty and its speaking silence; its
Knolls and valleys and lofty trees; its
Fragrant flowers and brisk brooks and
Singing birds.

Then I look beyond the wilderness and
Contemplate the sea with all the magical
Wonders and secrets of its depths, and
The foaming and raging waves of its
Surface. The depths are calm.

Then I gaze beyond the ocean and see the
Infinite sky with its glittering stars;
And its suns and moons and planets; its
Gigantic forces and its myriad elements
That comply unerringly with a great
Law possessing neither a beginning nor
An ending.

Upon these things I ponder from between
My walls, forgetting my twenty-five
Years and all the years which preceded
Them and all the centuries to come.

At this moment my own existence and
All of my environs seem as the weak
Sigh of a small child trembling in the
Deep and eternal emptiness of a supreme
And boundless space.

But this insignificant entity . . .
This self which is myself, and whose
Motion and clamour I hear constantly,
Is now lifting strengthening wings
Toward the spacious firmament,
Extending hands in all directions,
Swaying and shivering upon this day
Which brought me into life, and life
Into me.

And then a tremendous voice arises
From the Holy of Holies within me,
Saying, "Peace be with you, Life!
Peace be with you, Awakening!
Peace be with you, Revelation!

"Peace be with you, oh Day, who
Engulfs the darkness of the earth
With thy brilliant light!

"Peace be with you, oh Night,
Through whose darkness the lights
Of heaven sparkle!

"Peace be with you, Seasons of the
Year!
Peace be with you, Spring, who

Restores the earth to youth!
Peace be with you, Summer, who
Heralds the glory of the sun!
Peace be with you, Autumn, who
Gives with joy the fruits of
Labour and the harvest of toil!
Peace be with you, Winter, whose
Rage and tempest restore to
Nature her sleeping strength!

"Peace be with you, Years, who
Reveal what the years concealed!
Peace be with you, Ages, who
Build what the ages destroyed!
Peace be with you, Time, who leads
Us to the fullness of death!
Peace be with you, Heart, who
Throbs in peace while submerged
In tears!
Peace be with you, Lips, who
Utter joyous words of salaam while
Tasting the gall and the vinegar
Of life!
Peace be with you, Soul, who
Directs the rudder of life and
Death while hidden from us
Behind the curtain of the sun!"

BOOK
3

THE CRIMINAL

A YOUNG man of strong body, weakened by hunger, sat on the walker's portion of the street stretching his hand toward all who passed, begging and repeating the sad song of his defeat in life, while suffering from hunger and from humiliation.

When night came, his lips and tongue were parched, while his hand was still as empty as his stomach.

He gathered himself and went out from the city, where he sat under a tree and wept bitterly. Then he lifted his puzzled eyes to heaven while hunger was eating his inside, and he said, "Oh Lord, I went to the rich man and asked for employment, but he turned away because of my shabbiness; I knocked at the school door, but was forbidden solace because I was empty-handed; I sought any occupation that would give me bread, but all to no avail. In desperation I asked alms, but Thy worshippers saw me and said, "He is strong and lazy, and he should not beg."

"Oh Lord, it is Thy will that my mother gave

birth unto me, and now the earth offers me back to You before the Ending."

His expression then changed. He arose and his eyes now glittered in determination. He fashioned a thick and heavy stick from the branch of the tree, and pointed it toward the city, shouting, "I asked for bread with all the strength of my voice, and was refused. Now I shall obtain it by the strength of my muscles! I asked for bread in the name of mercy and love, but humanity did not heed. I shall take it now in the name of evil!"

The passing years rendered the youth a robber, killer, and destroyer of souls; he crushed all who opposed him; he amassed fabulous wealth with which he won himself over to those in power. He was admired by colleagues, envied by other thieves, and feared by the multitudes.

His riches and false position prevailed upon the Emir to appoint him deputy in that city—the sad process pursued by unwise governors. Thefts were then legalized; oppression was supported by authority; crushing of the weak became commonplace; the throngs curried and praised.

Thus does the first touch of humanity's selfishness make criminals of the humble, and make killers of the sons of peace; thus does the early greed of humanity grow and strike back at humanity a thousandfold!

HAVE MERCY ON ME, MY SOUL!

WHY ARE you weeping, my Soul?
Knowest thou my weakness?
Thy tears strike sharp and injure,
For I know not my wrong.
Until when shalt thou cry?
I have naught but human words
To interpret your dreams,
Your desires, and your instructions.

Look upon me, my Soul; I have
Consumed my full life heeding
Your teachings. Think of how
I suffer! I have exhausted my
Life following you.

My heart was glorying upon the
Throne, but is now yoked in slavery;
My patience was a companion, but
Now contends against me;
My youth was my hope, but
Now reprimands my neglect.

Why, my Soul, are you all-demanding?
I have denied myself pleasure
And deserted the joy of life
Following the course which you
Impelled me to pursue.
Be just to me, or call Death
To unshackle me,
For justice is your glory.

Have mercy on me, my Soul.
You have laden me with Love until
I cannot carry my burden. You and
Love are inseparable might; Substance
And I are inseparable weakness.
Will e'er the struggle cease
Between the strong and the weak?

Have mercy on me, my Soul.
You have shown me Fortune beyond
My grasp. You and Fortune abide on
The mountain top; Misery and I are
Abandoned together in the pit of
The valley. Will e'er the mountain
And the valley unite?

Have mercy on me, my Soul.
You have shown me Beauty, but then
Concealed her. You and Beauty live
In the light; Ignorance and I are
Bound together in the dark. Will
E'er the light invade darkness?

HAVE MERCY ON ME, MY SOUL!

Your delight comes with the Ending,
And you revel now in anticipation;
But this body suffers with life
While in life.
This, my Soul, is perplexing.

You are hastening toward Eternity,
But this body goes slowly toward
Perishment. You do not wait for him,
And he cannot go quickly.
This, my Soul, is sadness.

You ascend high, through heaven's
Attraction, but this body falls by
Earth's gravity. You do not console
Him, and he does not appreciate you.
This, my Soul, is misery.

You are rich in wisdom, but this
Body is poor in understanding.
You do not compromise
And he does not obey.
This, my Soul, is extreme suffering.

In the silence of the night you visit
The Beloved and enjoy the sweetness of
His presence. This body ever remains
The bitter victim of hope and separation.
This, my Soul, is agonizing torture.
Have mercy on me, my Soul!

THE WIDOW AND HER SON

Night fell over North Lebanon and snow was covering the villages surrounded by the Kadeesha Valley, giving the fields and prairies the appearance of a great sheet of parchment upon which the furious Nature was recording her many deeds. Men came home from the streets while silence engulfed the night.

In a lone house near those villages lived a woman who sat by her fireside spinning wool, and at her side was her only child, staring now at the fire and then at his mother.

A terrible roar of thunder shook the house and the little boy took fright. He threw his arms about his mother, seeking protection from Nature in her affection. She took him to her bosom and kissed him; then she sat him on her lap and said, "Do not fear, my son, for Nature is but comparing her great power to man's weakness. There is a Supreme Being beyond the falling snow and the heavy clouds and the blowing wind, and He knows the needs of the earth, for He made it; and He looks upon the weak with merciful eyes.

"Be brave, my boy. Nature smiles in Spring and laughs in Summer and yawns in Autumn, but now she is weeping; and with her tears she waters life, hidden under the earth.

"Sleep, my dear child; your father is viewing us from Eternity. The snow and thunder bring us closer to him at this time.

"Sleep, my beloved, for this white blanket which makes us cold, keeps the seeds warm, and these warlike things will produce beautiful flowers when Nisan comes.

"Thus, my child, man cannot reap love until after sad and revealing separation, and bitter patience, and desperate hardship. Sleep, my little boy; sweet dreams will find your soul who is unafraid of the terrible darkness of night and the biting frost."

The little boy looked upon his mother with sleep-laden eyes and said, "Mother, my eyes are heavy, but I cannot go to sleep without saying my prayer."

The woman looked at his angelic face, her vision blurred by misted eyes, and said, "Repeat with me, my boy—'God, have mercy on the poor and protect them from the winter; warm their thin-clad bodies with Thy merciful hands; look upon the orphans who are sleeping in wretched houses, suffering from hunger and cold. Hear, oh Lord, the call of widows who are helpless and shivering with fear for their young. Open, oh Lord, the hearts of all humans, that they may see the misery of the weak. Have mercy upon the sufferers who knock on doors, and lead the wayfarers into warm places. Watch, oh Lord, over the little birds and protect the trees and fields from the anger of the storm; for Thou art merciful and full of love.' "

As Slumber captured the boy's spirit, his mother placed him in the bed and kissed his eyes with quivering lips. Then she went back and sat by the hearth, spinning the wool to make him raiment.

EVENTIDE OF THE FEAST

NIGHT had fallen and obscurity engulfed the city while the lights glittered in the palaces and the huts and the shops. The multitudes, wearing their festive raiment, crowded the streets and upon their faces appeared the signs of celebration and contentment.

I avoided the clamour of the throngs and walked alone, contemplating the Man Whose greatness they were honouring, and meditating the Genius of the Ages Who was born in poverty, and lived virtuously, and died on the Cross.

I was pondering the burning torch which was lighted in this humble village in Syria by the Holy Spirit. . . . The Holy Spirit Who hovers over all the ages, and penetrates one civilization and then another through His truth.

As I reached the public garden, I seated myself on a rustic bench and commenced looking between the naked trees toward the crowded streets; I listened to the hymns and songs of the celebrants.

After an hour of deep thinking, I looked sidewise

and was surprised to find a man sitting by me, holding a short branch with which he engraved vague figures on the ground. I was startled, for I had not seen nor heard his approach, but I said within myself, "He is solitary, as I am." And after looking thoroughly at him, I saw that in spite of his old-fashioned raiment and long hair, he was a dignified man, worthy of attention. It seemed that he detected the thoughts within me, for in a deep and quiet voice he said, "Good evening, my son."

"Good evening to you," I responded with respect.

And he resumed his drawing while the strangely soothing sound of his voice was still echoing in my ears. And I spoke to him again, saying, "Are you a stranger in this city?"

"Yes, I am a stranger in this city and every city," he replied. I consoled him, adding, "A stranger should forget that he is an outsider in these holidays, for there is kindness and generosity in the people." He replied wearily, "I am more a stranger in these days than in any other." Having thus spoken, he looked at the clear skies; his eyes probed the stars and his lips quivered as if he had found in the firmament an image of a distant country. His queer statement aroused my interest, and I said, "This is the time of the year when the people are kind to all other people. The rich remember the poor and the strong have compassion for the weak."

He returned, "Yes, the momentary mercy of the rich upon the poor is bitter, and the sympathy of the strong toward the weak is naught but a reminder of superiority."

I affirmed, "Your words have merit, but the weak poor do not care to know what transpires in the heart of the rich, and the hungry never think of the method by which the bread he is craving is kneaded and baked."

And he responded, "The one who receives is not mindful, but the one who gives bears the burden of cautioning himself that it is with a view to brotherly love, and toward friendly aid, and not to self-esteem."

I was amazed at his wisdom, and again commenced to meditate upon his ancient appearance and strange garments. Then I returned mentally and said, "It appears that you are in need of help; will you accept a few coins from me?" And with a sad smile he answered me, saying, "Yes, I am in desperate need, but not of gold or silver."

Puzzled, I asked, "What is it that you require?"

"I am in need of shelter. I am in need of a place where I can rest my head and my thoughts."

"Please accept these two denars and go to the inn for lodging," I insisted.

Sorrowfully he answered, "I have tried every inn, and knocked at every door, but in vain. I have entered every food shop, but none cared to help me. I am hurt, not hungry; I am disappointed, not tired; I seek not a roof, but human shelter."

I said within myself, "What a strange person he

is! Once he talks like a philosopher and again like a madman!" As I whispered these thoughts into the ears of my inner self, he stared at me, lowered his voice to a sad level, and said, "Yes, I am a madman, but even a madman will find himself a stranger without shelter and hungry without food, for the heart of man is empty."

I apologized to him, saying, "I regret my unwitting thought. Would you accept my hospitality and take shelter in my quarters?"

"I knocked at your door and all the doors one thousand times, and received no answer," he answered severely.

Now I was convinced that he was truly a madman, and I suggested, "Let us go now, and proceed to my home."

He lifted his head slowly and said, "If you were aware of my identity you would not invite me to your home."

"Who are you?" I inquired, fearfully, slowly.

With a voice that sounded like the roar of the ocean, he thundered, bitterly, "I am the revolution who builds what the nations destroy. . . . I am the tempest who uproots the plants, grown by the ages. . . . I am the one who came to spread war on earth and not peace, for man is content only in misery!"

And, with tears coursing down his cheeks, he stood up high, and a mist of light grew about him, and he stretched forth his arms, and I saw the marks of the nails in the palms of his hands; I prostrated myself before him convulsively and cried out, saying, "Oh Jesus, the Nazarene!"

And He continued, in anguish, "The people are celebrating in My honour, pursuing the tradition woven by the ages around My name, but as to Myself, I am a stranger wandering from East to West upon this earth, and no one knows of Me. The foxes have their holes, and the birds of the skies their nests, but the Son of Man has no place to rest His head."

At that moment, I opened my eyes, lifted my head, and looked around, but found naught except a column of smoke before me, and I heard only the shivering voice of the silence of the night, coming from the depths of Eternity. I collected myself and looked again to the singing throngs in the distance, and a voice within me said, "The very strength that protects the heart from injury is the strength that prevents the heart from enlarging to its intended greatness within. The song of the voice is sweet, but the song of the heart is the pure voice of heaven."

SONG OF THE WAVE

The strong shore is my beloved
And I am his sweetheart.
We are at last united by love, and
Then the moon draws me from him.
I go to him in haste and depart
Reluctantly, with many
Little farewells.

I steal swiftly from behind the
Blue horizon to cast the silver of
My foam upon the gold of his sand, and
We blend in melted brilliance.

I quench his thirst and submerge his
Heart; he softens my voice and subdues
My temper.
At dawn I recite the rules of love upon
His ears, and he embraces me longingly.

At eventide I sing to him the song of
Hope, and then print smooth kisses upon
His face; I am swift and fearful, but he
Is quiet, patient, and thoughtful. His
Broad bosom soothes my restlessness.

As the tide comes we caress each other,
When it withdraws, I drop to his feet in
Prayer.

Many times have I danced around mermaids
As they rose from the depths and rested
Upon my crest to watch the stars;
Many times have I heard lovers complain
Of their smallness, and I helped them to sigh.

Many times have I teased the great rocks
And fondled them with a smile, but never
Have I received laughter from them;
Many times have I lifted drowning souls
And carried them tenderly to my beloved
Shore. He gives them strength as he
Takes mine.

Many times have I stolen gems from the
Depths and presented them to my beloved
Shore. He takes in silence, but still
I give for he welcomes me ever.

In the heaviness of night, when all
Creatures seek the ghost of Slumber, I
Sit up, singing at one time and sighing
At another. I am awake always.

Alas! Sleeplessness has weakened me!
But I am a lover, and the truth of love
Is strong.
I may weary, but I shall never die.

IRAM, CITY OF LOFTY PILLARS

TRANSLATOR'S PROLOGUE

"Seest thou not how thy God
Dealt with Ad of Iram, with
Lofty pillars, the like of
Which were not produced in
All of existence?"
The Holy Quran.

THE AD PEOPLE, with their Prophet Hud, are cited often in the Holy Quran, and their traditions belong to ancient Arabia. Their eponymous ancestor Ad was fourth in generation from Noah, having been a son of Aus, who was the son of Aram, who was the son of Shem, who was the first son of Noah.

They occupied a great tract of southern Arabia, extending from *Umman* at the mouth of the Persian Gulf to *Hadramaut* and *Yemen* at the southern end of the Red Sea, and the long, twisting areas of *ahqaf* (sands) in their domain were irrigated by canals.

The people were of great physical stature, and

were excellent masons and builders. However, as so often happens, their vast advancements resulted in the forsaking of the true God, and the leaders anguished the people with oppression in its most severe state.

A three year famine visited them, but they took no warning, and at length a terrible and tremendous blast of searing wind destroyed them and their civilization. A remnant, known as the Second Ad, or *Thamud,* salvaged itself and survived, but later suffered a similar fate, presumably because of the sins of the people.

The tomb of the Prophet Hud (*Qabr Nabi Hud*) is still shown to visitors in *Hadramaut,* latitude 16 degrees north, longitude 49½ degrees east, about 90 miles north of *Mukalla.* Ruins and inscriptions abound in the general vicinity, and there is an annual pilgrimage to this site in the month of *Rajab.**

Iram appears to have been an ancient Ad capital in southern Arabia, and it boasted lofty architecture. Controversially, some archaeologists and historians believe Iram to be the name of an individual hero of the Ad, and if this be true, the descriptive phrase "lofty pillars" applies not to the edifices, but to the people themselves, for the Ad were a tall race.

This sector, sometimes called *Arabia Felix,* is a source of interest, devotion and prosperity to many Arabs, for in its many ancient remains, numerous

* Bibliography: "Hadramaut—its Mysteries Unveiled," by D. Van Der Meulen and H. Von Wissman, Leyden, 1932. (*Editor's note.*)

objects of historical, religious, and monetary value have been found. In the time of *Muawiya* a rich cache of precious stones was discovered, and more recently some gold, silver, and bronze pieces of statuary bearing Sabaean inscriptions came to light in *Najram*. These have been described in detail in the British Museum Quarterly, Volume 4, September 1937.

The source of the foregoing lineage and geography is the Holy Quran. Kahlil Gibran probably based his play "Iram, the City of Lofty Pillars" on this information, or upon similar Eastern mythology pursuing the general vein of the following brief Arabian fantasy:

"When Shaddad, the son of Ad, became the Great King of the World, he commanded one thousand Emirs to seek for him a vast land abundant with water and pure air, that he might build in it a Golden City afar from the mountains. The rulers roamed throughout the world in quest of such land, and each Emir took with him one thousand men.

"And when it was found, the architects and builders erected within it a square city of forty leagues. They built a huge wall extending five hundred cubits, made of onyx stones, and covered it with sheets of gold that misted the eyes when the sun shone.

"And King Shaddad despatched his people to all parts of the world, and commanded them to dig out gold from the ground, to be used as mortar for the bricks. And he built inside the city walls one hundred thousand palaces for one hundred thousand officials of his kingdom. Each palace was erected upon columns of chrysolite and ruby blended with gold, and each column reached one hundred cubits toward heaven.

"And the rivers were brought through the city, and their tributaries through the palaces. The roadways of the city were gold and precious stones and ruby, and the palaces were adorned richly with gold and silver. Trees were imbedded along the banks of the river, and their branches were of living gold, and their leaves of silver, and their fruits of onyx and pearls. And the walls of the palaces were embellished with musk and ambergris.

"And King Shaddad built for himself a garden whose trees were of emerald and ruby, and upon the branches were singing birds of pure gold."

THE PLAY

IRAM, CITY OF LOFTY PILLARS

The locale of the play: A small forest of walnut, pomegranate and poplar trees. In this forest, between the Orantes River (Nahr el'Asi) and the village of Hermil, stands an old solitary house in a clearing.

The time of the play: Late afternoon in mid-July, 1883.

The characters of the play:

Zain Abedeen of Nahawand, forty years old, who is a Persian Dervish and a mystic.

Najeeb Rahmé, thirty years old, a Lebanese scholar.

Amena Divine, age unknown, prophetic and mysterious, known in the vicinity as the Houri of the Valley.

As the curtain rises, Zain Abedeen is seen leaning his head on one hand, under the trees, and with his long walking staff is inscribing circular figures upon the ground. Najeeb Rahmé enters the clearing on a horse a few moments thereafter. He dismounts, fastens the rein to the trunk of a tree, dusts his clothes and approaches Zain Abedeen.

NAJEEB: Peace be with you, Sir!

ZAIN: And with you be peace. (*He turns his face aside and whispers to himself*): Peace we shall accept . . . but superiority? That is a different matter.

NAJEEB: Is this the abiding place of Amena Divine?

ZAIN: This is but one of her several abodes. She lives in none, yet she exists in all.

NAJEEB: I have inquired of many, vet none knew Amena Divine had numerous dwellings.

ZAIN: This establishes that your informants are people who cannot see except with their eyes, nor hear except through their ears. Amena Divine is everywhere (*points to the east with his staff*) and she roams the knolls and the valleys.

NAJEEB: Will she return to this place today?

ZAIN: Heaven so willing, she will return here today.

NAJEEB: (*Seating himself upon a rock before Zain, and staring at him*): Your beard reveals to me that you are a Persian.

ZAIN: Yes, I was born in Nahawand, reared in Sheezar, and educated in Nisabour. I journeyed through the east and west of the world and returned, for I found myself a stranger to all places.

NAJEEB: We are often strangers to ourselves!

ZAIN: (*Disregarding Najeeb's comment*): Truly, I have encountered and conversed with thousands of men, and could find none but those who are content with their close environs, confining themselves to their small prisons which are the only ones they know and see in this vast world.

NAJEEB: (*Bewildered by Zain's words*): Is not man naturally attached to the place of his birth?

ZAIN: The person who is limited in heart and thought is inclined to love that which is limited in life, and the weak-sighted cannot see more than one cubit ahead upon the path he treads, nor more than one cubit of the wall upon which he rests his shoulder.

NAJEEB: Not all of us are enabled to see with our inner eyes the great depths of life, and it is cruel to demand that the weak-sighted see the dim and the far.

ZAIN: You are correct, but is it not also cruel to press wine from the green grape?

NAJEEB: (*After a brief, contemplative silence*): For many years I have been hearing tales of Amena Divine. I was fascinated with these stories, and determined to meet her and inquire into her secrets and mysteries.

ZAIN: There is no person in this world who is capable of possessing the secrets of Amena Divine, just as there is no human capable of roaming the bottom of the sea as if walking in a garden.

NAJEEB: I beg your pardon, Sir, for I have not rendered clear my purpose. I know that I am not capable of acquiring for myself the unrevealed mysteries of Amena Divine. My prime hope is that she will relate to me the story of her entry into Iram, the City of Lofty Pillars, and the manner of things she found in this Golden City.

ZAIN: You need merely to stand in sincerity at the door of her dream. If it opens, you will reach your goal, and if it does not open, then your own self must bear blame.

NAJEEB: I fail to comprehend your strange words.

ZAIN: They are simple . . . simple by comparison to your great reward should you succeed. Amena Divine knows more about the people than they know about themselves, and she can perceive in one glance all of that which is hidden within them. If she finds you worthy, she will be happy to converse with you and place you upon the true pathway to light. If not, she will ignore you with a strength bespeaking your non-existence.

NAJEEB: What shall I do and what shall I say in order to prove myself worthy?

ZAIN: It is vain and wasteful to endeavour an approach to Amena Divine through mere words or deeds, for she neither listens nor sees. But through the soul of her ear she will hear what you do not say, and through the soul of her eye she will see what you do not do.

NAJEEB: How wise and how beautiful are your words!

ZAIN: Were I to talk of Amena Divine for a century, all I would say would be naught but the humming of a mute who struggles to sing a song of beauty.

NAJEEB: Do you know where this strange woman was born?

ZAIN: Her body was born in the vicinity of Damascus, but all else, greater than substance, was born in the bosom of God.

NAJEEB: What of her parents?

ZAIN: Can that be of consequence? Can you study the element properly by examining its surface alone? Can you foretell the taste of the wine by gazing upon the vessel?

NAJEEB: You speak the truth. Nevertheless, there must be a bond between the spirit and the body, as there is a bond between the body and its immediate surroundings; and while I place no faith in chance, I believe that a knowledge of the background of Amena Divine will be of value to me in probing the secret of her life.

ZAIN: Well spoken! I know naught concerning her mother, except that she died upon the birth of Amena, her only child. Her father was Sheik Abdul Ghany, the famous blind prophet, who was thought to be divine, and recognized as the Imam of his time in mysticism. May his soul receive God's mercy! He was fanatically attached to his daughter, and educated her carefully and poured into her heart all of his heart. And as she grew, he sought that she take from him all of his knowledge and wisdom. In truth, his great learning was slight compared to that knowledge which God had already bestowed upon Amena. And of his daughter he said, "From my painful darkness there came a great light that illuminated my pathway through life." When Amena was twenty-three years old, her father took her with him on a pilgrimage, and when they crossed the Damascus Desert and made their way into the wasteland, and the lighted city disappeared behind them, the blind father became fevered and died. Amena buried him and watched over his grave for seven days and seven nights, calling to his spirit and inquiring into hidden secrets of his soul. And on the seventh night the spirit of her father dismissed her from her vigil and commanded her to travel to the southeast, whereupon she obeyed (*Zain ceases talking, gazes at the distant horizon, and after a few moments continues*): She resumed the journey and fought her way until she reached the heart of the desert, which they call Rabh el Khali, and which no caravan in my knowledge has ever crossed. A few wanderers are said to have reached this place in the early days of the Islamic religion. The pilgrims believed Amena to have been lost, and mourned her as having died in hunger, and upon their return, told the populace of Damascus of the tragedy. All those who had known Sheik Abdul Ghany and his strange daughter lamented them, but as the years passed, they were forgotten. Five years thereafter, Amena Divine appeared in Musil, and because of her supernatural wisdom, knowledge, and beauty, her presence enraptured the people like a silver chip of heaven's night falling from the blue tent.

NAJEEB: (*Interrupting, although obviously interested in Zain's story*): Did Amena reveal her identity to the people?

ZAIN: She disclosed nothing concerning herself. She stood with unveiled face before the Imams and scholars, speaking of divine and immortal things, and describing to them the City of Lofty Pillars in a manner so eloquent as to surprise and captivate her listeners, and the number of her followers increased with each day.

The wise men of the city became envious and complained to the Emir, who summoned her to appear before him, and upon her appearance, he placed in her hands a packet of gold and urged her to depart the borders of the city. She refused to accept the gold and, alone, left the city under the cover of night. She journeyed through Constantinople, Damascus, Homs, and Tripoli, and in every city she brought light into the hearts of the people who gathered about her, drawn by her magic power. However, the Imams of each city opposed her, and continual exile was her lot.

Finally, upon deciding to lead a solitary life, she came to this place a few years ago. She denied herself all things except the love of God and her meditations upon His mysteries. This is but a small picture of the history of Amena Divine. But the blessed power given me by God to understand something of her ideal existence is the same power which, in its overwhelming intoxication of heart, renders me unable to describe in earthly words the wonders of Amena Divine. What human is able to gather in one cup the total wisdom that surrounds this world in many cups?

NAJEEB: My gratitude, Sir, for the interesting and vital information you have offered. My anxiety to see her is now greater than ever!

ZAIN: (*Staring at Najeeb with piercing eyes*): You are a Christian, are you not?

NAJEEB: Yes, I was born a Christian. However, with all regard to my ancestors, who bequeathed to me a religion as well as a name, I must add that if we were to do away with the various religions, we would find ourselves united and enjoying one great faith and religion, abounding in brotherhood.

ZAIN: You speak wisely, and on the matter of a united faith, there is none more abundantly informed than Amena Divine. She is, to the multitudes of all beliefs and ancestries, like the dew of the morn that falls from high and becomes as glittering gems upon the colourful leaves of all of the flowers. Yes . . . she is like the morning dew. . . . (*Zain stops talking at this point, and looks toward the east, listening carefully. Then he stands up, cautioning Najeeb to be alert, and Zain warns in an excited whisper*): Amena Divine approaches! May good fortune be with you!

NAJEEB: (*In a faltering whisper*): My long months of anxiety may soon find reward! (*Najeeb places his hand upon his forehead, as if to calm his leaping nerves, and he senses a change in the character of the atmosphere. Recalling Zain's words of possible failure, his expression of joyful anticipation changes to one of deep concern, but he now remains as motionless as a statue of marble.*)

(*Amena Divine enters and stands before the two*

men. She is draped in long, silken robes, and her features, gestures, and raiment cause her to resemble one of those goddesses worshipped by the past ages, rather than an oriental woman of her actual time. It is impossible to speculate even generally upon her age, for her face, though youthful, is unrevealing, and her deep eyes reflect one thousand years of wisdom and suffering. Najeeb and Zain remain reverently motionless, as if in the presence of one of the prophets of God.)

AMENA: (*After staring at Najeeb as if penetrating his heart with her magnificent eyes; in a serene, confident voice*): You are here to learn about us, but you shall not know more about us than you know about yourself, and you shall hear from us only that which you hear from yourself.

NAJEEB: (*Perplexed, and exhibiting nervous fear*): I have already seen, heard, and believed. . . . I am contented.

AMENA: Be not satisfied with partial contentment, for he who engulfs the spring of life with one empty jar will depart with two full jars. (*Amena extends her hand toward him; he takes it in awe with both hands and kisses the ends of her fingers, impelled by a strong, unknown emotion. She then offers her other hand to Zain Abedeen, and he kisses it. Najeeb appears happy to have pursued the apparently correct procedure first. Amena Divine slowly withdraws herself.*)

AMENA: (*Sits upon a smooth rock and speaks to*

Najeeb): These are the chairs of God. Be seated. (*Najeeb seats himself nearby and Zain does likewise. Amena continues, again to Najeeb*): We see in your eyes the true light of God, and he who looks upon the true light of God will see in us our inner reality. You are sincere, and you love the truth, and therefore you desire to know more of truth. If you have words to say, you have but to speak and we will give heed, and if you have in your heart a question, ask and we will respond in truth.

NAJEEB: I come to inquire upon a matter that has been the consuming topic of conversation among the throngs. But when I found myself in your presence, I realized the enormity of the meaning of life, truth, and God, and now all else is unimportant. I am like the fisherman who threw his net into the sea hoping to find it laden with food for a day of his sustenance, but when he drew the net he found in it a heap of everlasting precious stones.

AMENA: I see in your heart that you have heard about our entry into Iram, the City of Lofty Pillars, and that you desire now to hear further of the Golden City.

NAJEEB: (*Ashamed, yet intensely interested*): Yes, since childhood the name Iram, the City of Lofty Pillars, has been embracing my dreams, preying upon my thoughts, and agitating my heart through its hidden meaning and tremendous significance.

AMENA: (*Lifts her head and closes her eyes, and in a voice that, to Najeeb, seems to be emanating from the very heart of space, she speaks solemnly*): Yes, we reached and entered the Golden City and sojourned there and filled our souls with its fragrance, and our hearts with its secrets, and our pouches with its pearls and its rubies, and our ears with its music, and our eyes with its beauty And he who doubts that which we have seen and heard and found there is doubting his very self before God and man.

NAJEEB: (*Slowly, and with difficulty and humility*): I am naught but an infant, lisping and faltering and unable to express myself. Will you be kind to me and explain further, and forgive my many questions?

AMENA: Ask as you wish, for God has made many doors opening into truth which He opens to all who knock upon them with hands of faith.

NAJEEB: Did you enter Iram, the City of Lofty Pillars, in body or in spirit? Is this Golden City built of the glittering elements of this world and erected in a precise part of this world, or is it an imaginary or spiritual city which only the prophets of God can reach in ecstasy when Providence brings upon their souls a veil of eternity?

AMENA: All on earth, seen and unseen, is spiritual only. I entered the Golden City with my bōdy, which is merely an earthly manifestation of my greater spirit, and which is, in all persons, a temporary vault for the safe-keeping of the spirit. I entered Iram with my body concealed within my spirit, for both are ever-present while on earth, and he who endeavours to cleave the body from the spirit, or the spirit from the body is directing his heart away from truth. The flower and its fragrance are one, and the blind who deny the colour and the image of the flower, believing that it possesses only a fragrance vibrating the ether, are like those with pinched nostrils who believe that flowers are naught but pictures and colours, possessing no fragrance.

NAJEEB: Then Iram, the City of Lofty Pillars, is a spiritual place only!

AMENA: (*Indulgently*): Time and place are spiritual states, and all that is seen and heard is spiritual. If you close your eyes you will perceive all things through the depths of your inner self, and you will see the world physical and ethereal, in its intended entirety, and you will acquaint yourself with its necessary laws and precautions, and you will understand the greatness that it possesses beyond its closeness. Yes . . . if you will close your eyes and open your heart and your inner perception you will discover the beginning and the end of existence . . . that beginning which in its turn becomes an ending, and that ending which must surely become a beginning.

NAJEEB: Is every human capable of thus closing his

eyes and seeing the unclothed truth of life and existence?

AMENA: Man is empowered by God to hope and hope fervently, until that for which he is hoping takes the cloak of oblivion from his eyes, whereupon he will at last view his real self. And he who sees his real self sees the truth of real life for himself, for all humanity, and for all things.

NAJEEB: (*Placing both hands upon his bosom*): Then all I can see and hear and touch and think of in this universe exists right here in my own heart!

AMENA: All things in this vast universe exist in you, with you, and for you.

NAJEEB: Then I may truthfully say that Iram, the City of Lofty Pillars, is not far distant, but is found within *me,* the entity existing as Najeeb Rahmé!

AMENA: All things in this creation exist within you, and all things in you exist in creation; there is no border between you and the closest things, and there is no distance between you and the farthest things, and all things, from the lowest to the loftiest, from the smallest to the greatest, are within you as equal things. In one atom are found all the elements of the earth; in one motion of the mind are found the motions of all the laws of existence; in one drop of water are found the secrets of all the endless oceans; in one aspect of *you* are found all the aspects of *existence.*

NAJEEB: (*Overwhelmed by the vastness of the subject, and after a brief pause, permitting full as-*

similation of his instruction): I was told that you journeyed many days before you reached the heart of the desert of Rabh el Khali, and that your father's spirit revealed itself to you and directed you in your wanderings until you reached the Golden City. If a person should desire to reach that city, need he be in the same spiritual state you possessed at that time, and is it required that he possess your wisdom in order to gain entrance into that celestial place you visited?

AMENA: We crossed the desert and suffered the pangs of hunger and the madness of thirst and the fears of the day and the horrors of the night and the frightening silence of eternity before we saw the walls of the Golden City. But many are those who reached the city of God before us without walking one cubit, and they reveled in its beauty and brightness without sorrowing in body or spirit. Truly I say unto you that many have visited the Sacred City although they never left the places of their birth.

(*Amena Divine interrupts herself and remains silent for a moment. Then she points at the trees and myrtles about her and continues*): For every seed that autumn drops into the heart of the earth, there exists a different manner of splitting the shell from the pulp; then are created the leaves, and then the flowers, and then the fruit. But regardless of the fashion in which this takes place, these plants must undertake one sole pilgrimage, and their great mission is to stand before the face of the sun.

ZAIN (*Moves gracefully back and forth, impressed by Amena as if in a supreme world. In an inspired voice he cries out prayerfully*): God is great! There is no God but Allah, the Merciful, who knows our needs!

AMENA: Allah is great . . . there is no God but Allah . . . there is nothing but Allah!

ZAIN: (*Repeats Amena's words in a scarcely audible whisper, with fervent, visible trembling*).

NAJEEB: (*Stares at Amena Divine as if in a trance, and in a strong, defiant voice says*): There is no God but *God*!

AMENA: (*Surprised*): There is no God but *Allah* . . . there is nothing but *Allah*. You may speak these words and remain a Christian, for a God Who is good knows of no segregations amongst words or names, and were a God to deny His blessing to those who pursue a different path to eternity, then there is no human who should offer worship.*

NAJEEB: (*Bends his head, closes his eyes and repeats Amena's words of prayer to Allah. He raises his head, saying*): I shall say the words to the God who offers me the true pathway to Him, and I shall continue to say them to Him until the end

* The zealous Christian in the Near East is taught that it is a sin to repeat any prayer belonging to the Islamic religion. (*Editor's note.*)

of my life, for I am in search of truth. And my prayers to God are to *The God,* wherever He may be and whatever He may be called. I love God . . . all of my life will I love God.

AMENA: Your life has no end, and you shall live forevermore.

NAJEEB: *Who* am I, and *what* am I, to live unto eternity?

AMENA: You are *you,* and as such, you are a creature of God, and you are therefore everything.

NAJEEB: Amena Divine, I know that the particles of which my own *self* is composed will remain as long as I remain, but will that *thought* which I call *myself* remain? Will this dim, new awakeness, garmented with the light slumber of dawn remain? Will these hopes and desires, sorrows and joys remain? Will these shivering fancies of my disturbed sleep, brilliant in truth's light, remain?

AMENA: (*Raises her eyes toward heaven, as if reaching for something in the great pocket of space. In a clear, strong voice she speaks*): Each thing that exists remains forever, and the very existence of existence is proof of its eternity. But without that realization, which is the knowledge of perfect being, man would never know whether there was existence or non-existence. If eternal existence is altered, then it must become more beautiful; and if it disappears, it must return with more sublime image; and if it sleeps, it must dream of a better awakening, for it is ever greater upon its rebirth.

I feel pity toward those who admit of the eternity of the elements of which the eye is made, but at the same time doubt the eternity of the various objects of sight which employ the eye as a medium.

I feel sympathy for the one who divides life into two parts, and at the same time places faith in one part and doubts the other.

I am saddened by the one who gazes upon the mountains and plains upon which the sun throws its rays, and who listens to the breeze singing the song of the thin branches, and who inhales the fragrance of the flowers and the jasmine, and then says within himself, "No . . . what I see and hear will pass away, and what I know and feel will vanish." This humble soul who sees and contemplates reverently the joys and sorrows about him, and then denies the perpetuity of their existence, must himself vanish like vapour in the air and disappear, for he is seeking darkness and placing his back to truth. Verily, he is a living soul denying *his* very existence, for he denies *other* of God's existing things.

NAJEEB: (*Excited*): Amena Divine, I believe in my existence, and he who listens to your words and does not believe is more the solid rock than a human in being.

AMENA: God has placed in each soul a true guide to the great light, but man struggles to find life outside himself, unaware that the life he is seeking is within him.

NAJEEB: Is there any light outside the body by which we can illuminate the way into our inner depths? Do we possess any power that will stir our spirits and awaken in us the realization of our living oblivion, and point the way to eternal knowledge? (*He becomes silent for a few moments, apparently fearful of proceeding. Then he continues, as if overcoming his reluctance*): Did not your father's soul reveal to you the secret of the earthly imprisonment of the soul?

AMENA: It is vain for the wayfarer to knock upon the door of the empty house. Man is standing mutely between the non-existence within him and the reality of his surroundings. If we did not possess what we have within ourselves we could not have the things we call our environs. My father's spirit called to me when my soul called to his soul, and revealed to my outer knowledge what my inner knowledge had already known.

Therefore, in simplicity, were it not for the hunger and thirst within me, I would not have obtained food and water from my environs; and were it not for the longing and affection within me, I would not have found the subject of my longing and affection about me in the Golden City.

NAJEEB: Is every person able to spin a thread from the sinews of his longing and affection and attach it between his soul and a departed soul? Is there any endowed people, empowered to talk to the spirits and understand their will and purpose?

AMENA: Between the people of eternity and the people of the earth there is a constant communication, and all comply with the will of that unseen power. Oftentimes an individual will perform an act, believing that it is born of his own free will, accord, and command, but in fact he is being guided and impelled with precision to do it. Many great men attained their glory by surrendering themselves in complete submission to the will of the spirit, employing no reluctance or resistance to its demands, as a violin surrenders itself to the complete will of a fine musician.

Between the spiritual world and the world of substance there is a path upon which we walk in a swoon of slumber. It reaches us and we are unaware of its strength, and when we return to ourselves we find that we are carrying with our real hands the seeds to be planted carefully in the good earth of our daily lives, bringing forth good deeds and words of beauty. Were it not for that path between our lives and the departed lives, no prophet or poet or learned man would have appeared among the people. (*Amena lowers her voice to a compelling whisper, and continues*): Truly I say unto you, and the outcome of time will prove it, that there are ties between the upper world and the lower world as surely as there is a binding tie between a mother and her child.

We are surrounded with an intuitive atmosphere that attracts our inner consciousness, and a knowledge that cautious our judgment, and a power that strengthens our own power. I say unto you that our doubt does not disprove or fortify our surrender to that which we doubt, and the fact of busying ourselves in self-gratification will not divert us from the accomplishment by the spirits of their purpose; and blinding ourselves to the reality of our spiritual being will not conceal our spiritual being from the eyes of the universe; and if we stop walking, we are still walking if they are walking . . . and if we remain motionless, we are still moving with their moving . . . and if we silence ourselves, we are still speaking with their voices.

Our sleep cannot drive the influence of their awakeness from us, nor can our awakeness divert their dreams from the stages of our fancies, for we and they are two worlds embraced by one world . . . we and they are two spirits wrapped within one spirit . . . we and they are two existences united by one Supreme and Eternal Consciousness which is above all and without beginning and without ending.

NAJEEB: (*Radiant, he is now thinking and feeling along the lines of Amena Divine's revelations*): Will ever the day arrive when man will discover through scientific knowledge and experience and earthly manifestation that which the spirits have always known through God, and which our hearts have known through longing? Must we await death in order to establish the eternity of our ideal selves? Will ever the day come when we will feel with the fingers of our hands those great secrets which we now feel only with the fingers of our faith?

AMENA: Yes, that day will come. But how ignorant are those who see, without question, the abstract existence with *some* of their senses, but insist upon doubting until that existence reveals itself to *all* their senses. Is not faith the sense of the heart as truly as sight is the sense of the eye? And how narrow is the one who hears the song of the blackbird and sees it hovering above the branches, but doubts that which he has seen and heard until he seizes the bird with his hands. Were not a *portion* of his senses sufficient? How strange is the one who dreams in truth of a beautiful reality, and then, when he endeavours to fashion it into form but cannot succeed, doubts the dream and blasphemes the reality and distrusts the beauty!

How blind is the one who fancies and plans a matter in all true form and angles, and when he cannot prove it completely with superficial measurement and word proofs, believes that his idea and imagination were empty objects! But if he contemplates with sincerity and meditates upon these happenings, he will understand with conviction that his idea is as much a reality as is the bird of the sky, but that it is not yet crystallized, and that the idea is a segment of knowledge that cannot be proved with figures and words, for it is too high and too spacious to be imprisoned at that moment; too deeply imbedded in the spiritual to submit yet to the real.

NAJEEB: (*Believing, yet curious*): Is there true being in all imagination, and real knowledge in every idea and fancy?

AMENA: Verily, it is impossible for the mirror of the soul to reflect in the imagination anything which does not stand before it. It is impossible for the calm lake to show in its depth the figure of any mountain or the picture of any tree or cloud that does not exist close by the lake. It is impossible for the light to throw upon the earth a shadow of an object that has no being. Nothing can be seen, heard, or otherwise sensed unless it has actual *being*. When you *know* a thing, you *believe* it, and the true believer sees with his *spiritual discernment* that which the surface investigator cannot see with the eyes of his head, and he understands through his *inner* thought that which the outside examiner cannot understand with his demanding, acquired process of thought.

The believer acquaints himself with the sacred realities through deep senses different from those used by others. A believer looks upon his senses as a great wall surrounding him, and when he walks upon the path he says, "This city has no exit, but it is perfect within." (*Amena stands, walks toward Najeeb and, after a pause, says*): The believer lives for all the days and the nights, and the unfaithful live but a few hours.

How small is the life of the person who places his hands between his face and the world, seeing naught but the narrow lines of his hands!

How unjust to themselves are those who turn their backs to the sun, and see naught except the shadows of their physical selves upon the earth!

NAJEEB: (*Standing, in preparation for departure*): Shall I tell the people that Iram, the City of Lofty Pillars, is a spiritual city of dreams, and that Amena Divine reached it through longing and affection for it, and through the door of faith?

AMENA: Tell them that Iram, the City of Lofty Pillars, is a true city, existing with the same visible existence of the oceans and the mountains and the forests and the deserts, for all in eternity is real. Tell them that Amena Divine reached it after she crossed the great desert and suffered the agonies of thirst, the torture of hunger, and the sorrows and horrors of aloneness. Tell them that the Golden City was erected by the giants of the ages from the glittering elements of existence, and concealed it not from the people, but the people cornered themselves from it. And tell them that the one who loses his way before reaching Iram must cast blame upon the guide, and not upon the rough, hard road. Tell them that the one who does not light his lamp of truth will find the road dark and impassable. (*Amena looks to heaven with love in her eyes, and her face emanates sweetness and peace*).

NAJEEB: (*Approaches Amena slowly, with head bent low, takes her hand and whispers*): It is eventide, and I must return to the dwellings of the people before darkness engulfs the road.

AMENA: Under God's direction, you will find your way in light.

NAJEEB: I shall walk in the light of the great torch you have placed in my trembling hand.

AMENA: Walk in the light of Truth, which cannot be extinguished by the tempest. (*Amena looks long and intently at Najeeb, her countenance bearing the love of a mother. Then she leaves to the east, and walks amid the trees until she disappears from view*).

ZAIN: May I accompany you to the vicinity of the people?

NAJEEB: With pleasure to me. I believed, however, that you lived close by Amena Divine. I envied you, saying within myself, "Would that I were to abide here."

ZAIN: We can live afar from the sun, but we cannot live close to the sun; yet, we need the sun. I come here often to be blessed and advised, and then I depart contented. (*Najeeb unties the rein and, leading his horse, walks off with Zain Abedeen*).

(*Curtain*)

THE CRUCIFIED

(WRITTEN ON GOOD FRIDAY)

TODAY, and on this same day of each year, man is startled from his deep slumber and stands before the phantoms of the Ages, looking with tearful eyes toward Mount Calvary to witness Jesus the Nazarene nailed on the Cross. . . . But when the day is over and eventide comes, human kinds return and kneel praying before the idols, erected upon every hilltop, every prairie, and every barter of wheat.

Today, the Christian souls ride on the wing of memories and fly to Jerusalem. There they will stand in throngs, beating upon their bosoms, and staring at Him, crowned with a wreath of thorns, stretching His arms before heaven, and looking from behind the veil of Death into the depths of Life. . . .

But when the curtain of night drops over the stage of the day and the brief drama is concluded, the Christians will go back in groups and lie down in the shadow of oblivion between the quilts of ignorance and slothfulness.

On this one day of each year, the philosophers leave their dark caves, and the thinkers their cold cells, and the poets their imaginary arbors, and all stand reverently upon that silent mountain, listening to the voice of a young man saying of His killers, "Oh Father, forgive them, for they know not what they are doing."

But as dark silence chokes the voices of the light, the philosophers and the thinkers and the poets return to their narrow crevices and shroud their souls with meaningless pages of parchment.

The women who busy themselves in the splendour of Life will bestir themselves today from their cushions to see the sorrowful woman standing before the Cross like a tender sapling before the raging tempest; and when they approach near to her, they will hear a deep moaning and a painful grief.

The young men and women who are racing with the torrent of modern civilization will halt today for a moment, and look backward to see the young Magdalen washing with her tears the blood stains from the feet of a Holy Man suspended between Heaven and Earth; and when their shallow eyes weary of the scene they will depart and soon laugh.

On this day of each year, Humanity wakes with the awakening of the Spring, and stands crying below the suffering Nazarene; then she closes her eyes and surrenders herself to a deep slumber. But

Spring will remain awake, smiling and progressing until merged into Summer, dressed in scented golden raiment. Humanity is a mourner who enjoys lamenting the memories and heroes of the Ages. . . . If Humanity were possessed of understanding, there would be rejoicing over their glory. Humanity is like a child standing in glee by a wounded beast. Humanity laughs before the strengthening torrent which carries into oblivion the dry branches of the trees, and sweeps away with determination all things not fastened to strength.

Humanity looks upon Jesus the Nazarene as a poor-born Who suffered misery and humiliation with all of the weak. And He is pitied, for Humanity believes He was crucified painfully. . . . And all that Humanity offers to Him is crying and wailing and lamentation. For centuries Humanity has been worshipping weakness in the person of the Saviour.

The Nazarene was not weak! He was strong and is strong! But the people refuse to heed the true meaning of strength.

Jesus never lived a life of fear, nor did He die suffering or complaining. . . . He lived as a leader; He was crucified as a crusader; He died with a heroism that frightened His killers and tormentors.

Jesus was not a bird with broken wings; He was a raging tempest who broke all crooked wings. He feared not His persecutors nor His enemies. He suffered not before His killers. Free and brave and daring He was. He defied all despots and oppressors.

He saw the contagious pustules and amputated them. . . . He muted Evil and He crushed Falsehood and He choked Treachery.

Jesus came not from the heart of the circle of Light to destroy the homes and build upon their ruins the convents and monasteries. He did not persuade the strong man to become a monk or a priest, but He came to send forth upon this earth a new spirit, with power to crumble the foundation of any monarchy built upon human bones and skulls. . . . He came to demolish the majestic palaces, constructed upon the graves of the weak, and crush the idols, erected upon the bodies of the poor. Jesus was not sent here to teach the people to build magnificent churches and temples amidst the cold wretched huts and dismal hovels. . . . He came to make the human heart a temple, and the soul an altar, and the mind a priest.

These were the missions of Jesus the Nazarene, and these are the teachings for which He was crucified. And if Humanity were wise, she would stand today and sing in strength the song of conquest and the hymn of triumph.

Oh, Crucified Jesus, Who are looking sorrowfully from Mount Calvary at the sad procession of the Ages, and hearing the clamour of the dark nations, and understanding the dreams of Eternity . . . Thou art, on the Cross, more glorious and dignified than one thousand kings upon one thousand thrones in one thousand empires. . . .

Thou art, in the agony of death, more powerful than one thousand generals in one thousand wars. . . .

With Thy sorrows, Thou art more joyous than Spring with its flowers. . . .

With Thy suffering, Thou art more bravely silent than the crying angels of heaven. . . .

Before Thy lashers, Thou art more resolute than the mountain of rock. . . .

Thy wreath of thorns is more brilliant and sublime than the crown of Bahram. . . . The nails piercing Thy hands are more beautiful than the sceptre of Jupiter. . . .

The spatters of blood upon Thy feet are more resplendent than the necklace of Ishtar.

Forgive the weak who lament Thee today, for they do not know how to lament themselves. . . .

Forgive them, for they do not know that Thou hast conquered death with death, and bestowed life upon the dead. . . .

Forgive them, for they do not know that Thy strength still awaits them. . . .

Forgive them, for they do not know that every day is Thy day.

BOOK 4

MY COUNTRYMEN

What do you seek, My Countrymen?
Do you desire that I build for
You gorgeous palaces, decorated
With words of empty meaning, or
Temples roofed with dreams? Or
Do you command me to destroy what
The liars and tyrants have built?
Shall I uproot with my fingers
What the hypocrites and the wicked
Have implanted? Speak your insane
Wish!

What is it you would have me do,
My Countrymen? Shall I purr like
The kitten to satisfy you, or roar
Like the lion to please myself? I
Have sung for you, but you did not
Dance; I have wept before you, but
You did not cry. Shall I sing and
Weep at the same time?

Your souls are suffering the pangs
Of hunger, and yet the fruit of

Knowledge is more plentiful than
The stones of the valleys.

Your hearts are withering from
Thirst, and yet the springs of
Life are streaming about your
Homes—why do you not drink?
The sea has its ebb and flow,
The moon has its fullness and
Crescents, and the Ages have
Their winter and summer, and all
Things vary like the shadow of
An unborn God moving between
Earth and sun, but Truth cannot
Be changed, nor will it pass away;
Why, then, do you endeavour to
Disfigure its countenance?

I have called you in the silence
Of the night to point out the
Glory of the moon and the dignity
Of the stars, but you startled
From your slumber and clutched
Your swords in fear, crying,
"Where is the enemy? We must kill
Him first!" At morningtide, when
The enemy came, I called to you
Again, but now you did not wake
From your slumber, for you were
Locked in fear, wrestling with

The processions of spectres in
Your dreams.

And I said unto you, "Let us climb
To the mountain top and view the
Beauty of the world." And you
Answered me, saying, "In the depths
Of this valley our fathers lived,
And in its shadows they died, and in
Its caves they were buried. How can
We depart this place for one which
They failed to honour?"
And I said unto you, "Let us go to
The plain that gives it bounty to
The sea." And you spoke timidly to
Me, saying, "The uproar of the abyss
Will frighten our spirits, and the
Terror of the depths will deaden
Our bodies."

I have loved you, My Countrymen, but
My love for you is painful to me
And useless to you; and today I
Hate you, and hatred is a flood
That sweeps away the dry branches
And quavering houses.

I have pitied your weakness, My
Countrymen, but my pity has but
Increased your feebleness, exalting

And nourishing slothfulness which
Is vain to Life. And today I see
Your infirmity which my soul loathes
And fears.

I have cried over your humiliation
And submission; and my tears streamed
Like crystalline, but could not sear
Away your stagnant weakness; yet they
Removed the veil from my eyes.

My tears have never reached your
Petrified hearts, but they cleansed
The darkness from my inner self.
Today I am mocking at your suffering,
For laughter is a raging thunder that
Precedes the tempest and never comes
After it.

What do you desire, My Countrymen?
Do you wish for me to show you
The ghost of your countenance on
The face of still water? Come,
Now, and see how ugly you are!

Look and meditate! Fear has
Turned your hair grey as the
Ashes, and dissipation has grown
Over your eyes and made them into
Obscured hollows, and cowardice
Has touched your cheeks that now
Appear as dismal pits in the

Valley, and Death has kissed
Your lips and left them yellow
As the Autumn leaves.

What is it that you seek, My
Countrymen? What ask you from
Life, who does not any longer
Count you among her children?

Your souls are freezing in the
Clutches of the priests and
Sorcerers, and your bodies
Tremble between the paws of the
Despots and the shedders of
Blood, and your country quakes
Under the marching feet of the
Conquering enemy; what may you
Expect even though you stand
Proudly before the face of the
Sun? Your swords are sheathed
With rust, and your spears are
Broken, and your shields are
Laden with gaps; why, then, do
You stand in the field of battle?

Hypocrisy is your religion, and
Falsehood is your life, and
Nothingness is your ending; why,
Then, are you living? Is not
Death the sole comfort of the
Miserables?

Life is a resolution that
Accompanies youth, and a diligence
That follows maturity, and a
Wisdom that pursues senility; but
You, My Countrymen, were born old
And weak. And your skins withered
And your heads shrank, whereupon
You became as children, running
Into the mire and casting stones
Upon each other.

Knowledge is a light, enriching
The warmth of life, and all may
Partake who seek it out; but you,
My Countrymen, seek out darkness
And flee the light, awaiting the
Coming of water from the rock,
And your nation's misery is your
Crime. . . . I do not forgive you
Your sins, for you know what you
Are doing.

Humanity is a brilliant river
Singing its way and carrying with
It the mountains' secrets into
The heart of the sea; but you,
My Countrymen, are stagnant
Marshes infested with insects
And vipers.

The Spirit is a sacred blue
Torch, burning and devouring

The dry plants, and growing
With the storm and illuminating
The faces of the goddesses; but
You, My Countrymen . . . your souls
Are like ashes which the winds
Scatter upon the snow, and which
The tempests disperse forever in
The valleys.

Fear not the phantom of Death,
My Countrymen, for his greatness
And mercy will refuse to approach
Your smallness; and dread not the
Dagger, for it will decline to be
Lodged in your shallow hearts.

I hate you, My Countrymen, because
You hate glory and greatness. I
Despise you because you despise
Yourselves. I am your enemy, for
You refuse to realize that you are
The enemies of the goddesses.

BEHIND THE GARMENT

RACHEL woke at mid-night and gazed intently at something invisible in the sky of her chamber. She heard a voice more soothing than the whispers of Life, and more dismal than the moaning call of the abyss, and softer than the rustling of white wings, and deeper than the message of the waves. . . . It vibrated with hope and with futility, with joy and with misery, and with affection for life, yet with desire for death. Then Rachel closed her eyes and sighed deeply, and gasped, saying, "Dawn has reached the extreme end of the valley; we should go toward the sun and meet him." Her lips were parted, resembling and echoing a deep wound in the soul.

At that moment the priest approached her bed and felt her hand, but found it as cold as the snow; and when he grimly placed his fingers upon her heart, he determined that it was as immobile as the ages, and as silent as the secret of his heart.

The reverend father bowed his head in deep despair. His lips quivered as if wanting to utter a divine word, repeated by the phantoms of the night in the distant and deserted valleys.

After crossing her arms upon her bosom, the priest looked toward a man sitting in an obscured corner of the room, and with a kind and merciful voice he said, "Your beloved has reached the great circle of light. Come, my brother, let us kneel and pray."

The sorrowful husband lifted his head; his eyes stared, gazing at the unseen, and his expression then changed as if he saw understanding in the ghost of an unknown God. He gathered the remnants of himself and walked reverently toward the bed of his wife, and knelt by the side of the clergyman who was praying and lamenting and making the sign of the cross.

Placing his hand upon the shoulder of the grief-stricken husband, the Father said quietly, "Go to the adjoining room, brother, for you are in great need of rest."

He rose obediently, walked to the room and threw his fatigued body upon a narrow bed, and in a few moments he was sailing in the world of sleep like a little child taking refuge in the merciful arms of his loving mother.

The priest remained standing like a statue in the center of the room, and a strange conflict gripped him. And he looked with tearful eyes first at the cold body of the young woman and then through the parted curtain at her husband, who had surrendered himself to the allure of slumber. An hour, longer than an age and more terrible than Death, had already passed, and the priest was still standing between two parted souls. One was dreaming as a field dreams of the coming Spring after the tragedy of Winter, and the other was resting eternally.

Then the priest came close to the body of the young woman and knelt as if worshipping before the altar; he held her cold hand and placed it against his trembling lips, and looked at her face that was adorned with the soft veil of Death. His voice was at the same time calm as the night and deep as the chasm and faltering as with the hopes of man. And in voice he wept, "Oh Rachel, bride of my soul, hear me! At last I am able to talk! Death has opened my lips so that I can now reveal to you a secret deeper than Life itself. Pain has unpinioned my tongue and I can disclose to you my suffering, more painful than pain. Listen to the cry of my soul, Oh Pure Spirit, hovering between the earth and the firmament. Give heed to the youth who waited for you to come from the field, gazing upon you from behind the trees, in fear of your beauty. Hear the priest, who is serving God, calling to you unashamed, after you have reached the City of God. I have proved the strength of my love by concealing it!"

Having thus opened his soul, the Father leaned over and printed three long, warm, and mute kisses upon her forehead, eyes and throat, pouring forth all his heart's secret of love and pain, and the anguish of the years. Then he suddenly withdrew to the dark corner and dropped in agony upon the floor, shaking like an Autumn leaf, as if the touch of her cold face had awakened within him the spirit to repent; whereupon he composed himself and knelt, hiding his face with his cupped hands, and he whispered softly, "God. . . . Forgive my sin; forgive my weakness, Oh Lord. I could no longer resist disclosing that which You knew. Seven years have I kept the deep secrets hidden in my heart from the spoken word, until Death came and tore them from me. Help me, Oh God, to hide this terrible and beautiful memory which brings sweetness from life and bitterness from You. Forgive me, My Lord, and forgive my weakness."

Without looking at the young woman's corpse, he continued suffering and lamenting until Dawn came and dropped a rosy veil upon those two still images, revealing the conflict of Love and Religion to one man; the peace of Life and Death to the other.

PEACE

THE TEMPEST calmed after bending the branches of the trees and leaning heavily upon the grain in the field. The stars appeared as broken remnants of the lightning, but now silence prevailed over all, as if Nature's war had never been fought.

At that hour a young woman entered her chamber and knelt by her bed sobbing bitterly. Her heart flamed with agony but she could finally open her lips and say, "Oh Lord, bring him home safely to me. I have exhausted my tears and can offer no more, oh Lord, full of love and mercy. My patience is drained and calamity is seeking possession of my heart. Save him, oh Lord, from the iron paws of War; deliver him from such unmerciful Death, for he is weak, governed by the strong. Oh Lord, save my beloved, who is Thine own son, from the foe, who is thy foe. Keep him from the forced pathway to Death's door; let him see me, or come and take me to him."

Quietly a young man entered. His head was wrapped in bandage soaked with escaping life.

He approached her with a greeting of tears and laughter, then took her hand and placed against it his flaming lips. And with a voice which bespoke past sorrow, and joy of union, and uncertainty of her reaction, he said, "Fear me not, for I am the object of your plea. Be glad, for Peace has carried me back safely to you, and humanity has restored what greed essayed to take from us. Be not sad, but smile, my beloved. Do not express bewilderment, for Love has power that dispels Death; charm that conquers the enemy. I am your one. Think me not a spectre emerging from the House of Death to visit your Home of Beauty.

"Do not be frightened, for I am now Truth, spared from swords and fire to reveal to the people the triumph of Love over War. I am Word uttering introduction to the play of happiness and peace."

Then the young man became speechless and his tears spoke the language of the heart; and the angels of Joy hovered about that dwelling, and the two hearts restored the singleness which had been taken from them.

At dawn the two stood in the middle of the field, contemplating the beauty of Nature injured by the tempest. After a deep and comforting silence, the soldier looked to the east and said to his sweetheart, "Look at the Darkness, giving birth to the Sun."

SONG OF THE SOUL

IN THE DEPTH of my soul there is
A wordless song—a song that lives
In the seed of my heart.
It refuses to melt with ink on
Parchment; it engulfs my affection
In a transparent cloak and flows,
But not upon my lips.

How can I sigh it? I fear it may
Mingle with earthly ether;
To whom shall I sing it? It dwells
In the house of my soul, in fear of
Harsh ears.

When I look into my inner eyes
I see the shadow of its shadow;
When I touch my fingertips
I feel its vibrations.

The deeds of my hands heed its
Presence as a lake must reflect
The glittering stars; my tears

Reveal it, as bright drops of dew
Reveal the secret of a withering rose.

It is a song composed by contemplation,
And published by silence,
And shunned by clamour,
And folded by truth,
And repeated by dreams,
And understood by love,
And hidden by awakening,
And sung by the soul.

It is the song of love;
What Cain or Esau could sing it?

It is more fragrant than jasmine;
What voice could enslave it?

It is heartbound, as a virgin's secret;
What string could quiver it?

Who dares unite the roar of the sea
And the singing of the nightingale?
Who dares compare the shrieking tempest
To the sigh of an infant?
Who dares speak aloud the words
Intended for the heart to speak?
What human dares sing in voice
The song of God?

LAUGHTER AND TEARS

As the Sun withdrew his rays from the garden, and the moon threw cushioned beams upon the flowers, I sat under the trees pondering upon the phenomena of the atmosphere, looking through the branches at the strewn stars which glittered like chips of silver upon a blue carpet; and I could hear from a distance the agitated murmur of the rivulet singing its way briskly into the valley.

When the birds took shelter among the boughs, and the flowers folded their petals, and tremendous silence descended, I heard a rustle of feet through the grass. I took heed and saw a young couple approaching my arbor. They sat under a tree where I could see them without being seen.

After he looked about in every direction, I heard the young man saying, "Sit by me, my beloved, and listen to my heart; smile, for your happiness is a symbol of our future; be merry, for the sparkling days rejoice with us.

"My soul is warning me of the doubt in your heart, for doubt in love is a sin.

"Soon you will be the owner of this vast land,

lighted by this beautiful moon; soon you will be the mistress of my palace, and all the servants and maids will obey your commands.

"Smile, my beloved, like the gold smiles from my father's coffers.

"My heart refuses to deny you its secret. Twelve months of comfort and travel await us; for a year we will spend my father's gold at the blue lakes of Switzerland, and viewing the edifices of Italy and Egypt, and resting under the Holy Cedars of Lebanon; you will meet the princesses who will envy you for your jewels and clothes.

"All these things I will do for you; will you be satisfied?"

In a little while I saw them walking and stepping on flowers as the rich step upon the hearts of the poor. As they disappeared from my sight, I commenced to make comparison between love and money, and to analyze their position in my heart.

Money! The source of insincere love; the spring of false light and fortune; the well of poisoned water; the desperation of old age!

I was still wandering in the vast desert of contemplation when a forlorn and spectre-like couple passed by me and sat on the grass; a young man and a young woman who had left their farming shacks in the nearby fields for this cool and solitary place.

After a few moments of complete silence, I heard the following words uttered with sighs from weather-bitten lips, "Shed not tears, my beloved; love that opens our eyes and enslaves our hearts can give us the blessings of patience. Be consoled in our delay, for we have taken an oath and entered Love's shrine; for our love will ever grow in adversity; for it is in Love's name that we are suffering the obstacles of poverty and the sharpness of misery and the emptiness of separation. I shall attack these hardships until I triumph and place in your hands a strength that will help over all things to complete the journey of life.

"Love—which is God—will consider our sighs and tears as incense burned at His altar and He will reward us with fortitude. Good-bye, my beloved; I must leave before the heartening moon vanishes."

A pure voice, combined of the consuming flame of love, and the hopeless bitterness of longing and the resolved sweetness of patience, said, "Good-bye, my beloved."

They separated, and the elegy to their union was smothered by the wails of my crying heart.

I looked upon slumbering Nature, and with deep reflection discovered the reality of a vast and infinite thing—something no power could demand, influence acquire, nor riches purchase. Nor could it be effaced by the tears of time or deadened by sorrow; a thing which cannot be discovered by the blue lakes of Switzerland or the beautiful edifices of Italy.

It is something that gathers strength with patience, grows despite obstacles, warms in winter, flourishes in spring, casts a breeze in summer, and bears fruit in autumn—I found Love.

ASHES OF THE AGES AND ETERNAL FIRE

PART ONE

Spring of the Year 116 B.C.

NIGHT had fallen and silence prevailed while life slumbered in the City of the Sun,* and the lamps were extinguished in the scattered houses about the majestic temples amidst the olive and laurel trees. The moon poured its silver rays upon the white marble columns that stood like giants in the silence of the night, guarding the god's temples and looking with perplexity toward the towers of Lebanon that sat bristling upon the foreheads of the distant hills.

At that hour, while souls succumbed to the allure of slumber, Nathan, the son of the High Priest, entered Ishtar's temple, bearing a torch in trembling

* Baalbek, or the City of Baal, called by the ancients "The City of the Sun," was built in honor of the Sun God Heliopolis, and historians assert that Baalbek was the most beautiful city in the Middle East. Its ruins, which we observe at present time, indicate that the architecture was largly influenced by the Romans during the occupation of Syria. (*Editor's note.*)

hands. He lighted the lamps and censers until the aromatic scent of myrrh and frankincense reached to the farthest corners; then he knelt before the altar, studded with inlays of ivory and gold, raised his hands toward Ishtar, and with a painful and choking voice he cried out, saying, "Have mercy upon me, O great Ishtar, goddess of Love and Beauty. Be merciful, and remove the hands of Death from my beloved, whom my soul has chosen by thy will. . . . The potions of the physicians and the wizards do not restore her life, neither the enchantments of the priests and the sorcerers. Naught is left to be done except thy holy will. Thou art my guide and my aid. Have mercy on me and grant my prayers! * Gaze upon my crushed heart and aching soul! Spare my beloved's life so that we may rejoice with the secrets of thy love, and glory in the beauty of youth that reveals the mystery of thy strength and wisdom. From the depths of my heart I cry unto thee, O exalted Ishtar, and from behind the darkness of the night I beg thy mercy; hear me, O Ishtar! I am thy good servant Nathan, the son of the High Priest Hiram, and I devote all of my deeds and words to thy greatness at thy altar.

"I love a maiden amongst all maidens and made

* Ishtar was the great goddess of the Phoenicians. They worshipped her in the cities of Tyre, Sidon, Sûr, Djabeil and Baalbek, and described her as the Burner of the Torch of Life, and Guardian of Youth. Greece adored her after Phoenicia, calling her the goddess of Love and Beauty. The Romans called her Venus. (*Editor's note.*)

her my companion, but the genii brides envied her and blew into her body a strange affliction and sent unto her the messenger of Death who is standing by her bed like a hungry spectre, spreading his black ribbed wings over her, stretching forth his sharp claws in readiness to prey upon her. I come here now beseeching you to have mercy upon me and spare that flower who has not yet rejoiced with the summer of Life.

"Save her from the grasp of Death so we may sing joyfully thy praise and burn incense in thine honour and offer sacrifices at thy altar, filling thy vases with perfumed oil and spreading roses and violets upon the portico of thy place of worship, burning frankincense before thy shrine. Save her, O Ishtar, goddess of miracles, and let Love overcome Death in this struggle of Joy against Sorrow." *

Nathan then became silent. His eyes were flooded with tears and his heart was uttering sorrowful sighs; then he continued, "Alas, my dreams are shattered, O Ishtar divine, and my heart is melted within; enliven me with thy mercy and spare my beloved."

At that moment one of his slaves entered the temple, hastened to Nathan, and whispered to him, "She has opened her eyes, Master, and looked about

* **During the Era of Ignorance, the Arabs believed that if a genie loved a human youth, she would prevent him from marrying, and if he did wed, she would bewitch the bride and cause her to die. This mythological superstition persists today in some small villages in Lebanon. (*Editor's note.*)**

her bed, but could not find you; then she called for you, and I used all speed to advise you."

Nathan departed hurriedly and the slave followed him.

When he reached his palace, he entered the chamber of the ailing maiden, leaned over her bed, held her frail hand, and printed several kisses upon her lips as if striving to breathe into her body a new life from his own life. She moved her head on the silk cushions and opened her eyes. And upon her lips appeared the phantom of a smile which was the faint residue of life in her wasted body . . . the echo of the calling of a heart which is racing toward a halt; and with a voice that bespoke the weakening cries of a hungry infant on the breast of a withered mother, she said, "The goddess has called me, Oh Life of my Soul, and Death has come to sever me from you; but fear not, for the will of the goddess is sacred, and the demands of Death are just. I am departing now, and I hear the rustle of the whiteness descending, but the cups of Love and Youth are still full in our hands, and the flowered paths of beautiful Life are extended before us. I am embarking, My Beloved, upon an ark of the spirit, and I shall come back to this world, for great Ishtar will bring back to life those souls of loving humans who departed to Eternity before they enjoyed the sweetness of Love and the happiness of Youth.

"We shall meet again, Oh Nathan, and drink together the dew of the dawn from the cupped petals of the lilies, and rejoice with the birds of the fields over the colours of the rainbow. Until then, My Forever, farewell." *

Her voice lowered and her lips trembled like a lone flower before the gusts of dawn. Nathan embraced her with pouring tears, and as he pressed his lips upon her lips, he found them cold as the stone of the field. He uttered a terrible cry and commenced tearing his raiment; he threw himself upon her dead body while his shivering soul was sailing fitfully between the mountain of Life and the precipice of Death.

In the silence of the night, the slumbering souls were awakened. Women and children were frightened as they heard mighty rumbling and painful wailing and bitter lamentation coming from the corners of the palace of the High Priest of Ishtar.

When the tired morn arrived, the people asked about Nathan to offer their sympathy, but were told that he had disappeared. And after a fortnight, the chief of a caravan arriving from the East related that he had seen Nathan in the distant wilderness, wandering with a flock of gazelles.

The ages passed, crushing with their invisible feet the feeble acts of the civilizations, and the goddess of Love and Beauty had left the country. A strange

* Many Asiatics pursue this belief with conviction, having derived it from their holy writings. Mohammed said, "You were dead and He brought you back to life, and He will deaden you again and

and fickle goddess took her place. She destroyed the magnificent temples of the City of the Sun and demolished its beautiful palaces. The blooming orchards and fertile prairies were laid waste and nothing was left in that spot save ruins commemorating to the aching souls the ghosts of Yesterday, repeating to the sorrowful spirits only the echo of the hymns of glory.

But the severe ages that crushed the deeds of man could not destroy his dreams; nor could they weaken his love, for dreams and affections are ever-living with the Eternal Spirit. They may disappear for a time, pursuing the sun when the night comes, and the stars when morning appears, but like the lights of heaven, they must surely return.

PART TWO

Spring of the Year 1890 A.D.

The day was over, Nature was making her many preparations for slumber, and the sun withdrew its golden rays from the plains of Baalbek. Ali El Hosseini * brought his herd back to the shed in the

then will enliven you, whereupon you shall go back to Him." Buddha said, "Yesterday we existed in this life, and now we came, and we will continue to go back until we become perfect like the God." (*Editor's note.*)

* The Hosseinese are groups comprising an Arabian tribe, at present living in tents pitched in the plains surrounding the ruins of Baalbek. (*Editor's note.*)

midst of the ruins of the temples. He sat there near the ancient columns which symbolized the bones of countless soldiers left behind in the field of battle. The sheep folded around him, charmed with the music of his flute.

Midnight came, and heaven sowed the seeds of the following day in the deep furrows of the darkness. Ali's eyes became tired of the phantoms of awakeness, and his mind was wearied by the procession of ghosts marching in horrible silence amidst the demolished walls. He leaned upon his arm, and sleep captured his senses with the extreme end of its plaited veil, like a delicate cloud touching the face of a calm lake. He forgot his actual self and encountered his invisible self, rich with dreams and ideals higher than the laws and teachings of man. The circle of vision broadened before his eyes, and Life's hidden secrets gradually became apparent to him. His soul abandoned the rapid parade of time rushing toward nothingness; it stood alone before symmetrical thoughts and crystal ideas. For the first time in his life, Ali was aware of the causes for the spiritual famine that had accompanied his youth. . . . The famine which levels away the pit between the sweetness and the bitterness of Life. . . . That thirst which unites into contentment the sighs of Affection and the silence of Satisfaction. . . . That longing which cannot be vanquished by the glory of the world nor twisted by the passing of the ages. Ali felt the surge of a strange affection and a kind tenderness within himself which was Memory, enlivening itself like incense placed upon white firebrands. . . . It was a magic love whose soft fingers had touched Ali's heart as a musician's delicate fingers touch quivering strings. It was a new power emanating from nothingness and growing forcefully, embracing his real self and filling his spirit with ardent love, at once painful and sweet.

Ali looked toward the ruins and his heavy eyes became alert as he fancied the glory of those devastated shrines that stood as mighty, impregnable, and eternal temples long before. His eyes became motionless and the breathing of his heart quickened. And like a blind man whose sight has suddenly been restored, he commenced to see, think and meditate. . . . He recollected the lamps and the silver censers that surrounded the image of an adored and revered goddess. . . . He remembered the priests offering sacrifices before an altar built of ivory and gold. . . . He envisioned the dancing maidens, and the tambourine players, and the singers who chanted the praise of the goddess of Love and Beauty; he saw all this before him, and felt the impression of their obscurity in the choking depths of his heart.

But memory alone brings naught save echoes of voices heard in the depths of the long ago. What, then, is the bizarre relationship between these powerful, weaving memories and the past actual life of a simple youth who was born in a tent and who spent the spring of his life grazing sheep in the valleys?

Ali gathered himself and walked amidst the ruins, and the gnawing memories suddenly tore the veil of oblivion from his thoughts. As he reached the great and cavernous entrance to the temple, he halted as if a magnetic power gripped him and fastened his feet. As he looked downward, he found a smashed statue on the ground. He broke from the grasp of the Unseen and at once his soul's tears unleashed and poured like blood issuing from a deep wound; his heart roared in ebb and flow like the welling waves of the sea. He sighed bitterly and cried painfully, for he felt a stabbing aloneness and a destructive remoteness standing as an abyss between his heart and the heart from whom he was torn before he entered upon this life. He felt that his soul's element was but a flame from the burning torch which God had separated from Himself before the passing of the Ages. He perceived the feathery touch of delicate wings rustling about his flaming heart, and a great love possessing him. . . . A love whose power separates the mind from the world of quantity and measurement. . . . A love that talks when the tongue of Life is muted. . . . A love that stands as a blue beacon to point out the path, guiding with no visible light. That love or that God who descended in that quiet hour upon Ali's heart had seared into his being a bitter and sweet affection, like thorns growing by the side of the flourishing flowers.

But who is this Love and whence did he come? What does he desire of a shepherd kneeling in the midst of those ruins? Is it a seed sown without awareness in the domain of the heart by a Bedouin maiden? Or a beam appeared from behind the dark cloud to illuminate life? Is it a dream that crept close in the silence of the night to ridicule him? Or is it Truth that existed since the Beginning, and shall continue to exist until the Ending?

Ali closed his tearful eyes and stretched forth his arms like a beggar, and exclaimed, "Who are you, standing close to my heart but away from my sight, yet acting as a great wall between me and my real self, binding my today with my forgotten past? Are you the phantom of a spectre from Eternity to show me the vanity of Life and the weakness of mankind? Or the spirit of a genie appeared from the earth's crevices to enslave me and render me an object of mockery amongst the youths of my tribe? Who are you and what is this strange power which at one time deadens and enlivens my heart? Who am I and what is this strange self whom I call "Myself?" Has the Water of Life which I drank made of me an angel, seeing and hearing the mysterious secrets of the Universe, or is it merely an evil wine that intoxicated me and blinded me from myself?"

He became silent, while his anxiety grew and his spirit exulted. Then he continued, "Oh, that which the soul reveals, and the night conceals. . . . Oh, beautiful spirit, hovering in the sky of my dream;

you have awakened in me a dormant fullness, like healthy seeds hidden under the blankets of snow; you have passed me like a frolicsome breeze carrying to my hungry self the fragrance of the flowers of heaven; you have touched my senses and agitated and quivered them like the leaves of the trees. Let me look upon you now if you are a human, or command Slumber to shut my eyes so I can view your vastness through my inner being. Let me touch you; let me hear your voice. Tear away this veil that conceals my entire purpose, and destroy this wall that hides my deity from my clearing eyes, and place upon me a pair of wings so I may fly behind you to the halls of the Supreme Universe. Or bewitch my eyes so I may follow you to the ambush of the genii if you are one of their brides. If I am worthy, place your hand upon my heart and possess me."

Ali was whispering these words into the mystic darkness, and before him crept the ghosts of night, as if they were vapour coming from his boiling tears. Upon the walls of the temple he fancied magical pictures painted with the brush of the rainbow.

Thus did one hour pass, with Ali shedding tears and reveling in his miserable plight and hearing the beats of his heart, looking beyond the objects as if he were observing the images of Life vanishing slowly and being replaced with a dream, strange in its beauty and terrible in enormity. Like a prophet who meditates the stars of heaven awaiting the Descent and Revelation, he pondered the power existing beyond these contemplations. He felt that his spirit left him and probed through the temples for a priceless but unknown segment of himself, lost among the ruins.

Dawn had appeared and silence roared with the passing of the breeze; the first rays of light raced through, illuminating the particles of the ether, and the sky smiled like a dreamer viewing his beloved's phantom. The birds probed from their sanctuary in the crevices of the walls and emerged into the halls of the columns, singing their morning prayers.

Ali placed his cupped hand over his forehead, looking downward with glazed eyes. Like Adam, when God opened his eyes with Almighty breath, Ali saw new objects, strange and fantastic. Then he approached his sheep and called to them, whereupon they followed him quietly toward the lush fields. He led them, as he gazed at the sky like a philosopher divining and meditating the secrets of the Universe. He reached a brook whose murmuring was soothing to the spirit, and he sat by the edge of the spring under the willow tree, whose branches dipped over the water as if drinking from the cool depths. The dew of dawn glistened upon the sheep's wool as they grazed amid flowers and green grass.

In a few moments Ali again felt that his heartbeats were increasing rapidly and his spirit commenced to vibrate violently, almost visibly. Like a mother suddenly awakened from her slumber by the scream of her child, he bolted from his position, and as his eyes were compelled to her, he saw a beautiful maiden carrying an earthenware container upon her shoulder, slowly approaching the far side of the brook. As she reached the edge and leaned forward to fill the jar, she glanced across, and her eyes met Ali's eyes. As if in insanity she cried out, dropped the jar, and withdrew swiftly. Then she turned, gazing at Ali with anxious, agonizing disbelief.

A minute passed, whose seconds were glittering lamps illuminating their hearts and spirits, and silence brought vague remembrance, revealing to them images and scenes far away from that brook and those trees. They heard each other in the understanding silence, listening tearfully to each other's sighs of heart and soul until complete knowing prevailed between the two.

Ali, still compelled by a mysterious power, leaped across the brook and approached the maiden, embraced her and printed a long kiss upon her lips. As if the sweetness of Ali's caress had usurped her will, she did not move, and the kind touch of Ali's arms had stolen her strength. She yielded to him as the fragrance of jasmine concedes to the vibration of the breeze, carrying it into the spacious firmament.

She placed her head upon his chest like a tortured person who has found rest. She sighed deeply . . . a sigh that announced the rebirth of happiness in a torn heart and proclaimed a revolution of wings that had ascended after having been injured and committed to earth.

She raised her head and looked at him with her soul . . . the look of a human which, in mighty silence, belittles the conventional words used amongst mankind; the expression which offers myriads of thoughts in the unspoken language of the hearts. She bore the look of a person who accepts Love not as a spirit in a body of words, but as a reunion occurring long after two souls were divided by earth and joined by God.

The enamoured couple walked amidst the willow trees, and the singleness of two selves was a speaking tongue for their unification; a seeing eye for the glory of Happiness; a silent listener to the tremendous revelation of Love.

The sheep continued grazing, and the birds of the sky still hovered above their heads, singing the song of Dawn, following the emptiness of night. As they reached the end of the valley the sun appeared, spreading a golden garment upon the knolls and the hills, and they sat by the side of a rock where the violets hid. The maiden looked into Ali's black eyes while the breeze caressed her hair, as if the shimmering wisps were fingertips craving for sweet kisses. She felt as though some magic and strong gentleness were touching her lips in spite of her will, and with a serene and charming voice she said, "Ishtar has restored both of our spirits to this life from another, so we may not be denied the joy of Love and the glory of Youth, my beloved."

Ali closed his eyes, as if her musical voice brought to him images of a dream he had seen, and he felt an invisible pair of wings carrying him from that place and depositing him in a strange chamber by the side of a bed upon which lay the corpse of a maiden whose beauty had been claimed by Death. He cried fearfully, then opened his eyes and found that same maiden sitting by his side, and upon her lips appeared a smile. Her eyes shone with the rays of Life. Ali's face brightened and his heart was refreshed. The phantom of his vision withdrew slowly until he forgot completely the past and its cares. The two lovers embraced and drank the wine of sweet kisses together until they became intoxicated. They slumbered, wrapped between each other's arms, until the last remnant of the shadow was dispersed by the Eternal Power which had awakened them.

BETWEEN NIGHT AND MORN

BE SILENT, my heart, for the space cannot
Hear you; be silent, for the ether is
Laden with cries and moans, and cannot
Carry your songs and hymns.

Be silent, for the phantoms of the night
Will not give heed to the whispering of
Your secrets; nor will the processions
Of darkness halt before your dreams.

Be silent, my heart, until Dawn comes,
For he who patiently awaits the morn
Will meet him surely, and he who loves
The light will be loved by the light.

Be silent, my heart, and hearken to my
Story; in my dream I saw a nightingale
Singing over the throat of a fiery
Volcano, and I saw a lily raising her
Head above the snow, and a naked Houri
Dancing in the midst of the graves, and
An infant playing with skulls while
Laughing.

I saw all these images in my dream, and
When I opened my eyes and looked about
Me, I saw the volcano still raging, but
No longer heard the nightingale sing;
Nor did I see him hovering.

I saw the sky spreading snow upon the
Fields and valleys, and concealing under
White shrouds the stilled bodies of the
Lilies. I saw a row of graves before
The silence of the Ages, but there was
No person dancing or praying in their
Midst. I saw a heap of skulls, but no
One was there to laugh, save the wind.

In my awakeness I saw grief and sorrow;
What became of the joy and sweetness of
My dream? Where has the beauty of my
Dream gone, and in what manner did the
Images disappear?

How can the soul be patient until Slumber
Restores the happy phantoms of hope and
Desire?

Give heed, my heart, and hear my story;
Yesterday my soul was like an old and
Strong tree, whose roots grasped into the
Depths of the earth, and whose branches
Reached the Infinite. My soul blossomed
In Spring, and gave fruit in Summer, and

When Autumn came, I gathered the fruit on
A silver tray and placed it by the
Walker's portion of the street; and all
Who passed partook willingly and continued
To walk.

And when Autumn passed away, and submerged
His rejoicing under wailing and lamentation,
I looked upon my tray and found but one
Fruit remaining; I took it and placed it
Into my mouth, but found it bitter as gall,
And sour as the hard grapes, and I said to
Myself, "Woe to me, for I have placed a
Curse in the mouths of the people, and an
Ailment in their bodies. What have you
Done, my soul, with the sweet sap which
Your roots have sucked from the earth, and
The fragrance which you have drawn from
The sky?" In anger did I tear the strong
And old tree of my soul, with each of the
Struggling roots, from the depths of the
Earth.

I uprooted it from the past, and took
From it the memories of one thousand
Springs and one thousand Autumns, and I
Planted the tree of my soul in another
Place. It was now in a field afar from
The path of Time; and I tended it in day
And in night, saying within me, "Wakefulness
Will bring us closer to the stars."

I watered it with blood and tears, saying,
"There is a flavour in blood, and a
Sweetness in tears." When Spring returned,
My tree bloomed again, and in the Summer it
Bore fruit. And when Autumn came, I gathered
All the ripe fruit upon a golden plate and
Offered it in the public path, and the people
Passed but none desired my fruit.

Then I took one fruit and brought it to my
Lips, and it was sweet as the honeycomb
And exhilarating as the wine of Babylon
And fragrant as the jasmine. And I cried
Out, saying, "The people do not want a
Blessing in their mouths, nor a truth in
Their hearts, for Blessing is the daughter
Of Tears, and Truth is the son of Blood."

I left the noisome city to sit in the shadow
Of the solitary tree of my soul, in a
Field far from life's path.

Be silent, my heart, until Dawn comes;
Be silent and attend my story;
Yesterday my thoughts were a boat sailing
Amidst the waves in the sea, and moving
With the winds from one land to another.
And my boat was empty except of seven
Jars of rainbow colours; and the time
Came when I grew weary of moving about
On the face of the sea, and I said to

Myself, "I shall return with the empty
Boat of my thoughts to the harbour of the
Isle of my birth."

And I prepared by colouring my boat yellow
Like the sunset, and green like the heart
Of Spring, and blue like the sky, and red
Like the anemone. And on the masts and
On the rudder I drew strange figures that
Compelled the attention and dazzled the
Eye. And as I ended my task, the boat of
My thoughts seemed as a prophetic vision,
Sailing between the two infinities, the
Sea and the sky.

I entered the harbour of the isle of my
Birth, and the people surged to meet me
With singing and merriment. And the
Throngs invited me to enter the city;
And they were plucking their instruments
And sounding their tambourines.

Such welcome was mine because my boat
Was beautifully decorated, and none
Entered and saw the interior of the
Boat of my thoughts, nor asked what
I had brought from beyond the seas. Nor
Could they observe that I had brought
My boat back empty, for its brilliance
Had rendered them blind. Thereupon I
Said within myself, "I have led the

People astray, and with seven jars of
Colours I have cheated their eyes."

Thereafter, I embarked in the boat of
My thoughts, again to set sail. I
Visited the East Islands and gathered
Myrrh, frankincense and sandalwood, and
Placed them in my boat. . . . I roamed the
West Islands and brought ivory and ruby
And emerald and many rare gems. . . . I
Journeyed the South Islands and carried
Back with me beautiful armours and
Glittering swords and spears and all
Varieties of weapons. . . . I filled the
Boat of my thoughts with the choicest
And most precious things on earth, and
Returned to the harbour of the isle of
My birth, saying, "The people shall again
Glorify me, but with honesty, and they
Shall again invite me to enter their
City, but with merit."

And when I reached the harbour, none
Came to meet me. . . . I walked the streets
Of my earlier glory but no person looked
Upon me. . . . I stood in the market place
Shouting to the people of the treasures
In my boat, and they mocked at me and
Heeded not.

I returned to the harbour with spiritless
Heart and disappointment and confusion.

And when I gazed upon my boat, I observed
A thing which I had not seen during my
Voyage, and I exclaimed, "The waves of
The sea have done away with the colours and
The figures on my boat and caused it to look
Like a skeleton." The winds and the spray
Together with the burning sun had effaced
The brilliant hues and my boat looked now
Like tattered grey raiment. I could not
Observe these changes from amid my treasures,
For I had blinded my eyes from the inside.

I had gathered the most precious things on
Earth and placed them in a floating chest
Upon the face of the water and returned to
My people, but they cast me away and could
Not see me, for their eyes had been allured
By empty, shimmering objects.

At that hour I left the boat of my thoughts
For the City of the Dead, and sat in the
Midst of the trim graves, contemplating
Their secrets.

Be silent, my heart, until Dawn comes; be
Silent, for the raging tempest is ridiculing
Your inner whispering, and the caves of
The valleys do not echo the vibration of
Your strings.

Be silent, my heart, until Morn comes,
For he who awaits patiently the coming

Of Dawn will be embraced longingly by
Morningtide.

Dawn is breaking. Speak if you are able,
My heart. Here is the procession of
Morningtide. . . .Why do you not speak?
Has not the silence of the night left
A song in your inner depths with which
You may meet Dawn?

Here are the swarms of doves and the
Nightingales moving in the far portion
Of the valley. Are you capable of flying
With the birds, or has the horrible night
Weakened your wings? The shepherds are
Leading the sheep from their folds; has
The phantom of the night left strength
In you so you may walk behind them to
The green prairies? The young men and
Women are walking gracefully toward the
Vineyards. Will you be able to stand
And walk with them? Rise, my heart, and
Walk with Dawn, for the night has passed,
And the fear of darkness has vanished with
Its black dreams and ghastly thoughts and
Insane travels.

Rise, my heart, and raise your voice with
Music, for he who shares not Dawn with
His songs is one of the sons of ever-
Darkness.

HONEYED POISON

It was a beautiful morn of dizzying brilliance in North Lebanon when the people of the village of Tula gathered around the portico of the small church that stood in the midst of their dwellings. They were discussing busily the sudden and unexplained departure of Farris Rahal, who left behind his bride of but half a year.

Farris Rahal was the Sheik and leader of the village, and he had inherited this honourable status from his ancestors who had ruled over Tula for centuries. Although he was not quite twenty-seven years of age, he possessed an outstanding ability and sincerity that won the admiration, reverence, and respect of all the fellahin. When Farris married Susan, the people commented upon him, saying, "What a fortunate man is Farris Rahal! He has attained all that man can hope for in the bounty of life's happiness, and he is but a youth!"

That morning, when all of Tula arose from slumber and learned that the Sheik had gathered his gold, mounted his steed and left the village bidding none farewell, curiosity and concern prevailed, and inquiries were many as to the cause that prompted him to desert his wife and his home, his lands and his vineyards.

By reason of tradition and geography, life in North Lebanon is highly sociable, and the people share their joys and sorrows, provoked by humble spirit and instinctive clannishness. Upon any occurrence, the entire populace of the village convenes to inquire upon the incident, offers all possible assistance, and returns to labour until fate again offers a congregant mission.

It was such a matter that drew the people of Tula from their work that day, and caused them to gather about the church of Mar Tula discussing the departure of their Sheik and exchanging views upon its singularity.

It was at this time that Father Estephan, head of the local church, arrived, and upon his drawn countenance one could read the unmistakable signs of deep suffering, the signs of a painfully wounded spirit. He contemplated the scene for a moment and then spoke. "Do not ask . . . do not ask any question of me! Before daybreak this day, Sheik Farris knocked upon the door of my house, and I saw him holding the rein of his horse, and from his face emanated grave sorrow and agonized grief. Upon my remark as to the strangeness of the hour, he replied, 'Father, I come to bid you farewell, for I am sailing beyond the oceans and will never again return to this land.' And he handed to me a sealed envelope, addressed to his dearest friend Nabih Malik, asking me to deliver it. He mounted his steed and sped off to the east, affording me no further opportunity to understand the purpose of his unusual departure."

One of the villagers observed, "Undoubtedly the missive will reveal to us the secret of his going, for Nabih is his closest friend." Another added, "Have you seen his bride, Father?" The priest replied, saying, "I visited her after the morning prayer and found her standing at the window, staring with unseeing eyes at something invisible, appearing as one who has lost all senses, and when I endeavoured to ask concerning Farris she merely said, 'I do not know! I do not know!' Then she wept like a child who suddenly becomes an orphan."

As the father concluded talking, the group tightened with fear at the startling report of a gunshot coming from the east portion of the village, and it was followed immediately by the bitter wailing of a woman. The throng was in a dismayed trance of immobility for a moment, and then, men, women and children, all ran toward the scene, and upon their faces there was a dark mask of fear and evil omen. As they reached the garden that surrounded the Sheik's residence, they became witness to a most horrible drama, portrayed with death. Nabih Malik was lying on the ground, a stream of blood issuing from his breast, and by him stood Susan, wife of the Sheik Farris Rahal, tearing her hair and shredding her raiment and flailing her arms about and shrieking wildly, "Nabih . . . Nabih . . . why did you do it!"

The onlookers were astounded, and it was as though the unseen hands of fate had clutched with icy fingers at their hearts. The priest found in the dead Nabih's right hand the note he had delivered that morning, and he placed it deftly into his robe without notice by the milling multitude.

Nabih was carried to his miserable mother, who, upon seeing the lifeless body of her only son, lost her sanity in shock and soon joined him in Eternity. Susan was led slowly into her home, wavering between faltering life and grasping death.

As Father Estephan reached his home, under bent shoulders, he fastened the door, adjusted his reading glasses, and in a quivering whisper commenced reading to himself the message he had taken from the hand of the departed Nabih.

"My Dearest Friend Nabih,

"I must leave this village of my fathers, for my continued presence is casting misery upon you and upon my wife and upon myself. You are noble in spirit, and scorn the betrayal of friend or neighbour, and although I know that Susan is innocent and virtuous, I know also that the true love which unites your heart and her heart is beyond your power and beyond my hopes. I cannot struggle longer against the mighty will of God, as I cannot halt the strong flow of the great Kadeesha River.

"You have been my sincere friend, Nabih, since we played as children in the fields; and before God, believe me, you remain my friend, I beg you to ponder with good thoughts upon me in the future as you did in the past. Tell Susan that I love her and that I wronged her by taking her in empty marriage. Tell her that my heart bled in burning pain each time I turned from restless sleep in the silence of the night and observed her kneeling before the shrine of Jesus, weeping and beating upon her bosom in anguish.

"There is no punishment so severe as that suffered by the woman who finds herself imprisoned between a man she loves and another man who loves her. Susan suffered through a constant and painful conflict, but performed sorrowfully and honourably and silently her duties as a wife. She tried, but could not choke her honest love for you.

"I am leaving for distant lands and will never again return, for I can no longer act as barrier to a genuine and eternal love, embraced by the enfolded arms of God; and may God, in his inscrutable wisdom, protect and bless both of you.

FARRIS"

Father Estephan folded the letter, returned it to his pocket, and sat by the window that opened upon the distant valley. He sailed long and deep in a great ocean of contemplation, and after wise and intense meditation, he stood suddenly, as if he had found between the plaited folds of his intricate thoughts a delicate and horrible secret, disguised with diabolical slyness, and wrapped with elaborate cunning! He cried out, "How sagacious you are, Farris! How massive, yet simple, is your crime! You sent to him honey blended with fatal poison, and enclosed death in a letter! And when Nabih pointed the weapon at his heart, it was your finger that discharged the missile, and it was your will that engulfed his will. . . . How clever you are, Farris!"

He returned quivering to his chair, shaking his head and combing his beard with his fingers, and upon his lips appeared a smile whose meaning was more terrible than the tragedy itself. He opened his prayer book and commenced reading and pondering, and at intervals he raised his head to hear the wailing and lamentation of the women, coming from the heart of the village of Tula, close by the Holy Cedars of Lebanon.

BOOK 5

MADAME ROSE HANIE

PART ONE

MISERABLE is the man who loves a woman and takes her for a wife, pouring at her feet the sweat of his skin and the blood of his body and the life of his heart, and placing in her hands the fruit of his toil and the revenue of his diligence; for when he slowly wakes up, he finds that the heart, which he endeavoured to buy, is given freely and in sincerity to another man for the enjoyment of its hidden secrets and deepest love. Miserable is the woman who arises from the inattentiveness and restlessness of youth and finds herself in the home of a man showering her with his glittering gold and precious gifts and according her all the honors and grace of lavish entertainment but unable to satisfy her soul with the heavenly wine which God pours from the eyes of a man into the heart of a woman.

I knew Rashid Bey Namaan since I was a youngster; he was a Lebanese, born and reared in the City of Beyrouth. Being a member of an old and rich family which preserved the tradition and glory of his ancestry, Rashid was fond of citing incidents that dealt mainly with the nobility of his forefathers. In his routine life he followed their beliefs and customs which, at that time, prevailed in the Middle East.

Rashid Bey Namaan was generous and good-hearted, but like many of the Syrians, looked only at the superficial things instead of reality. He never hearkened to the dictates of his heart, but busied himself in obeying the voices of his environment. He amused himself with shimmering objects that blinded his eyes and heart to life's secrets; his soul was diverted away from an understanding of the law of nature, and to a temporary self-gratification. He was one of those men who hastened to confess their love or disgust to the people, then regretted their impulsiveness when it was too late for recall. And then shame and ridicule befell them, instead of pardon or sanction.

These are the characteristics that prompted Rashid Bey Namaan to marry Rose Hanie far before her soul embraced his soul in the shadow of the true love that makes union a paradise.

After a few years of absence, I returned to the City of Beyrouth. As I went to visit Rashid Bey Namaan, I found him pale and thin. On his face one could see the spectre of bitter disappointment; his sorrowful eyes bespoke his crushed heart and melancholy soul. I was curious to find the cause for his miserable plight; however, I did not hesitate to ask for explanation and said, "What became of you, Rashid? Where is the radiant smile and the happy countenance that accompanied you since childhood? Has death taken away from you a dear friend? Or have the black nights stolen from you the gold you have amassed during the white days? In the name of friendship, tell me what is causing this sadness of heart and weakness of body?"

He looked at me ruefully, as if I had revived to him some secluded images of beautiful days. With a distressed and faltering voice he responded, "When a person loses a friend, he consoles himself with the many other friends about him, and if he loses his gold, he meditates for a while and casts misfortune from his mind, especially when he finds himself healthy and still laden with ambition. But when a man loses the ease of his heart, where can he find comfort, and with what can he replace it? What mind can master it? When Death strikes close by, you will suffer. But when the day and night pass, you will feel the smooth touch of the soft fingers of Life; then you will smile and rejoice.

"Destiny comes suddenly, bringing concern; she stares at you with horrible eyes and clutches you at the throat with sharp fingers and hurls you to the ground and tramples upon you with ironclad feet: then she laughs and walks away, but later regrets her actions and asks you through good fortune to forgive her. She stretches forth her silky hand and lifts you high and sings to you the Song of Hope and causes you to lose your cares. She creates in you a new zest for confidence and ambition. If your lot in life is a beautiful bird that you love dearly, you gladly feed to him the seeds of your inner self, and make your heart his cage and your soul his nest. But while you are affectionately admiring him and looking upon him with the eyes of love, he escapes from your hands and flies very high; then he descends and enters into another cage and never comes back to you. What can you do? Where can you find patience and condolence? How can you revive your hopes and dreams? What power can still your turbulent heart?"

Having uttered these words with a choking voice and suffering spirit, Rashid Bey Namaan stood shaking like a reed between the north and south wind. He extended his hands as if to grasp something with his bent fingers and destroy it. His wrinkled face was livid, his eyes grew larger as he stared a few moments, and it seemed to him as if he saw a demon appearing from nonexistence to take him away; then he fixed his eyes on mine and his appearance suddenly changed; his anger was converted into keen suffering and distress, and he cried out saying, "It is the woman whom I rescued from between the deathly paws of poverty; I opened my coffers to her and made her envied by all women for the beautiful raiment and precious gems and magnificent carriages drawn by spirited horses; the woman whom my heart has loved and at whose feet I poured my affection; the woman, to whom I was a true friend, sincere companion and a faithful husband; the woman who betrayed me and departed me for another man to share with him destitution and partake his evil bread, kneaded with shame and mixed with disgrace. The woman I loved; the beautiful bird whom I fed, and to whom I made my heart a cage, and my soul a nest, has escaped from my hands and entered into another cage; that pure angel, who resided in the paradise of my affection and love, now appears to me as a horrible demon, descended into the darkness to suffer for her sin and cause me to suffer on earth for her crime."

He hid his face with his hands as if wanting to protect himself from himself, and became silent for a moment. Then he sighed and said, "This is all I can tell you; please do not ask anything further. Do not make a crying voice of my calamity, but let it rather be mute misfortune; perhaps it will grow in silence and deaden me away so that I may rest at last with peace."

I rose with tears in my eyes and mercy in my heart, and silently bade him goodbye; my words had no power to console his wounded heart, and my knowledge had no torch to illuminate his gloomy self.

PART TWO

A few days thereafter I met Madame Rose Hanie for the first time, in a poor hovel, surrounded by flowers and trees. She had heard of me through Rashid Bey Namaan, the man whose heart she had crushed and stamped upon and left under the terrible hoofs of Life. As I looked at her beautiful bright eyes, and heard her sincere voice, I said to myself, "Can this be the sordid woman? Can this clear face hide an ugly soul and a criminal heart? Is this the unfaithful wife? Is this the woman of whom I have spoken evil and imagined as a serpent disguised in the form of a beautiful bird?" Then I whispered again to myself saying, "Is it this beautiful face that made Rashid Bey Namaan miserable? Haven't we heard that obvious beauty is the cause of many hidden distresses and deep suffering? Is not the beautiful moon, that inspires the poets, the same moon that angers the silence of the sea with a terrible roar?"

As we seated ourselves, Madame Hanie seemed to have heard and read my thoughts and wanted not to prolong my doubts. She leaned her beautiful head upon her hands and with a voice sweeter than the sound of the lyre, she said, "I have never met you, but I heard the echoes of your thoughts and dreams from the mouths of the people, and they convinced me that you are merciful and have understanding for the oppressed woman—the woman whose heart's secrets you have discovered and whose affections you have known. Allow me to reveal to you the full contents of my heart so you may know that Rose Hanie never was an unfaithful woman.

"I was scarcely eighteen years of age when fate led me to Rashid Bey Namaan, who was then forty years old. He fell in love with me, according to what the people say, and took me for a wife and put me in his magnificent home, placing at my disposal servants and maids and dressing me with expensive clothes and precious gems. He exhibited me as a strange rarity at the homes of his friends and family; he smiled with triumph when he saw his contemporaries looking upon me with surprise and admiration; he lifted his chin high with pride when he heard the ladies speak of me with praise and affection. But never could he hear the whispers, 'Is this the wife of Rashid Bey Namaan, or his adopted daughter?' And another one commenting, 'If he had married at the proper age, his first born would have been older than Rose Hanie.'

"All that happened before my life had awakened from the deep swoon of youth, and before God inflamed my heart with the torch of love, and before the growth of the seeds of my affections. Yes, all this transpired during the time when I believed that real happiness came through beautiful clothes and magnificent mansions. When I woke up from the slumber of childhood, I felt the flames of sacred fire burning in my heart, and a spiritual hunger gnawing at my soul, making it suffer. When I opened my eyes, I found my wings moving to the right and left, trying to ascend into the spacious firmament of love, but shivering and dropping under the gusts of the shackles of laws that bound my body to a man before I knew the true meaning of that law. I felt all these things and knew that a woman's happiness does not come through man's glory and honour, nor through his generosity and affection, but through love that unites both of their hearts and affections, making them one member of life's body and one word upon the lips of God. When Truth showed herself to me, I found myself imprisoned by law in the mansion of Rashid Bey Nemaan, like a thief stealing his bread and hiding in the dark and friendly corners of the night. I knew that every hour spent with him was a terrible lie written upon my forehead with letters of fire before heaven and earth. I could not give him my love and affection in reward for his generosity and sincerity. I tried in vain to love him, but love is a power that makes our hearts, yet our hearts cannot make that power. I prayed and prayed in the silence of the night before God to create in the depths of my heart a spiritual attachment that would carry me closer to the man who had been chosen for me as a companion through life.

"My prayers were not granted, because Love descends upon our souls by the will of God and not by the demand or the plea of the individual. Thus I remained for two years in the home of that man, envying the birds of the field their freedom while my friends envied me my painful chains of gold. I was like a woman who is torn from her only child; like a lamenting heart, existing without attachment;

like an innocent victim of the severity of human law. I was close to death from spiritual thirst and hunger.

"One dark day, as I looked behind the heavy skies, I saw a gentle light pouring from the eyes of a man who was walking forlornly on the path of life; I closed my eyes to that light and said to myself, 'Oh, my soul, darkness of the grave is thy lot, do not be greedy for the light.' Then I heard a beautiful melody from heaven that revived my wounded heart with its purity, but I closed my ears and said, 'Oh, my soul, the cry of the abyss is thy lot, do not be greedy for heavenly songs.' I closed my eyes again so I could not see, and shut my ears so I could not hear, but my closed eyes still saw that gentle light, and my ears still heard that divine sound. I was frightened for the first time and felt like the beggar who found a precious jewel near the Emir's palace and could not pick it up on account of fear, or leave it because of poverty. I cried–a cry of a thirsty soul who sees a brook surrounded by wild beasts, and falls upon the ground waiting and watching fearfully."

Then she turned her eyes away from me as if she remembered the past that made her ashamed to face me, but she continued, "Those people who go back to eternity before they taste the sweetness of real life are unable to understand the meaning of a woman's suffering. Especially when she devotes her soul to a man she loves by the will of God, and her body to another whom she caresses by the enforcement of earthly law. It is a tragedy written with the woman's blood and tears which the man reads with ridicule because he cannot understand it; yet, if he does understand, his laughter will turn into scorn and blasphemy that act like fire upon her heart. It is a drama enacted by the black nights upon the stage of a woman's soul, whose body is tied up into a man, known to her as husband, ere she perceives God's meaning of marriage. She finds her soul hovering about the man whom she adores by all agencies of pure and true love and beauty. It is a terrible agony that began with the existence of weakness in a woman and the commencement of strength in a man. It will not end unless the days of slavery and superiority of the strong over the weak are abolished. It is a horrible war between the corrupt law of humanity and the sacred affections and holy purpose of the heart. In such a battlefield I was lying yesterday, but I gathered the remnants of my strength, and unchained my irons of cowardice, and untied my wings from the swaddles of weakness and arose into the spacious sky of love and freedom.

"Today I am one with the man I love; he and I sprang out as one torch from the hand of God before the beginning of the world. There is no power under the sun that can take my happiness from me, because it emanated from two embraced spirits, engulfed by understanding, radiated by Love, and protected by heaven."

She looked at me as if she wanted to penetrate

my heart with her eyes in order to discover the impression of her words upon me, and to hear the echo of her voice from within me; but I remained silent and she continued. Her voice was full of bitterness of memory and sweetness of sincerity and freedom when she said, "The people will tell you that Rose Hanie is an heretic and unfaithful woman who followed her desires by leaving the man who elated her into him and made her the elegance of his home. They will tell you that she is an adulteress and prostitute who destroyed with her filthy hands the wreath of a sacred marriage and replaced it with a besmirched union woven of the thorns of hell. She took off the garment of virtue and put on the cloak of sin and disgrace. They will tell you more than that, because the ghosts of their fathers are still living in their bodies. They are like the deserted caves of the mountains that echo voices whose meanings are not understood. They neither understand the law of God, nor comprehend the true intent of veritable religion, nor distinguish between a sinner and an innocent. They look only at the surface of objects without knowing their secrets. They pass their verdicts with ignorance, and judge with blindness, making the criminal and the innocent, the good and the bad, equal. Woe to those who prosecute and judge the people. . . .

"In God's eyes I was unfaithful and an adulteress only while at the home of Rashid Bey Namaan, because he made me his wife according to the customs and traditions and by the force of haste, before heaven had made him mine in conformity with the spiritual law of Love and Affection. I was a sinner in the eyes of God and myself when I ate his bread and offered him my body in reward for his generosity. Now I am pure and clean because the law of Love has freed me and made me honourable and faithful. I ceased selling my body for shelter and my days for clothes. Yes, I was an adulteress and a criminal when the people viewed me as the most honourable and faithful wife; today I am pure and noble in spirit, but in their opinion I am polluted, for they judge the soul by the outcome of the body and measure the spirit by the standard of matter."

Then she looked through the window and pointed out with her right hand toward the city as if she had seen the ghost of corruption and the shadow of shame among its magnificent buildings. She said pityingly, "Look at those majestic mansions and sublime palaces where hypocrisy resides; in those edifices and between their beautifully decorated walls resides Treason beside Putridity; under the ceiling painted with melted gold lives Falsehood beside Pretension. Notice those gorgeous homes that represent happiness, glory and domination; they are naught but caverns of misery and distress. They are plastered graves in which Treason of the weak woman hides behind her kohled eyes and crimsoned lips; in their corners selfishness exists, and the animality of man through his gold and silver rules supreme.

"If those high and impregnable buildings scented the odor of hatred, deceit and corruption, they would have cracked and fallen. The poor villager looks upon those residences with tearful eyes, but when he finds that the hearts of the occupants are empty of that pure love that exists in the heart of his wife and fills its domain, he will smile and go back to his fields contented."

And then she took hold of my hand and led me to the side of the window and said, "Come, I will show you the unveiled secrets of those people whose path I refused to follow. Look at that palace with giant columns. In it lives a rich man who inherited his gold from his father. After having led a life of filth and putrefaction, he married a woman about whom he knew nothing except that her father was one of the Sultan's dignitaries. As soon as the wedding trip was over he became disgusted and commenced associations with women who sell their bodies for pieces of silver. His wife was left alone in that palace like an empty bottle left by a drunkard. She cried and suffered for the first time; then she realized that her tears were more precious than her degenerate husband. Now she is busying herself in the love and devotion of a young man upon whom she showers her joyous hours, and into whose heart she pours her sincere love and affection.

"Let me take you now to that gorgeous home surrounded by beautiful gardens. It is the home of a man who comes from a noble family which ruled the country for many generations, but whose standards, wealth, and prestige have declined due to their indulgence in mad spending and slothfulness. A few years ago this man married an ugly but rich woman. After he acquired her fortune, he ignored her completely and commenced devoting himself to an attractive young woman. His wife today is devoting her time to curling her hair, painting her lips and perfuming her body. She wears the most expensive clothes and hopes that some young man will smile and come to visit her, but it is all in vain, for she cannot succeed except in receiving a smile from her ugly self in the mirror.

"Observe that big manor, encircled with marble statuary; it is the home of a beautiful woman who possesses strange character. When her first husband died, she inherited all his money and estates; then she selected a man with a weak mind and feeble body and became his wife to protect herself from the evil tongues, and to use him as a shield for her abominations. She is now among her admirers like a bee that sucks the sweetest and most delicious flowers.

"That beautiful home next to it was built by the greatest architect in the province; it belongs to a greedy and substantial man who devotes all of his time to amassing gold and grinding the faces of the poor. He has a wife of supernatural beauty, bodily and spiritually, but she is like the rest, a victim of early marriage. Her father committed a crime by giving her away to a man before she attained understanding age, placing on her neck the heavy yoke of corrupt marriage. She is thin and pale now, and cannot find an outlet for her imprisoned affection. She is sinking slowly and craving for death to free her from the mesh of slavery and deliver her from a man who spends his life gathering gold and cursing the hour he married a barren woman who could not bring him a child to carry on his name and inherit his money.

"In that home among those orchards lives an ideal poet; he married an ignorant woman who ridicules his works because she cannot understand them, and laughs at his conduct because she cannot adjust herself to his sublime way of life. That poet found freedom from despair in his love for a married woman who appreciates his intelligence and inspires him by kindling in his heart the torch of affections, and revealing to him the most beautiful and eternal sayings by means of her charm and beauty."

Silence prevailed for a few moments, and Madame Hanie seated herself on a sofa by the window as if her soul were tired of roaming those quarters. Then she slowly continued, "These are the residences in which I refused to live; these are the graves in which I, too, was spiritually buried. Those people from whom I have freed myself are the ones who become attracted by the body and repelled by the spirit, and who know naught of Love and Beauty. The only mediator between them and God is God's pity for their ignorance of the law of God. I cannot judge, for I was one of them, but I sympathize with all my heart. I do not hate them, but I hate their surrender to weakness and falsehood. I have said all these things to show you the reality of people from whom I have escaped against their will. I was trying to explain to you the life of persons who speak every evil against me because I have lost their friendship and finally gained my own. I emerged from their dark dungeon and directed my eyes towards the light where sincerity, truth and justice prevail. They have exiled me now from their society and I am pleased, because humanity does not exile except the one whose noble spirit rebels against despotism and oppression. He who does not prefer exile to slavery is not free by any measure of freedom, truth and duty.

"Yesterday I was like a tray containing all kinds of palatable food, and Rashid Bey Namaan never approached me unless he felt a need for that food; yet both of our souls remained far apart from us like two humble, dignified servants. I have tried to reconcile myself to what people call misfortune, but my spirit refused to spend all its life kneeling with me before a horrible idol erected by the dark ages and called LAW. I kept my chains until I heard Love calling me and saw my spirit preparing to embark. Then I broke them and walked out from Rashid Bey Namaan's home like a bird freed from his iron cage and leaving behind me all the gems, clothes and servants. I came to live with my beloved, for I knew that what I was doing was honest. Heaven does not want me to weep and suffer. Many times at night I prayed for dawn to come and when dawn came, I prayed for the day to be over. God does not want me to lead a miserable life, for He placed in the depths of my heart a desire for happiness; His glory rests in the happiness of my heart.

"This is my story and this my protest before heaven and earth; this is what I sing and repeat while the people are closing their ears for fear of hearing me and leading their spirits into rebellion that would crumble the foundation of their quavering society.

"This is the rough pathway I have carved until I reached the mountain peak of my happiness. Now if death comes to take me away, I will be more than willing to offer myself before the Supreme Throne of Heaven without fear or shame. I am ready for the day of judgment and my heart is white as the snow. I have obeyed the will of God in everything I have done and followed the call of my heart while listening to the angelic voice of heaven. This is my drama which the people of Beyrouth call 'A curse upon the lips of life,' and 'An ailment in the body of society.' But one day love will arouse their hearts like the sun rays that bring forth the flowers even from contaminated earth. One day the wayfarers will stop by my grave and greet the earth that enfolds my body and say, 'Here lies Rose Hanie who freed herself from the slavery of decayed human laws in order to comply with God's law of pure love. She turned her face toward the sun so she would not see the shadow of her body amongst the skulls and thorns.' "

The door was opened and a man entered. His eyes were shining with magic rays and upon his lips appeared a wholesome smile. Madame Hanie rose, took the young man's arm and introduced him to me, then gave him my name with flattering words. I knew that he was the one for whose sake she denied the whole world and violated all earthly laws and customs.

As we sat down, silence controlled. Each one of us was engrossed in deep thought. One minute worthy of silence and respect had passed when I looked at the couple sitting side by side. I saw something I had never seen before, and realized instantly the meaning of Madame Hanie's story. I comprehended the secret of her protest against the society which persecutes those who rebel against confining laws and customs before determining the cause for the rebellion. I saw one heavenly spirit before me, composed of two beautiful and united persons, in the midst of which stood the god of Love stretching his wings over them to protect them from evil tongues. I found a complete understanding emanating from two smiling faces, illuminated by sincerity and surrounded by virtue. For the first time in my life I found the phantom of happiness standing between a man and a woman, cursed by religion and opposed by the law. I rose and bade them goodbye and left that poor hovel which Affection had erected as an altar to Love and Understanding. I walked past the buildings which Madame Hanie pointed out to me. As I reached the end of these quarters I remembered Rashid Bey Namaan and meditated his miserable plight and said to myself, "He is oppressed; will heaven ever listen to him if he complains about Madame Hanie? Had that woman done wrong when she left him and followed the freedom of her heart? Or did he commit a crime by subduing her body in marriage before subduing her heart in love? Which of the two is the oppressed and which is the oppressor? Who is the criminal and who is the innocent?"

Then I resumed talking to myself after a few moments of deep thinking. "Many times deception had tempted woman to leave her husband and follow wealth, because her love for riches and beautiful raiment blinds her and leads her into shame. Was Madame Hanie deceitful when she left her rich husband's palace for a poor man's hut? Many times ignorance kills a woman's honour and revives her passion; she grows tired and leaves her husband, prompted by her desires, and follows a man to whom she lowers herself. Was Madame Hanie an ignorant woman following her physical desires when she declared publicly her independence and joined her beloved young man? She could have satisfied herself secretly while at her husband's home, for many men were willing to be the slaves of her beauty and martyrs of her love. Madame Hanie was a miserable woman. She sought only happiness, found it, and embraced it. This is the very truth which society disrespects." Then I whispered through the ether and inquired of myself, "Is it permissible for a woman to buy her happiness with her husband's misery?" And my soul added, "Is it lawful for a man to enslave his wife's affection when he realizes he will never possess it?"

I continued walking and Madame Hanie's voice was still sounding in my ears when I reached the extreme end of the city. The sun was disappearing and silence ruled the fields and prairies while the birds commenced singing their evening prayers. I stood there meditating, and then I sighed and said, "Before the throne of Freedom, the trees rejoice with the frolicsome breeze and enjoy the rays of the sun and the beams of the moon. Through the ears of Freedom these birds whisper and around Freedom they flutter to the music of the brooks. Throughout the sky of Freedom these flowers breathe their fragrance and before Freedom's eyes they smile when dawn comes.

"Everything on earth lives according to the law of nature, and from that law emerges the glory and joy of liberty; but man is denied this fortune, because he set for the God-given soul a limited and earthly law of his own. He made for himself strict rules. Man built a narrow and painful prison in which he secluded his affections and desires. He dug out a deep grave in which he buried his heart and its purpose. If an individual, through the dictates of his soul, declares his withdrawal from society and violates the law, his fellowmen will say he is a rebel worthy of exile, or an infamous creature worthy only of execution. Will man remain a slave of self-confinement until the end of the world? Or will he be freed by the passing of time and live in the Spirit for the Spirit? Will man insist upon staring downward and backward at the earth? Or will he turn his eyes toward the sun so he will not see the shadow of his body amongst the skulls and thorns?"

LEAVE ME, MY BLAMER

Leave me, my blamer,
For the sake of the love
Which unites your soul with
That of your beloved one;
For the sake of that which
Joins spirit with mother's
Affection, and ties your
Heart with filial love. Go,
And leave me to my own
Weeping heart.

Let me sail in the ocean of
My dreams; wait until Tomorrow
Comes, for Tomorrow is free to
Do with me as he wishes. Your
Flaying is naught but shadow
That walks with the spirit to
The tomb of abashment, and shows
Her the cold, solid earth.

I have a little heart within me
And I like to bring him out of

His prison and carry him on the
Palm of my hand to examine him
In depth and extract his secret.
Aim not your arrows at him, lest
He take fright and vanish ere he
Pours the secret's blood as a
Sacrifice at the altar of his
Own faith, given him by Deity
When He fashioned him of Love and Beauty.

The sun is rising and the nightingale
Is singing, and the myrtle is
Breathing its fragrance into space.
I want to free myself from the
Quilted slumber of wrong. Do not
Detain me, my blamer!

Cavil me not by mention of the
Lions of the forest or the
Snakes of the valley, for
My soul knows no fear of earth and
Accepts no warning of evil before
Evil comes.

Advise me not, my blamer, for
Calamities have opened my heart and
Tears have cleansed my eyes, and
Errors have taught me the language
Of the hearts.

Talk not of banishment, for Conscience
Is my judge and he will justify me

And protect me if I am innocent, and
Will deny me of life if I am a criminal.

Love's procession is moving;
Beauty is waving her banner;
Youth is sounding the trumpet of joy;
Disturb not my contrition, my blamer.
Let me walk, for the path is rich
With roses and mint, and the air
Is scented with cleanliness.

Relate not the tales of wealth and
Greatness, for my soul is rich
With bounty and great with God's glory.

Speak not of peoples and laws and
Kingdoms, for the whole earth is
My birthplace and all humans are
My brothers.

Go from me, for you are taking away
Life-giving repentance and bringing
Needless words.

VISION

THERE in the middle of the field, by the side of a crystalline stream, I saw a bird-cage whose rods and hinges were fashioned by an expert's hands. In one corner lay a dead bird, and in another were two basins—one empty of water and the other of seeds. I stood there reverently, as if the lifeless bird and the murmur of the water were worthy of deep silence and respect—something worthy of examination and meditation by the heart and conscience.

As I engrossed myself in view and thought, I found that the poor creature had died of thirst beside a stream of water, and of hunger in the midst of a rich field, cradle of life; like a rich man locked inside his iron safe, perishing from hunger amid heaps of gold.

Before my eyes I saw the cage turned suddenly into a human skeleton, and the dead bird into a man's heart which was bleeding from a deep wound that looked like the lips of a sorrowing woman. A voice came from that wound saying, "I am the human heart, prisoner of substance and victim of earthly laws.

"In God's field of Beauty, at the edge of the stream of life, I was imprisoned in the cage of laws made by man.

"In the center of beautiful Creation I died neglected because I was kept from enjoying the freedom of God's bounty.

"Everything of beauty that awakens my love and desire is a disgrace, according to man's conceptions; everything of goodness that I crave is but naught, according to his judgment.

"I am the lost human heart, imprisoned in the foul dungeon of man's dictates, tied with chains of earthly authority, dead and forgotten by laughing humanity whose tongue is tied and whose eyes are empty of visible tears."

All these words I heard, and I saw them emerging with a stream of ever-thinning blood from that wounded heart.

More was said, but my misted eyes and crying soul prevented further sight or hearing.

SONG OF THE FLOWER

I AM A KIND WORD uttered and repeated
By the voice of Nature;
I am a star fallen from the
Blue tent upon the green carpet.
I am the daughter of the elements
With whom Winter conceived;
To whom Spring gave birth; I was
Reared in the lap of Summer and I
Slept in the bed of Autumn.

At dawn I unite with the breeze
To announce the coming of light;
At eventide I join the birds
In bidding the light farewell.

The plains are decorated with
My beautiful colours, and the air
Is scented with my fragrance.

As I embrace Slumber the eyes of
Night watch over me, and as I
Awaken I stare at the sun, which is
The only eye of the day.

I drink dew for wine, and hearken to
The voices of the birds, and dance
To the rhythmic swaying of the grass.

I am the lover's gift; I am the wedding wreath;
I am the memory of a moment of happiness;
I am the last gift of the living to the dead;
I am a part of joy and a part of sorrow.

But I look up high to see only the light,
And never look down to see my shadow.
This is wisdom which man must learn.

SOCIETY

THE SUFFERINGS of the multitudes are as the agonies of gnawing pain, and in the mouth of society there are many decayed and ailing teeth. But society declines the careful and patient remedy, satisfying itself with polishing the exteriors and stuffing them with resplendent, glittering gold that blinds the eye to the decay beyond. But the patient cannot blind himself to the continuing pain.

Many are the social dentists who endeavour to administer to the evils of the world, offering fillings of beauty, and many are the sufferers who yield to the will of the reformers and thereby increase their own suffering, draw deeper of their waning strength, and deceive themselves more surely into the abyss of death.

The decayed teeth of Syria are found in her schools, wherein today's youth is taught to be tomorrow's sorrow; and in her courts of justice, wherein the judges twist and play with the law as a tiger plays with its prey; and in the palaces, wherein falsehood and hypocrisy prevail; and in the huts of the poor, wherein fear, ignorance, and cowardice abide

The political dentists of soft fingers pour honey into the ears of the people, shouting that they are filling the crevices of the nation's weakness. Their song is made to sound higher than the sound of the grinding millstone, but in truth it is no nobler than the croaking of the frogs in the stagnant marsh.

Many are the thinkers and idealists in this world of emptiness . . . and how faint are their dreams!

SONG OF MAN

I WAS HERE from the moment of the
Beginning, and here I am still. And
I shall remain here until the end
Of the world, for there is no
Ending to my grief-stricken being.

I roamed the infinite sky, and
Soared in the ideal world, and
Floated through the firmament. But
Here I am, prisoner of measurement.

I heard the teachings of Confucius;
I listened to Brahma's wisdom;
I sat by Buddha under the Tree of Knowledge.
Yet here am I, existing with ignorance
And heresy.

I was on Sinai when Jehovah approached Moses;
I saw the Nazarene's miracles at the Jordan;
I was in Medina when Mohammed visited.
Yet here I am, prisoner of bewilderment.

Then I witnessed the might of Babylon;
I learned of the glory of Egypt;
I viewed the warring greatness of Rome.
Yet my earlier teachings showed the
Weakness and sorrow of those achievements.

I conversed with the magicians of Ain Dour;
I debated with the priests of Assyria;
I gleaned depth from the prophets of Palestine.
Yet, I am still seeking the truth.

I gathered wisdom from quiet India;
I probed the antiquity of Arabia;
I heard all that can be heard.
Yet, my heart is deaf and blind.

I suffered at the hands of despotic rulers;
I suffered slavery under insane invaders;
I suffered hunger imposed by tyranny;
Yet, I still possess some inner power
With which I struggle to greet each day.

My mind is filled, but my heart is empty;
My body is old, but my heart is an infant.
Perhaps in youth my heart will grow, but I
Pray to grow old and reach the moment of
My return to God. Only then will my heart fill!

I was here from the moment of the
Beginning, and here I am still. And
I shall remain here until the end
Of the world, for there is no
Ending to my grief-stricken being.

BOOK 6

KHALIL THE HERETIC

PART ONE

Sheik Abbas was looked upon as a prince by the people of a solitary village in North Lebanon. His mansion stood in the midst of those poor villagers' huts like a healthy giant amidst sickly dwarfs. He lived amid luxury while they pursued an existence of penury. They obeyed him and bowed reverently before him as he spoke to them. It seemed as though the power of mind had appointed him its official interpreter and spokesman. His anger would make them tremble and scatter like autumn leaves before a strong wind. If he were to slap one's face, it would be heresy on the individual's part to move or lift his head or make any attempt to discover why the blow had come. If he smiled at a man, the villagers would consider the person thus honoured as the most fortunate. The people's fear and surrender to Sheik Abbas were not due to weakness; however, their poverty and need of him had brought about this state of continual humiliation. Even the huts they lived in and the fields they cultivated were owned by Sheik Abbas who had inherited them from his ancestors.

The farming of the land and the sowing of the seeds and the gathering of wheat were all done under the supervision of the Sheik who, in reward for their toil, compensated them with a small portion of the crop which barely kept them from falling as victims of gnawing starvation.

Often many of them were in need of bread before the crop was reaped, and they came to Sheik Abbas and asked him with pouring tears to advance them a few piastres or a bushel of wheat, and the Sheik gladly granted their request for he knew that they would pay their debts doubly when harvest time came. Thus those people remained obligated all their lives, left a legacy of debts to their children and were submissive to their master whose anger they had always feared and whose friendship and good will they had constantly but unsuccessfully endeavoured to win.

PART TWO

Winter came and brought heavy snow and strong winds; the valleys and the fields became empty of all things except leafless trees which stood as spectres of death above the lifeless plains.

Having stored the products of the land in the Sheik's bins and filled his vases with the wine of the vineyards, the villagers retreated to their huts to spend a portion of their lives idling by the fireside and commemorating the glory of the past ages and relating to one another the tales of weary days and long nights.

The old year had just breathed its last into the grey sky. The night had arrived during which the New Year would be crowned and placed upon the throne of the Universe. The snow began to fall heavily and the whistling winds were racing from the lofty mountains down to the abyss and blowing the snow into heaps to be stored away in the valleys.

The trees were shaking under the heavy storms and the fields and knolls were covered with a white floor upon which Death was writing vague lines and effacing them. The mists stood as partitions between the scattered villages by the sides of the valleys. The lights that flickered through the windows of those wretched huts disappeared behind the thick veil of Nature's wrath.

Fear penetrated the fellahin's hearts and the animals stood by their mangers in the sheds, while the dogs were hiding in the corners. One could hear the voices of the screaming winds and thundering of the storms resounding from the depths of the valleys. It seemed as if Nature were enraged by the passing of the old year and trying to wrest revenge from those peaceful souls by fighting with weapons of cold and frost.

That night under the raging sky, a young man was attempting to walk the winding trail that connected Deir Kizhaya * with Sheik Abbas' village. The youth's limbs were numbed with cold, while pain and hunger usurped him of his strength. The black raiment he wore was bleached with the falling snow, as if he were shrouded in death before the hour of his death had come. He was struggling against the wind. His progress was difficult, and he took but a few steps forward with each effort. He called for help and then stood silent, shivering in the cold night. He had slim hope, withering between great despair and deep sorrow. He was like a bird with a broken wing, who fell in a stream whose whirlpools carried him down to the depths.

The young man continued walking and falling until his blood stopped circulating and he collapsed. He uttered a terrible sound . . . the voice of a soul who encountered the hollow face of Death . . . a voice of dying youth, weakened by man and trapped by nature . . . a voice of the love of existence in the space of nothingness.

PART THREE

On the north side of that village, in the midst of the wind-torn fields, stood the solitary home of a woman named Rachel, and her daughter Miriam who had not then attained the age of eighteen. Rachel was the

* One of the richest and most famous convents in Lebanon. Kizhaya is a Syriac word meaning "Paradise of Life." (*Editor's note.*)

widow of Samaan Ramy, who was found slain six years earlier, but the law of man did not find the murderer.

Like the rest of the Lebanese widows, Rachel sustained life through long, hard work. During the harvest season, she would look for ears of corn left behind by others in the field, and in Autumn she gathered the remnants of some forgotten fruits in the gardens. In Winter she spun wool and made raiment for which she received a few piastres or a bushel of grain. Miriam, her daughter, was a beautiful girl who shared with her mother the burden of toil.

That bitter night the two women were sitting by the fireplace whose warmth was weakened by the frost and whose firebrands were buried beneath the ashes. By their side was a flickering lamp that sent its yellow, dimmed rays into the heart of darkness like prayer that sends phantoms of hope into the hearts of the sorrowful.

Midnight had come and they were listening to the wailing winds outside. Every now and then Miriam would get up, open the small transom and look toward the obscured sky, and then she would return to her chair worried and frightened by the raging elements. Suddenly Miriam started, as if she had awakened from a swoon of deep slumber. She looked anxiously toward her mother and said, "Did you hear that, Mother? Did you hear a voice calling for help?" The mother listened a moment and said,

"I hear nothing except the crying wind, my daughter." Then Miriam exclaimed, "I heard a voice deeper than the thundering heaven and more sorrowful than the wailing of the tempest."

Having uttered these words, she stood up and opened the door and listened for a moment. Then she said, "I hear it again, Mother!" Rachel hurried toward the frail door and after a moment's hesitation she said, "And I hear it, too. Let us go and see."

She wrapped herself with a long robe, opened the door and walked out cautiously, while Miriam stood at the door, the wind blowing her long hair.

Having forced her way a short distance through the snow, Rachel stopped and shouted out, "Who is calling . . . where are you?" There was no answer; then she repeated the same words again and again, but she heard naught except thunder. Then she courageously advanced forward, looking in every direction. She had walked for some time, when she found some deep footprints upon the snow; she followed them fearfully and in a few moments found a human body lying before her on the snow, like a patch on a white dress. As she approached him and leaned his head over her knees, she felt his pulse that bespoke his slowing heart beats and his slim chance in life. She turned her face toward the hut and called, "Come, Miriam, come and help me, I have found him!" Miriam rushed out and followed her mother's footprints, while shivering with cold and trembling with fear. As she reached the place and saw the youth lying motionless, she cried with an aching voice. The mother put her hands under his armpits, calmed Miriam and said, "Fear not, for he is still living; hold the lower edge of his cloak and let us carry him home."

Confronted with the strong wind and heavy snow, the two women carried the youth and started toward the hut. As they reached the little haven, they laid him down by the fireplace. Rachel commenced rubbing his numbed hands and Miriam drying his hair with the end of her dress. The youth began to move after a few minutes. His eyelids quivered and he took a deep sigh—a sigh that brought the hope of his safety into the hearts of the merciful women. They removed his shoes and took off his black robe. Miriam looked at her mother and said, "Observe his raiment, Mother; these clothes are worn by the monks." After feeding the fire with a bundle of dry sticks, Rachel looked at her daughter with perplexity and said, "The monks do not leave their convent on such a terrible night." And Miriam inquired, "But he has no hair on his face; the monks wear beards." The mother gazed at him with eyes full of mercy and maternal love; then she turned to her daughter and said, "It makes no difference whether he is a monk or a criminal; dry his feet well, my daughter." Rachel opened a closet, took from it a jar of wine and poured some in an earthenware bowl. Miriam held his head while the mother gave him some of it to stimulate his heart. As he sipped the wine he opened his eyes for the first time and gave his rescuers a sorrowful look mingled with tears of gratitude—the look of a human who felt the smooth touch of life after having been gripped in the sharp claws of death—a look of great hope after hope had died. Then he bent his head, and his lips trembled when he uttered the words, "May God bless both of you." Rachel placed her hand upon his shoulder and said, "Be calm, brother. Do not tire yourself with talking until you gain strength." And Miriam added, "Rest your head on this pillow, brother, and we will place you closer to the fire." Rachel refilled the bowl with wine and gave it to him. She looked at her daughter and said, "Hang his robe by the fire so it will dry." Having executed her mother's command, she returned and commenced looking at him mercifully, as if she wanted to help him by pouring into his heart all the warmth of her soul. Rachel brought two loaves of bread with some preserves and dry fruits; she sat by him and began to feed him small morsels, as a mother feeds her little child. At this time he felt stronger and sat up on the hearth mat while the red flames of fire reflected upon his sad face. His eyes brightened and he shook his head slowly, saying, "Mercy and cruelty are both wrestling in the human heart like the mad elements in the sky of this terrible night, but mercy shall overcome cruelty because it is divine, and the terror alone, of this night, shall pass away when daylight comes." Silence prevailed for a minute and then he added with a whispering voice, "A human hand drove me into desperation and a human hand rescued me; how severe man is, and how merciful man is!" And Rachel inquired, "How ventured you, brother, to leave the convent on such a terrible night, when even the beasts do not venture forth?"

The youth shut his eyes as if he wanted to restore his tears back into the depths of his heart, whence they came, and he said, "The animals have their caves, and the birds of the sky their nests, but the son of man has no place to rest his head." Rachel retorted, "That is what Jesus said about himself." And the young man resumed, "This is the answer for every man who wants to follow the Spirit and the Truth in this age of falsehood, hypocrisy and corruption."

After a few moments of contemplation, Rachel said, "But there are many comfortable rooms in the convent, and the coffers are full of gold, and all kinds of provisions. The sheds of the convent are stocked with fat calves and sheep; what made you leave such haven in this deathly night?" The youth sighed deeply and said, "I left that place because I hated it." And Rachel rejoined, "A monk in a convent is like a soldier in the battlefield who is required to obey the orders of his leader regardless of their nature. I heard that a man could not become a monk unless he did away with his will, his thoughts, his desires, and all that pertains to the mind. But a good head priest does not ask his monks to do unreasonable things. How could the head priest of Deir Kizhaya ask you to give up your life to the storms and snow?" And he remarked, "In the opinion of the head priest, a man cannot become a monk unless he is blind and ignorant, senseless and dumb. I left the convent because I am a sensible man who can see, feel, and hear."

Miriam and Rachel stared at him as if they had found in his face a hidden secret; after a moment of meditation the mother said, "Will a man who sees and hears go out on a night that blinds the eyes and deafens the ears?" And the youth stated quietly, "I was expelled from the convent." "Expelled!" exclaimed Rachel; and Miriam repeated the same word in unison with her mother.

He lifted his head, regretting his words, for he was afraid lest their love and sympathy be converted into hatred and disrespect; but when he looked at them and found the rays of mercy still emanating from their eyes, and their bodies vibrating with anxiety to learn further, his voice choked and he continued, "Yes, I was expelled from the convent because I could not dig my grave with my own hands, and my heart grew weary of lying and pilfering. I was expelled from the convent because my soul refused to enjoy the bounty of a people who surrendered themselves to ignorance. I was driven away because I could not find rest in the comfortable rooms, built with the money of the poor fellahin. My stomach could not hold bread baked with the tears of orphans. My lips could not utter prayers sold for gold and food by the heads to the simple and faithful people. I was expelled from the convent like a filthy leper because I was repeating to the monks the rules that qualified them to their present position."

Silence prevailed while Rachel and Miriam were contemplating his words and gazing at him, when they asked, "Are your father and mother living?" And he responded, "I have no father or mother nor a place that is my home." Rachel drew a deep sigh and Miriam turned her face toward the wall to hide her merciful and loving tears.

As a withering flower is brought back to life by dew drops that dawn pours into its begging petals, so the youth's anxious heart was enlivened by his benefactors' affection and kindness. He looked at them as a soldier looks upon his liberators who rescue him from the grip of the enemy, and he resumed, "I lost my parents before I reached the age of seven. The village priest took me to Deir Kizhaya and left me at the disposal of the monks who were happy to take me in and put me in charge of the cows and sheep, which I led each day to the pasture. When I attained the age of fifteen, they put on me this black robe and led me into the altar whereupon the head priest addressed me saying, "Swear by the name of God and all saints, and make a vow to live a virtuous life of poverty and obedience." I repeated the words before I realized their significance or comprehended his own interpretation of poverty, virtue and obedience.

"My name was Khalil, and since that time the monks addressed me as Brother Mobaarak,* but they never did treat me as a brother. They ate the most palatable foods and drank the finest wine, while I lived on dry vegetables and water, mixed with tears. They slumbered in soft beds while I slept on a stone slab in a dark and cold room by the shed. Oftentimes I asked myself, 'When will I become a monk and share with those fortunate priests their bounty? When will my heart stop craving for the food they eat and the wine they drink? When will I cease to tremble with fear before my superiors?' But all my hopes were in vain, for I was kept in the same state; and in addition to caring for the cattle, I was obliged to move heavy stones on my shoulders and to dig pits and ditches. I sustained life on a few morsels of bread given to me in reward for my toil. I knew of no other place to which I might go, and the clergymen at the convent had caused me to abhor everything they were doing. They had poisoned my mind until I commenced to think that the whole world was an ocean of sorrows and miseries and that the convent was the only port of salvation. But when I discovered the source of their food and gold, I was happy that I did not share it."

* Coincidentally, Mobaarak was the name of the Right Reverend Maronite Archbishop who officiated at Kahlil Gibran's last rites. (*Editor's note.*)

Khalil straightened himself and looked about with wonder, as if he had found something beautiful standing before him in that wretched hut. Rachel and Miriam remained silent and he proceeded, "God, who took my father and exiled me as an orphan to the convent, did not want me to spend all my life walking blindly toward a dangerous jungle; nor did He wish me to be a miserable slave for the rest of my life. God opened my eyes and ears and showed me the bright light and made me hear Truth when Truth was talking."

Rachel thought aloud, "Is there any light, other than the sun, that shines over all the people? Are human beings capable of understanding the Truth?" Khalil returned, "The true light is that which emanates from within man, and reveals the secrets of the heart to the soul, making it happy and contented with life. Truth is like the stars; it does not appear except from behind obscurity of the night. Truth is like all beautiful things in the world; it does not disclose its desirability except to those who first feel the influence of falsehood. Truth is a deep kindness that teaches us to be content in our everyday life and share with the people the same happiness."

Rachel rejoined, "Many are those who live according to their goodness, and many are those who believe that compassion to others is the shadow of the law of God to man; but still, they do not rejoice in life, for they remain miserable until death." Khalil replied, "Vain are the beliefs and teachings that make man miserable, and false is the goodness that leads him into sorrow and despair, for it is man's purpose to be happy on this earth and lead the way to felicity and preach its gospel wherever he goes. He who does not see the kingdom of heaven in this life will never see it in the coming life. We came not into this life by exile, but we came as innocent creatures of God, to learn how to worship the holy and eternal spirit and seek the hidden secrets within ourselves from the beauty of life. This is the truth which I have learned from the teachings of the Nazarene. This is the light that came from within me and showed me the dark corners of the convent that threatened my life. This is the deep secret which the beautiful valleys and fields revealed to me when I was hungry, sitting lonely and weeping under the shadow of the trees.

"This is the religion as the convent should impart it; as God wished it; as Jesus taught it. One day, as my soul became intoxicated with the heavenly intoxication of Truth's beauty, I stood bravely before the monks who were gathering in the garden, and criticized their wrong deeds saying, 'Why do you spend your days here and enjoy the bounty of the poor, whose bread you eat was made with the sweat of their bodies and the tears of their hearts? Why are you living in the shadow of parasitism, segregating yourselves from the people who are in need of knowledge? Why are you depriving the country of your help? Jesus has sent you as lambs amongst the wolves; what has made you as wolves amongst the lambs? Why are you fleeing from mankind and from God who created you? If you are better than the people who walk in the procession of life, you should go to them and better their lives; but if you think they are better than you, you should desire to learn from them. How do you take an oath and vow to live in poverty, then forget what you have said and live in luxury? How do you swear an obedience to God and then revolt against all that religion means? How do you adopt virtue as your rule when your hearts are full of lusts? You pretend that you are killing your bodies, but in fact you are killing your souls. You feign to abhor the earthly things, but your hearts are swollen with greed. You have the people believe in you as religious teachers; truly speaking you are like busy cattle who divert themselves from knowledge by grazing in a green and beautiful pasture. Let us restore to the needy the vast land of the convent and give back to them the silver and gold we took from them. Let us disperse from our aloofness and serve the weak who made us strong, and cleanse the country in which we live. Let us teach this miserable nation to smile and rejoice with heaven's bounty and glory of life and freedom.

" 'The people's tears are more beautiful and God-joined than the ease and tranquillity to which you have accustomed yourselves in this place. The sympathy that touches the neighbour's heart is more supreme than the hidden virtue in the unseen corners of the convent. A word of compassion to the weak criminal or prostitute is nobler than the long prayer which we repeat emptily every day in the temple.' "

At this time Khalil took a deep breath. Then he lifted his eyes toward Rachel and Miriam saying, "I was saying all of these things to the monks and they were listening with an air of perplexity, as if they could not believe that a young man would dare stand before them and utter such bold words. When I finished, one of the monks approached and angrily said to me, 'How dare you talk in such fashion in our presence?' And another one came laughing and added, 'Did you learn all this from the cows and pigs you tended in the fields?' And a third one stood up and threatened me saying, 'You shall be punished, heretic!' Then they dispersed as though running away from a leper. Some of them complained to the head priest who summoned me before him at eventide. The monks took delight in anticipation of my suffering, and there was glee on their faces when I was ordered to be scourged and put into prison for forty days and nights. They led me into the dark cell where I spent the time lying in that grave without seeing the light. I could not tell the end of the night from the beginning of the day, and could feel nothing but crawling insects and the earth under me. I could hear naught save the tramping of their feet when my morsel of bread and dish of water mixed with vinegar were brought to me at great intervals.

"When I came out of the prison I was weak and frail, and the monks believed that they had cured me of thinking, and that they had killed my soul's desire. They thought that hunger and thirst had choked the kindness which God placed in my heart. In my forty days of solitude I endeavoured to find a method by which I could help these monks to see the light and hear the true song of life, but all of my ponderings were in vain, for the thick veil which the long ages had woven around their eyes could not be torn away in a short time; and the mortar with which ignorance had cemented their ears was hardened and could not be removed by the touch of soft fingers."

Silence prevailed for a moment, and then Miriam looked at her mother as if asking permission to speak. She said, "You must have talked to the monks again, if they selected this terrible night in which to banish you from the convent. They should learn to be kind even to their enemies."

Khalil returned, "This evening, as the thunder storms and warring elements raged in the sky, I withdrew myself from the monks who were crouching about the fire, telling tales and humourous stories. When they saw me alone they commenced to place their wit at my expense. I was reading my Gospel and contemplating the beautiful sayings of Jesus that made me forget for the time the enraged nature and belligerent elements of the sky, when they approached me with a new spirit of ridicule.

I ignored them by occupying myself and looking through the window, but they became furious because my silence dried the laughter of their hearts and the taunting of their lips. One of them said, 'What are you reading, GreatReformer?' In response to his inquiry, I opened my book and read aloud the following passage, 'But when he saw many of the Pharisees and Saducees come to his baptism, he said unto them, "O generation of vipers, who hath warned you to flee from the wrath to come? Bring forth therefore fruits for repentance; And think not to say within yourselves, 'We have Abraham to our father;' " 'for I say unto you, that God is able of these stones to raise children unto Abraham. And now also the axe is laid unto the root of the trees; therefore every tree which bringeth not forth good fruit is hewn down, and cast into the fire.'

"As I read to them these words of John the Baptist, the monks became silent as if an invisible hand strangled their spirits, but they took false courage and commenced laughing. One of them said, 'We have read these words many times, and we are not in need of a cow grazier to repeat them to us.'

"I protested, 'If you had read these words and comprehended their meaning, these poor villagers would not have frozen or starved to death.' When I said this, one of the monks slapped my face as if I had spoken evil of the priests; another kicked me and a third took the book from me and a fourth one called the head priest who hurried to the scene shaking with anger. He cried out, 'Arrest this rebel and drag him from this sacred place, and let the storm's fury teach him obedience. Take him away and let nature do unto him the will of God, and then wash your hands of the poisonous germs of heresy infesting his raiment. If he should return pleading for forgiveness, do not open the door for him, for the viper will not become a dove if placed in a cage, nor will the briar bear figs if planted in the vineyards.'

"In accordance with the command, I was dragged out by the laughing monks. Before they locked the door behind me, I heard one saying, 'Yesterday you were king of cows and pigs, and today you are dethroned, Oh Great Reformer; go now and be the king of wolves and teach them how to live in their lairs.' "

Khalil sighed deeply, then turned his face and looked toward the flaming fire. With a sweet and loving voice, and with a pained countenance he said, "Thus was I expelled from the convent, and thus did the monks deliver me over to the hands of Death. I fought through the night blindly; the heavy wind was tearing my robe and the piling snow was trapping my feet and pulling me down until I fell, crying desperately for help. I felt that no one heard me except Death, but a power which is all knowledge and mercy had heard my cry. That power did not want me to die before I had learned what is left of life's secrets. That power sent you both to me to save my life from the depth of the abyss and non-existence."

Rachel and Miriam felt as if their spirits understood the mystery of his soul, and they became his partners in feeling and understanding. Notwithstanding her will, Rachel stretched forth and gently touched his hand while tears coursed down from her eyes, and she said, "He who has been chosen by heaven as a defender of Truth will not perish by heaven's own storms and snow." And Miriam added, "The storms and snow may kill the flowers, but cannot deaden the seeds, for the snow keeps them warm from the killing frost."

Khalil's face brightened upon hearing those words of encouragement, and he said, "If you do not look upon me as a rebel and an heretic as the monks did, the persecution which I have sustained in the convent is the symbol of an oppressed nation that has not yet attained knowledge; and this night in which I was on the verge of death is like a revolution that precedes full justice. And from a sensitive woman's heart springs the happiness of mankind, and from the kindness of her noble spirit comes mankind's affection."

He closed his eyes and leaned down on the pillow; the two women did not bother him with further conversation for they knew that the weariness caused by long exposure had allured and captured his eyes. Khalil slept like a lost child who had finally found safety in his mother's arms.

Rachel and her daughter slowly walked to their bed and sat there watching him as if they had found in his trouble-torn face an attraction bringing their souls and hearts closer to him. And the mother whispered, saying, "There is a strange power in his closed eyes that speaks in silence and stimulates the soul's desires."

And Miriam rejoined, "His hands, Mother, are like those of Christ in the Church." The mother replied, "His face possesses at the same time a woman's tenderness and a man's boldness."

And the wings of slumber carried the women's spirits into the world of dream, and the fire went down and turned into ashes, while the light of the oil lamp dimmed gradually and disappeared. The fierce tempest continued its roar, and the obscured sky spread layers of snow, and the strong wind scattered them to the right and left.

PART FOUR

Five days passed, and the sky was still heavy with snow, burying the mountains and prairies relentlessly. Khalil made three attempts to resume his journey toward the plains, but Rachel restrained him each time, saying, "Do not give up your life to the blind elements, brother; remain here, for the bread that suffices two will also feed three, and the fire will still be burning after your departure as it was before your arrival. We are poor, brother, but like the rest of the people, we live our lives before the face of the sun and mankind, and God gives us our daily bread."

And Miriam was begging him with her kind glances, and pleading with her deep sighs, for since he entered the hut she felt the presence of a divine power in her soul sending forth life and light into her heart and awakening new affection in the Holy of Holies of her spirit. For the first time she experienced the feeling which made her heart like a white rose that sips the dew drops from the dawn and breathes its fragrance into the endless firmament.

There is no affection purer and more soothing to the spirit than the one hidden in the heart of a maiden who awakens suddenly and fills her own spirit with heavenly music that makes her days like poets' dreams and her nights prophetic. There is no secret in the mystery of life stronger and more beautiful than that attachment which converts the silence of a virgin's spirit into a perpetual awareness that makes a person forget the past, for it kindles fiercely in the heart the sweet and overwhelming hope of the coming future.

The Lebanese woman distinguishes herself from the woman of other nations by her simplicity. The manner in which she is trained restricts her progress educationally, and stands as a hindrance to her future. Yet for this reason, she finds herself inquiring of herself as to the inclination and mystery of her heart. The Lebanese young woman is like a spring that comes out from the heart of the earth and follows its course through winding depressions, but since it cannot find an outlet to the sea, it turns into a calm lake that reflects upon its growing surface the glittering stars and the shining moon. Khalil felt the vibration of Miriam's heart twining steadily about his soul, and he knew that the divine torch that illuminated his heart had also touched her heart. He rejoiced for the first time, like a parched brook greeting the rain, but he blamed himself for his haste, believing that this spiritual understanding would pass like a cloud when he departed from that village. He often spoke to himself saying, "What is this mystery that plays so great a part in our lives? What is this Law that drives us into a rough road and stops us just before we reach the face of the sun where we might rejoice? What is this power that elevates our spirits until we reach the mountain top, smiling and glorying, then suddenly we are cast to the depths of the valley, weeping and suffering? What is this life that embraces us like a lover one day, and fights us like an enemy the second day? Was I not persecuted yesterday? Did I not survive hunger and thirst and suffering and mockery for the sake of the Truth which heaven had awakened in my heart? Did I not tell the monks that happiness through Truth is the will and the purpose of God in man? Then what is this fear? And why do I close my eyes to the light that emanates from that young woman's eyes? I am expelled and she is poor, but is it on bread only that man can live? Are we not, between famine and plenty, like trees between winter and summer? But what would Rachel say if she knew that my heart and her daughter's heart came to an understanding in silence, and approached close to each other and neared the circle of the Supreme Light? What would she say if she discovered that the young man whose life she saved longed to gaze upon her daughter? What would the simple villagers say if they knew that a young man, reared in the convent, came to their village by necessity and expulsion, and desired to live near a beautiful maiden? Will they listen to me if I tell them that he who leaves the convent to live amongst them is like a bird that flies from the bruising walls of the cage to the light of freedom? What will Sheik Abbas say if he hears my story? What will the priest of the village do if he learns of the cause of my expulsion?"

Khalil was talking to himself in this fashion while sitting by the fireplace, meditating the flames, symbol of his love; and Miriam was stealing a glance now and then at his face and reading his dreams through his eyes, and hearing the echo of his thoughts, and feeling the touch of his love, even though no word was uttered.

One night, as he stood by the small transom that faced the valleys where the trees and rocks were shrouded with white coverings, Miriam came and stood by him, looking at the sky. As their eyes turned and met, he drew a deep sigh and shut his eyes as if his soul were sailing in the spacious sky looking for a word. He found no word necessary, for the silence spoke for them. Miriam ventured, "Where will you go when the snow meets the stream and the paths are dry?" His eyes opened, looking beyond the horizon, and he explained, "I shall follow the path to wherever my destiny and my mission for Truth shall take me." Miriam sighed sadly and offered, "Why will you not remain here and live close to us? Is it that you are obliged to go elsewhere?" He was moved by her kindness and sweet words, but protested, "The villagers here will not accept an expelled monk as their neighbour, and will not permit him to breathe the air they breathe because they believe that the enemy of the convent is an infidel, cursed by God and His saints." Miriam resorted to silence, for the Truth that pained her prevented further talk. Then Khalil turned aside and explained, "Miriam, these villagers are taught by those in authority to hate everyone who thinks freely; they are trained to remain afar from those whose minds soar aloft; God does not like to be worshipped by an ignorant man who imitates someone else; if I remained in this village and asked the people to worship as they please, they would say that I am an infidel disobeying the authority that was given to the priest by God. If I asked them to listen and hear the voices of their hearts and do according to the will of the spirit within, they would say that I am an evil man who wants them to do away with the clergy that God placed between heaven and earth." Khalil looked straight into Miriam's eyes, and with a voice that bespoke the sound of silver strings said, "But, Miriam, there is a magic power in this village that possesses me and engulfs my soul; a power so divine that it causes me to forget my pain. In this village I met Death to his very face, and in this place my soul embraced God's spirit. In this village there is a beautiful flower grown over the lifeless grass; its beauty attracts my heart and its fragrance fills its domain. Shall I leave this important flower and go out preaching the ideas that caused my expulsion from the convent, or shall I remain by the side of that flower and dig a grave and bury my thoughts and truths among its neighbouring thorns? What shall I do, Miriam?" Upon hearing these words, she shivered like a lily before the frolicsome breeze of the dawn. Her heart glowed through her eyes when she faltered, "We are both in the hands of a mysterious and merciful power. Let it do its will."

At that moment the two hearts joined and thereafter both spirits were one burning torch illuminating their lives.

PART FIVE

Since the beginning of the creation and up to our present time, certain clans, rich by inheritance, in co-operation with the clergy, had appointed themselves the administrators of the people. It is an old, gaping wound in the heart of society that cannot be removed except by intense removal of ignorance.

The man who acquires his wealth by inheritance builds his mansion with the weak poor's money. The clergyman erects his temple upon the graves and bones of the devoted worshippers. The prince grasps the fellah's arms while the priest empties his pocket; the ruler looks upon the sons of the fields with frowning face, and the bishop consoles them with his smile, and between the frown of the tiger and the smile of the wolf the flock is perished; the ruler claims himself as king of the law, and the priest as the representative of God, and between these two, the bodies are destroyed and the souls wither into nothing.

In Lebanon, that mountain rich in sunlight and poor in knowledge, the noble and the priest joined hands to exploit the farmer who ploughed the land and reaped the crop in order to protect himself from the sword of the ruler and the curse of the priest. The rich man in Lebanon stood proudly by his palace and shouted at the multitudes saying, "The Sultan had appointed me as your lord." And the priest stands before the altar saying, "God has delegated me as an executive of your souls." But the Lebanese resorted to silence, for the dead could not talk.

Sheik Abbas had friendship in his heart for the clergymen, because they were his allies in choking the people's knowledge and reviving the spirit of stern obedience among his workers.

That evening, when Khalil and Miriam were approaching the throne of Love, and Rachel was looking upon them with the eyes of affection, Father Elias informed Sheik Abbas that the head priest had expelled a rebellious young man from the convent and that he had taken refuge at the house of Rachel, the widow of Samaan Ramy. And the priest was not satisfied with the little information he gave the Sheik, but commented, "The demon they chased out of the convent cannot become an angel in this village, and the fig tree which is hewn and cast into the fire, does not bear fruit while burning. If we wish to clean this village of the filth of this beast, we must drive him away as the monks did." And the Sheik inquired, "Are you certain that the young man will be a bad influence upon our people? Is it not better for us to keep him and make him a worker in our vineyards? We are in need of strong men."

The priest's face showed his disagreement. Combing his beard with his fingers, he said shrewdly, "If he were fit to work, he would not have been expelled from the convent. A student who works in the convent, and who happened to spend last night at my house, informed me that this young man had violated the rules of the head priest by preaching danger-ridden ideas among the monks, and he quoted him as saying, 'Restore the fields and the vineyards and the silver of the convent to the poor and scatter it in all directions; and help the people who are in need of knowledge; by thus doing, you will please your Father in Heaven.' "

On hearing these words, Sheik Abbas leaped to his feet, and like a tiger making ready to strike the victim, he walked to the door and called to the servants, ordering them to report immediately. Three men entered, and the Sheik commanded, "In the house of Rachel, the widow of Samaan Ramy, there is a young man wearing a monk's raiment. Tie him and bring him here. If that woman objects to his arrest, drag her out by her braided hair over the snow and bring her with him, for he who helps evil is evil himself." The men bowed obediently and hurried to Rachel's home while the priest and the Sheik discussed the type of punishment to be awarded to Khalil and Rachel.

PART SIX

The day was over and the night had come spreading its shadow over those wretched huts, heavily laden with snow. The stars finally appeared in the sky, like hopes in the coming eternity after the suffering of death's agony. The doors and windows were closed and the lamps were lighted. The fellahin sat by the fireside warming their bodies. Rachel, Miriam and Khalil were seated at a rough wooden table eating their evening meal when there was a knock at the door and three men entered. Rachel and Miriam were frightened, but Khalil remained calm, as if he awaited the coming of those men. One of the Sheik's servants walked toward Khalil, laid his hand upon his shoulder and asked, "Are you the one who was expelled from the convent?" And Khalil responded, "Yes, I am the one, what do you want?" The man replied, "We are ordered to arrest you and take you with us to Sheik Abbas' home, and if you object we shall drag you out like a butchered sheep over the snow."

Rachel turned pale as she exclaimed, "What crime has he committed, and why do you want to tie him and drag him out?" The two women pleaded with tearful voices, saying, "He is one individual in the hands of three and it is cowardly of you to make him suffer." The men became enraged and shouted, "Is there any woman in this village who opposes the Sheik's order?" And he drew forth a rope and started to tie Khalil's hands. Khalil lifted his head proudly, and a sorrowful smile appeared on his lips when he said, "I feel sorry for you men, because you are a strong and blind instrument in the hands of a man who oppresses the weak with the strength of your arms. You are slaves of ignorance. Yesterday I was a man like you, but tomorrow you shall be free in mind as I am now. Between us there is a deep precipice that chokes my calling voice and hides my reality from you, and you cannot hear or see. Here I am, tie my hands and do as you please." The three men were moved by his talk and it seemed that his voice had awakened in them a new spirit, but the voice of Sheik Abbas still rang in their minds, warning them to complete the mission. They bound his hands and led him out silently with a heavy conscience. Rachel and Miriam followed them to the Sheik's home, like the daughters of Jerusalem who followed Christ to Mount Calvary.

PART SEVEN

Regardless of its import, news travels swiftly among the fellahin in the small villages, because their absence from the realm of society makes them anxious and busy in discussing the happenings of their limited environs. In winter, when the fields are slumbering under the quilts of snow, and when human life is taking refuge and warming itself by the fireside, the villagers become most inclined to learn of current news in order to occupy themselves.

It was not long after Khalil was arrested, when the story spread like a contagious disease amongst the villagers. They left their huts and hurried like an army from every direction into the home of Sheik Abbas. When Khalil's feet stepped into the Sheik's home, the residence was crowded with men, women and children who were endeavouring for a glance at the infidel who was expelled from the convent. They were also anxious to see Rachel and her daughter, who had helped Khalil in spreading the hellish disease of heresy in the pure sky of their village.

The Sheik took the seat of judgment and beside

him sat Father Elias, while the throng was gazing at the pinioned youth who stood bravely before them. Rachel and Miriam were standing behind Khalil and trembling with fear. But what could fear do to the heart of a woman who found Truth and followed him? What could the scorn of the crowd do to the soul of a maiden who had been awakened by Love? Sheik Abbas looked at the young man, and with a thundering voice he interrogated him saying, "What is your name, man?" "Khalil is my name," answered the youth. The Sheik returned, "Who are your father and mother and relatives, and where were you born?" Khalil turned toward the fellahin, who looked upon him with hateful eyes, and said, "The oppressed poor are my clan and my relatives, and this vast country is my birthplace."

Sheik Abbas, with an air of ridicule, said, "Those people whom you claim as kin demand that you be punished, and the country you assert as your birthplace objects to your being a member of its people." Khalil replied, "The ignorant nations arrest their good men and turn them into their despots; and a country, ruled by a tyrant, persecutes those who try to free the people from the yoke of slavery. But will a good son leave his mother if she is ill? Will a merciful man deny his brother who is miserable? Those poor men who arrested me and brought me here today are the same ones who surrendered their lives to you yesterday. And this vast earth that disapproves my existence is the one that does not yawn and swallow the greedy despots."

The Sheik uttered a loud laugh, as if wanting to depress the young man's spirit and prevent him from influencing the audience. He turned to Khalil and said impressively, "You cattle grazier, do you think that we will show more mercy than did the monks, who expelled you from the convent? Do you think that we feel pity for a dangerous agitator?" Khalil responded, "It is true that I was a cattle grazier, but I am glad that I was not a butcher. I led my herds to the rich pastures and never grazed them on arid land. I led my animals to pure springs and kept them from contaminated marshes. At eventide I brought them safely to their shed and never left them in the valleys as prey for the wolves. Thus I have treated the animals; and if you had pursued my course and treated human beings as I treated my flock, these poor people would not live in wretched huts and suffer the pangs of poverty, while you are living like Nero in this gorgeous mansion."

The Sheik's forehead glittered with drops of perspiration, and his smirk turned into anger, but he tried to show only calm by pretending that he did not heed Khalil's talk, and he expostulated, pointing at Khalil with his finger, "You are a heretic, and we shall not listen to your ridiculous talk; we summoned you to be tried as a criminal, and you realize that you are in the presence of the Lord of this village who is empowered to represent his Excellency

Emir Ameen Shebab. You are standing before Father Elias, the representative of the Holy Church whose teachings you have opposed. Now, defend yourself, or kneel down before these people and we will pardon you and make you a cattle grazier, as you were in the convent." Khalil calmly returned, "A criminal is not to be tried by another criminal, as an atheist will not defend himself before sinners." And Khalil looked at the audience and spoke to them saying, "My brethren, the man whom you call the Lord of your fields, and to whom you have yielded thus long, has brought me to be tried before you in this edifice which he built upon the graves of your forefathers. And the man who became a pastor of your church through your faith, has come to judge me and help you to humiliate me and increase my sufferings. You have hurried to this place from every direction to see me suffer and hear me plead for mercy. You have left your huts in order to witness your pinioned son and brother. You have come to see the prey trembling between the paws of a ferocious beast. You came here tonight to view an infidel standing before the judges. I am the criminal and I am the heretic who has been expelled from the convent. The tempest brought me into your village. Listen to my protest, and do not be merciful, but be just, for mercy is bestowed upon the guilty criminal, while justice is all that an innocent man requires.

"I select you now as my jury, because the will of

the people is the will of God. Awaken your hearts and listen carefully and then prosecute me according to the dictates of your conscience. You have been told that I am an infidel, but you have not been informed of what crime or sin I have committed. You have seen me tied like a thief, but you have not yet heard about my offenses, for wrongdoings are not revealed in this court, while punishment comes out like thunder. My crime, dear fellowmen, is my understanding of your plight, for I felt the weight of the irons which have been placed upon your necks. My sin is my heartfelt sorrows for your women; it is my sympathy for your children who suck life from your breast mixed with the shadow of death. I am one of you, and my forefathers lived in these valleys and died under the same yoke which is bending your heads now. I believe in God who listens to the call of your suffering souls, and I believe in the Book that makes all of us brothers before the face of heaven. I believe in the teachings that make us all equal, and that render us unpinioned upon this earth, the stepping place of the careful feet of God.

"As I was grazing my cows at the convent, and contemplating the sorrowful condition you tolerate, I heard a desperate cry coming from your miserable homes—a cry of oppressd souls—a cry of broken hearts which are locked in your bodies as slaves to the lord of these fields. As I looked, I found me in the convent and you in the fields, and I saw you as a flock of lambs following a wolf to the lair; and as I stopped in the middle of the road to aid the lambs, I cried for help and the wolf snapped me with his sharp teeth.

"I have sustained imprisonment, thirst, and hunger for the sake of Truth that hurts only the body. I have undergone suffering beyond endurance because I turned your sad sighs into a crying voice that rang and echoed in every corner of the convent. I never felt fear, and my heart never tired, for your painful cry was injecting a new strength into me every day, and my heart was healthy. You may ask yourself now saying, 'When did we ever cry for help, and who dares open his lips?' But I say unto you, your souls are crying every day, and pleading for help every night, but you cannot hear them, for the dying man cannot hear his own heart rattling, while those who are standing by his bedside can surely hear. The slaughtered bird, in spite of his will, dances painfully and unknowingly, but those who witness the dance know what caused it. In what hour of the day do you sigh painfully? Is it in the morning, when love of existence cries at you and tears the veil of slumber off your eyes and leads you like slaves into the fields? Is it at noon, when you wish to sit under a tree to protect yourself from the burning sun? Or at eventide, when you return home hungry, wishing for sustaining food instead of a meagre morsel and impure water? Or at night when fatigue throws you upon your rough bed, and as soon as slumber closes your eyes, you sit up with open eyes, fearing that the Sheik's voice is ringing in your ears?

"In what season of the year do you not lament yourselves? Is it in Spring, when nature puts on her beautiful dress and you go to meet her with tattered raiment? Or in Summer, when you harvest the wheat and gather the sheaves of corn and fill the shelves of your master with the crop, and when the reckoning comes you receive naught but hay and tare? Is it in Autumn, when you pick the fruits and carry the grapes into the wine-press, and in reward for your toil you receive a jar of vinegar and a bushel of acorns? Or in Winter, when you are confined to your huts laden with snow, do you sit by the fire and tremble when the enraged sky urges you to escape from your weak minds?

"This is the life of the poor; this is the perpetual cry I hear. This is what makes my spirit revolt against the oppressors and despise their conduct. When I asked the monks to have mercy upon you, they thought that I was an atheist, and expulsion was my lot. Today I came here to share this miserable life with you, and to mix my tears with yours. Here I am now, in the grip of your worst enemy. Do you realize that this land you are working like slaves was taken from your fathers when the law was written on the sharp edge of the sword? The monks deceived your ancestors and took all their fields and vineyards when the religious rules were written on the lips of the priests. Which man or woman is not influenced by the lord of the fields to do according to the will of the priests? God said, 'With the sweat of thy brow, thou shall eat thy bread.' But Sheik Abbas is eating his bread baked in the years of your lives and drinking his wine mixed with your tears. Did God distinguish this man from the rest of you while in his mother's womb? Or is it your sin that made you his property? Jesus said, 'Gratis you have taken and gratis you shall give. . . . Do not possess gold, nor silver, neither copper.' Then what teachings allow the clergymen to sell their prayers for pieces of gold and silver? In the silence of the night you pray saying, 'Give us today our daily bread.' God has given you this land from which to draw your daily bread, but what authority has He given the monks to take this land and this bread away from you?

"You curse Judas because he sold his Master for a few pieces of silver, but you bless those who sell Him every day. Judas repented and hanged himself for his wrongdoing, but these priests walk proudly, dressed with beautiful robes, resplendent with shining crosses hanging over their chests. You teach your children to love Christ and at the same time you instruct them to obey those who oppose His teachings and violate His law.

"The apostles of Christ were stoned to death in order to revive in you the Holy Spirit, but the monks and the priests are killing that spirit in you so they may live on your pitiful bounty. What persuades you to live such a life in this universe, full of misery and oppression? What prompts you to kneel before that horrible idol which has been erected upon the bones of your fathers? What treasure are you reserving for your posterity?

"Your souls are in the grip of the priests, and your bodies are in the closing jaws of the rulers. What thing in life can you point at and say 'this is mine!' My fellowmen, do you know the priest you fear? He is a traitor who uses the Gospel as a threat to ransom your money . . . a hypocrite wearing a cross and using it as a sword to cut your veins . . . a wolf disguised in lambskin . . . a glutton who respects the tables more than the altars . . . a gold-hungry creature who follows the Denar to the farthest land . . . a cheat pilfering from widows and orphans. He is a queer being, with an eagle's beak, a tiger's clutches, a hyena's teeth and a viper's clothes. Take the Book away from him and tear his raiment off and pluck his beard and do whatever you wish unto him; then place in his hand one Denar, and he will forgive you smilingly.

"Slap his face and spit on him and step on his neck; then invite him to sit at your board. He will immediately forget and untie his belt and gladly fill his stomach with your food.

"Curse him and ridicule him; then send him a jar of wine or a basket of fruit. He will forgive you your sins. When he sees a woman, he turns his face, saying, 'Go from me, Oh, daughter of Babylon.' Then he whispers to himself saying, 'Marriage is better than coveting.' He sees the young men and women walking in the procession of Love, and he lifts his eyes toward heaven and says, 'Vanity of vanities, all is vanity.' And in his solitude he talks to himself saying, 'May the laws and traditions that deny me the joys of life, be abolished.'

"He preaches to the people saying, 'Judge not, lest ye be judged.' But he judges all those who abhor his deeds and sends them to hell before Death separates them from this life.

"When he talks he lifts his head toward heaven, but at the same time, his thoughts are crawling like snakes through your pockets.

"He addresses you as beloved children, but his heart is empty of paternal love, and his lips never smile at a child, nor does he carry an infant between his arms.

"He tells you, while shaking his head, 'Let us keep away from earthly things, for life passes like a cloud.' But if you look thoroughly at him, you will find that he is gripping on to life, lamenting the passing of yesterday, condemning the speed of today, and waiting fearfully for tomorrow.

"He asks you for charity when he has plenty to give; if you grant his request, he will bless you publicly, and if you refuse him, he will curse you secretly.

"In the temple he asks you to help the needy, and

about his house the needy are begging for bread, but he cannot see or hear.

"He sells his prayers, and he who does not buy is an infidel, excommunicated from Paradise.

"This is the creature of whom you are afraid. This is the monk who sucks your blood. This is the priest who makes the sign of the Cross with the right hand, and clutches your throat with the left hand.

"This is the pastor whom you appoint as your servant, but he appoints himself as your master.

"This is the shadow that embraces your souls from birth until death.

"This is the man who came to judge me tonight because my spirit revolted against the enemies of Jesus the Nazarene Who loved all and called us brothers, and Who died on the Cross for us."

Khalil felt that there was understanding in the villagers' hearts; his voice brightened and he resumed his discourse saying, "Brethren, you know that Sheik Abbas has been appointed as Master of this village by Emir Shehab, the Sultan's representative and Governor of the Province, but I ask you if anyone has seen that power appoint the Sultan as the god of this country. That Power, my fellowmen, cannot be seen, nor can you hear it talk, but you can feel its existence in the depths of your hearts. It is that Power which you worship and pray for every day saying, 'Our Father which art in heaven.' Yes, your Father Who is in heaven is the one Who appoints kings and princes, for He is powerful and above all. But do you think that your Father, Who loved you and showed you the right path through His prophets, desires for you to be oppressed? Do you believe that God, Who brings forth the rain from heaven, and the wheat from the hidden seeds in the heart of the earth, desires for you to be hungry in order that but one man will enjoy His bounty? Do you believe that the Eternal Spirit Who reveals to you the wife's love, the children's pity and the neighbor's mercy, would have upon you a tyrant to enslave you through your life? Do you believe that the Eternal Law that made life beautiful, would send you a man to deny you of that happiness and lead you into the dark dungeon of painful Death? Do you believe that your physical strength, provided you by nature, belongs beyond your body to the rich?

"You cannot believe in all these things, because if you do you will be denying the justice of God who made us all equal, and the light of Truth that shines upon all peoples of the earth. What makes you struggle against yourselves, heart against body, and help those who enslave you while God has created you free on this earth?

"Are you doing yourselves justice when you lift your eyes towards Almighty God and call him Father, and then turn around, bow your heads before a man, and call him Master?

"Are you contented, as sons of God, with being slaves of man? Did not Christ call you brethren?

Yet Sheik Abbas calls you servants. Did not Jesus make you free in Truth and Spirit? Yet the Emir made you slaves of shame and corruption. Did not Christ exalt you to heaven? Then why are you descending to hell? Did He not enlighten your hearts? Then why are you hiding your souls in darkness? God has placed a glowing torch in your hearts that glows in knowledge and beauty, and seeks the secrets of the days and nights; it is a sin to extinguish that torch and bury it in ashes. God has created your spirits with wings to fly in the spacious firmament of Love and Freedom; it is pitiful that you cut your wings with your own hands and suffer your spirits to crawl like insects upon the earth."

Sheik Abbas observed in dismay the attentiveness of the villagers, and attempted to interrupt, but Khalil, inspired, continued, "God has sown in your hearts the seeds of Happiness; it is a crime that you dig those seeds out and throw them wilfully on the rocks so the wind will scatter them and the birds will pick them. God has given you children to rear, to teach them the truth and fill their hearts with the most precious things of existence. He wants you to bequeath upon them the joy of Life and the bounty of Life; why are they now strangers to their place of birth and cold creatures before the face of the Sun? A father who makes his son a slave is the father who gives his child a stone when he asks for bread. Have you not seen the birds of the sky training their young ones to fly? Why, then, do you teach your children to drag the shackles of slavery? Have you not seen the flowers of the valleys deposit their seeds in the sun-heated earth? Then why do you commit your children to the cold darkness?"

Silence prevailed for a moment, and it seemed as if Khalil's mind were crowded with pain. But now with a low and compelling voice he continued, "The words which I utter tonight are the same expressions that caused my expulsion from the convent. If the lord of your fields and the pastor of your church were to prey upon me and kill me tonight, I will die happy and in peace because I have fulfilled my mission and revealed to you the Truth which demons consider a crime. I have now completed the will of Almighty God."

There had been a magic message in Khalil's voice that forced the villagers' interest. The women were moved by the sweetness of his words and looked upon him as a messenger of peace, and their eyes were rich with tears.

Sheik Abbas and Father Elias were shaking with anger. As Khalil finished, he walked a few steps and stopped near Rachel and Miriam. Silence dominated the courtroom, and it seemed as if Khalil's spirit hovered in that vast hall and diverted the souls of the multitude from fearing Sheik Abbas and Father Elias, who sat trembling in annoyance and guilt.

The Sheik stood suddenly and his face was pale. He looked toward the men who were standing about him as he said, "What has become of you, dogs? Have your hearts been poisoned? Has your blood stopped running and weakened you so that you cannot leap upon this criminal and cut him to pieces? What awful thing has he done to you?" Having finished reprimanding the men, he raised a sword and started toward the fettered youth, whereupon a strong villager walked to him, gripped his hand and said, "Lay down your weapon, Master, for he who draws the sword to kill, shall, by the sword, be killed!"

The Sheik trembled visibly and the sword fell from his hand. He addressed the man saying, "Will a weak servant oppose his Master and benefactor?" And the man responded, "The faithful servant does not share his Master in the committing of crimes; this young man has spoken naught but the truth." Another man stepped forward and assured, "This man is innocent and is worthy of honour and respect." And a woman raised her voice saying, "He did not swear at God or curse any saint; why do you call him heretic?" And Rachel asked, "What is his crime?" The Sheik shouted, "You are rebellious, you miserable widow; have you forgotten the fate of your husband who turned rebel six years ago?" Upon hearing these impulsive words, Rachel shivered with painful anger, for she had found the murderer of her husband. She choked her tears and looked upon the throng and cried out, "Here is the criminal you have been trying for six years to find; you hear him now confessing his guilt. He is the killer who has been hiding his crime. Look at him and read his face; study him well and observe his fright; he shivers like the last leaf on winter's tree. God has shown you that the Master whom you have always feared is a murderous criminal. He caused me to be a widow amongst these women, and my daughter an orphan amidst these children." Rachel's utterance fell like thunder upon the Sheik's head, and the uproar of men and exaltation of women fell like firebrands upon him.

The priest assisted the Sheik to his seat. Then he called the servants and ordered them saying, "Arrest this woman who has falsely accused your Master of killing her husband; drag her and this young man into a dark prison, and any who oppose you will be criminals, excommunicated as he was from the Holy Church." The servants gave no heed to his command, but remained motionless staring at Khalil who was still bound with rope. Rachel stood at his right and Miriam at his left like a pair of wings ready to soar aloft into the spacious sky of Freedom.

His beard shaking with anger, Father Elias said, "Are you denying your Master for the sake of an infidel criminal and a shameless adulteress?" And the oldest one of the servants answered him saying, "We have served Sheik Abbas long for bread and shelter, but we have never been his slaves." Having thus spoken, the servant took off his cloak and turban and threw them before the Sheik and added, "I shall no longer require this raiment, nor do I wish my soul to suffer in the narrow house of a criminal." And all the servants did likewise and joined the crowd whose faces radiated with joy, symbol of Freedom and Truth. Father Elias finally saw that his authority had declined, and he left the place cursing the hour that brought Khalil to the village. A strong man strode to Khalil and untied his hands, looked at Sheik Abbas who fell like a corpse upon his seat, and boldly addressed him saying, "This fettered youth, whom you have brought here tonight to be tried as a criminal, has lifted our depressed spirits and enlightened our hearts with Truth and Knowledge. And this poor widow whom Father Elias referred to as a false accuser has revealed to us the crime you committed six years past. We came here tonight to witness the trial of an innocent youth and a noble soul. Now, heaven has opened our eyes and has shown us your atrocity; we shall leave you and ignore you and allow heaven to do its will."

Many voices were raised in that hall, and one could hear a certain man saying, "Let us leave this ill-famed residence for our homes." And another one remarking, "Let us follow this young man to Rachel's home and listen to his wise sayings and consoling wisdom." And a third one saying, "Let us seek his advice, for he knows our needs." And a fourth one calling out, "If we are seeking justice, let us complain to the Emir and tell him of Abbas' crime." And many were saying, "Let us petition the

Emir to appoint Khalil as our Master and ruler, and tell the Bishop that Father Elias was a partner in these crimes." While the voices were rising and falling upon the Sheik's ears like sharp arrows, Khalil lifted his hands and calmed the villagers saying, "My brethren, do not seek haste, but rather listen and meditate. I ask you, in the name of my love and friendship for you, not to go to the Emir, for you will not find justice. Remember that a ferocious beast does not snap another one like him, neither should you go to the Bishop, for he knows well that the house cloven amid itself shall be ruined. Do not ask the Emir to appoint me as the Sheik in this village, for the faithful servant does not like to be an aid to the evil Master. If I deserve your kindness and love, let me live amongst you and share with you the happiness and sorrows of Life. Let me join hands and work with you at home and in the fields, for if I could not make myself one of you, I would be a hypocrite who does not live according to his sermon. And now, as the axe is laid unto the root of the tree, let us leave Sheik Abbas alone in the courtroom of his conscience and before the Supreme Court of God whose sun shines upon the innocent and the criminal."

Having thus spoken, he left the place, and the multitude followed him as if there were a divine power in him that attracted their hearts. The Sheik remained alone with the terrible silence, like a destroyed tower, suffering his defeat quietly like a surrendering commander. When the multitude reached the church yard and the moon was just showing from behind the cloud, Khalil looked at them with the eyes of love like a good shepherd watching over his herd. He was moved with sympathy upon those villagers who symbolized an oppressed nation; and he stood like a prophet who saw all the nations of the East walking in those valleys and dragging empty souls and heavy hearts.

He raised both hands toward heaven and said, "From the bottom of these depths we call thee, Oh, Liberty. Give heed to us! From behind the darkness we raise our hands to thee, Oh, Liberty. Look upon us! Upon the snow, we worship before thee, Oh, Liberty. Have mercy on us! Before thy great throne we stand, hanging on our bodies the blood-stained garments of our forefathers, covering our heads with the dust of the graves mixed with their remains, carrying the swords that stabbed their hearts, lifting the spears that pierced their bodies, dragging the chains that slowed their feet, uttering the cry that wounded their throats, lamenting and repeating the song of our failure that echoed throughout the prison, and repeating the prayers that came from the depths of our fathers' hearts. Listen to us, Oh Liberty, and hear us. From the Nile to the Euphrates comes the wailing of the suffering souls, in unison with the cry of the abyss; and from the end of the East to the mountains of Lebanon, hands are stretched to you, trembling with the presence of

Death. From the shores of the sea to the end of the desert, tear-flooded eyes look beseechingly toward you. Come, Oh Liberty, and save us.

"In the wretched huts standing in the shadow of poverty and oppression, they beat at their bosoms, soliciting thy mercy; watch us, Oh Liberty, and have mercy on us. In the pathways and in the houses miserable youth calls thee; in the churches and the mosques, the forgotten Book turns to thee; in the courts and in the palaces the neglected Law appeals to thee. Have mercy on us, Oh Liberty, and save us. In our narrow streets the merchant sells his days in order to make tribute to the exploiting thieves of the West, and none would give him advice. In the barren fields the fellah tills the soil and sows the seeds of his heart and nourishes them with his tears, but he reaps naught except thorns, and none would teach him the true path. In our arid plains the Bedouin roams barefoot and hungry, but none would have mercy on him; speak, Oh Liberty, and teach us! Our sick lambs are grazing upon the grassless prairie, our calves are gnawing on the roots of the trees, and our horses are feeding on dry plants. Come, Oh Liberty, and help us. We have been living in darkness since the beginning, and like prisoners they take us from one prison to another, while time ridicules our plight. When will dawn come? Until when shall we bear the scorn of the ages? Many a stone have we been dragging, and many a yoke has been placed upon our necks. Until when shall we bear this human outrage? The Egyptian slavery, the Babylonian exile, the tyranny of Persia, the despotism of the Romans, and the greed of Europe . . . all these things we have suffered. Where are we going now, and when shall we reach the sublime end of the rough roadway? From the clutches of Pharaoh to the paws of Nebuchadnezzar, to the iron hands of Alexander, to the swords of Herod, to the talons of Nero, and the sharp teeth of Demon . . . into whose hands are we now to fall, and when will Death come and take us, so we may rest at last?

"With the strength of our arms we lifted the columns of the temple, and upon our backs we carried the mortar to build the great walls and the impregnable pyramids for the sake of glory. Until when shall we continue building such magnificent palaces and living in wretched huts? Until when shall we continue filling the bins of the rich with provisions, while sustaining weak life on dry morsels? Until when shall we continue weaving silk and wool for our lords and masters while we wear naught except tattered swaddles?

"Through their wickedness we were divided amongst ourselves; and the better to keep their thrones and be at ease, they armed the Druze to fight the Arab, and stirred up the Shiite to attack the Sunnite, and encouraged the Kurdish to butcher the Bedouin, and cheered the Mohammedan to dispute with the Christian. Until when shall a brother continue killing his own brother upon his mother's bosom? Until when shall the Cross be kept apart from the Crescent * before the eyes of God? Oh Liberty, hear us, and speak in behalf of but one individual, for a great fire is started with a small spark. Oh Liberty, awaken but one heart with the rustling of thy wings, for from one cloud alone comes the lightning which illuminates the pits of the valleys and the tops of the mountains. Disperse with thy power these black clouds and descend like thunder and destroy the thrones that were built upon the bones and skulls of our ancestors."

"Hear us, Oh Liberty;
Bring mercy, Oh Daughter of Athens;
Rescue us, Oh Sister of Rome;
Advise us, Oh Companion of Moses;
Help us, Oh Beloved of Mohammed;
Teach us, Oh Bride of Jesus;
Strengthen our hearts so we may live,
Or harden our enemies so we may perish
And live in peace eternally."

As Khalil was pouring forth his sentiment before heaven, the villagers were gazing at him in reverence, and their love was springing forth in unison with the song of his voice until they felt that he became part of their hearts. After a short silence,

* The crescent is the emblem of the Mohammedan flag, flown over Svria during the Turkish rule. (*Editor's note.*)

Khalil brought his eyes upon the multitude and quietly said, "Night has brought us to the house of Sheik Abbas in order to realize the daylight; oppression has arrested us before the cold Space, so we may understand one another and gather like chicks under the wings of the Eternal Spirit. Now let us go to our homes and sleep until we meet again tomorrow."

Having thus spoken, he walked away, following Rachel and Miriam to their poor hovel. The throng departed and each went to his home, contemplating what he had seen and heard that memorable night. They felt that a burning torch of a new spirit had scoured their inner selves and led them into the right path. In an hour all the lamps were extinguished and Silence engulfed the whole village while Slumber carried the fellahin's souls into the world of strong dreams; but Sheik Abbas found no sleep all night, as he watched the phantoms of darkness and the horrible ghosts of his crimes in procession.

PART EIGHT

Two months had already passed and Khalil was still preaching and pouring his sentiments in the villagers' hearts, reminding them of their usurped rights and showing them the greed and oppression of the rulers and the monks. They listened to him with care, for he was a source of pleasure; his words fell upon their hearts like rain upon thirsty land.

In their solitude, they repeated Khalil's sayings as they did their daily prayers. Father Elias commenced fawning upon them to regain their friendship; he became docile since the villagers found out that he was the Sheik's ally in crime, and the fellahin ignored him.

Sheik Abbas had a nervous suffering, and walked through his mansion like a caged tiger. He issued commands to his servants, but no one answered except the echo of his voice inside the marble walls. He shouted at his men, but no one came to his aid except his poor wife who suffered the pang of his cruelty as much as the villagers did. When Lent came and Heaven announced the coming of Spring, the days of the Sheik expired with the passing of Winter. He died after a long agony, and his soul was carried away on the carpet of his deeds to stand naked and shivering before that high Throne whose existence we feel, but cannot see. The fellahin heard various tales about the manner of Sheik Abbas' death; some of them related that the Sheik died insane, while others insisted that disappointment and despair drove him to death by his own hand. But the women who went to offer their sympathies to his wife reported that he died from fear, because the ghost of Samaan Ramy hunted him and drove him every midnight out to the place where Rachel's husband was found slain six years before.

The month of Nisan proclaimed to the villagers the love secrets of Khalil and Miriam. They rejoiced the good tidings which assured them that Khalil would thereby remain in their village. As the news reached all the inhabitants of the huts, they congratulated one another upon Khalil's becoming their beloved neighbour.

When harvest time came, the fellahin went to the fields and gathered the sheaves of corn and bundles of wheat to the threshing floor. Sheik Abbas was not there to take the crop and have it carried to his bins. Each fellah harvested his own crop; the villagers' huts where filled with wheat and corn; their vessels were replenished with good wine and oil. Khalil shared with them their toils and happiness; he helped them in gathering the crop, pressing the grapes and picking the fruits. He never distinguished himself from any one of them except by his excess of love and ambition. Since that year and up to our present time, each fellah in that village commenced to reap with joy the crop which he sowed with toil and labour. The land which the fellahin tilled and the vineyards they cultivated became their own property.

Now, half a century has passed since this incident, and the Lebanese have awakened.

On his way to the Holy Cedars of Lebanon, a traveller's attention is caught by the beauty of that village, standing like a bride at the side of the valley. The wretched huts are now comfortable and happy homes surrounded by fertile fields and blooming orchards. If you ask any one of the residents about Sheik Abbas' history, he will answer you, pointing with his finger to a heap of demolished stones and destroyed walls saying, "This is the Sheik's palace, and this is the history of his life." And if you inquire about Khalil, he will raise his hand toward heaven saying, "There resides our beloved Khalil, whose life's history was written by God with glittering letters upon the pages of our hearts, and they cannot be effaced by the ages."

THE POET

He is link between this and the coming world.
  He is
A pure spring from which all thirsty souls may
  drink.

He is a tree watered by the River of Beauty, bearing
Fruit which the hungry heart craves;
He is a nightingale, soothing the depressed
Spirit with his beautiful melodies;
He is a white cloud appearing over the horizon,
Ascending and growing until it fills the face of the
  sky.
Then it falls on the flowers in the Field of Life,
Opening their petals to admit the light.

He is an angel, sent by the goddess to
Preach the Deity's gospel;
He is a brilliant lamp, unconquered by darkness
And inextinguishable by the wind. It is filled with
Oil by Ishtar of Love, and lighted by Apollon of
  Music.

He is a solitary figure, robed in simplicity and
Kindness; He sits upon the lap of Nature to draw his
Inspiration, and stays up in the silence of the night,
Awaiting the descending of the spirit.

He is a sower who sows the seeds of his heart in the
Prairies of affection, and humanity reaps the
Harvest for her nourishment.

This is the poet—whom the people ignore in this
life,
And who is recognized only after he bids the earthly
World farewell and returns to his arbor in heaven.

This is the poet—who asks naught of
Humanity but a smile.
This is the poet—whose spirit ascends and
Fills the firmament with beautiful sayings;
Yet the people deny themselves his radiance.

Until when shall the people remain asleep?
Until when shall they continue to glorify those
Who attained greatness by moments of advantage?
How long shall they ignore those who enable
Them to see the beauty of their spirit,
Symbol of peace and love?
Until when shall human beings honor the dead
And forget the living, who spend their lives
Encircled in misery, and who consume themselves
Like burning candles to illuminate the way
For the ignorant and lead them into the path of
light?

THE POET

Poet, you are the life of this life, and you have
Triumphed over the ages despite their severity.

Poet, you will one day rule the hearts, and
Therefore, your kingdom has no ending.

Poet, examine your crown of thorns; you will
Find concealed in it a budding wreath of laurel.

YOUTH AND BEAUTY

Beauty belongs to youth, but the youth for whom this earth was made is naught but a dream whose sweetness is enslaved to a blindness that renders its awareness too late. Will ever the day come when the wise will band together the sweet dreams of youth and the joy of knowledge? Each is but naught when in solitary existence. Will ever the day come when Nature will be the teacher of man, and Humanity his book of devotions, and Life his daily school?

Youth's purpose of joy—capable in its ecstasy and mild in its responsibility—cannot seek fulfillment until knowledge heralds the dawn of that day.

Many are the men who curse with venom the dead days of their youth; many are the women who execrate their wasted years with the fury of the lioness who has lost her cubs; and many are the youths and maidens who are using their hearts only to sheath the daggers of the bitter memories of the future, wounding themselves through ignorance with the sharp and poisoned arrows of seclusion from happiness.

Old age is the snow of the earth; it must, through light and truth, give warmth to the seeds of youth below, protecting them and fulfilling their purpose until Nisan comes and completes the growing pure life of youth with new awakening.

We are walking too slowly toward the awakening of our spiritual elevation, and only that plane, as endless as the firmament, is the understanding of the beauty of existence through our affection and love for that beauty.

SONG OF LOVE

I AM the lover's eyes, and the spirit's
Wine, and the heart's nourishment.
I am a rose. My heart opens at dawn and
The virgin kisses me and places me
Upon her breast.

I am the house of true fortune, and the
Origin of pleasure, and the beginning
Of peace and tranquility. I am the gentle
Smile upon the lips of beauty. When youth
Overtakes me he forgets his toil, and his
Whole life becomes reality of sweet dreams.

I am the poet's elation,
And the artist's revelation,
And the musician's inspiration.

I am a sacred shrine in the heart of a
Child, adored by a merciful mother.

I appear to a heart's cry; I shun a demand;
My fullness pursues the heart's desire;
It shuns the empty claim of the voice.

I appeared to Adam through Eve
And exile was his lot;
Yet I revealed myself to Solomon, and
He drew wisdom from my presence.

I smiled at Helena and she destroyed Tarwada;
Yet I crowned Cleopatra and peace dominated
The Valley of the Nile.

I am like the ages—building today
And destroying tomorrow;
I am like a god, who creates and ruins;
I am sweeter than a violet's sigh;
I am more violent than a raging tempest.

Gifts alone do not entice me;
Parting does not discourage me;
Poverty does not chase me;
Jealousy does not prove my awareness;
Madness does not evidence my presence.

Oh seekers, I am Truth, beseeching Truth;
And your Truth in seeking and receiving
And protecting me shall determine my
Behaviour.

CONTEMPLATIONS IN SADNESS

Fate carried me by the painful current of modern, narrow civilization, taking me from between the arms of Nature in her cool green arbour, and placing me roughly under the feet of the throngs, where I fell as suffering prey to the tortures of the city.

No punishment more severe has befallen a child of God; no exile so bitter has become the lot of one who loves one blade of the earth's grass with a fervency that causes every fibre of his being to tremble; no confinement imposed upon a criminal has approached in closeness the misery of my imprisonment, for the narrow walls of my cell are bruising my heart.

We may be wealthier than the villagers in gold, but they are infinitely richer in fullness of true existence. We sow in plenty, but reap naught; they reap the glorious bounty awarded by Nature to the diligent children of God. We calculate every barter with slyness; they take Nature's products with honesty and peace. We sleep fitfully, seeing spectres of the morrow; they sleep as a child upon its mother's bosom, knowing that Nature will never refuse her accustomed yield.

We are the slaves of gain; they are the masters of contentment. We drink bitterness and despair and fear and weariness from the cup of life; they drink the purest nectar of God's blessings.

Oh, Giver of Graces, hidden from me behind these edifices of the throngs which are naught but idols and images . . . hear the anguished cries of my imprisoned soul! Hear the agonies of my bursting heart! Have mercy and return Your straying child to the mountainside, which is Thy edifice!

BOOK 7

THE CRY OF THE GRAVES

PART ONE

THE EMIR walked into the court room and took the central chair while at his right and left sat the wise men of the country. The guards, armed with swords and spears, stood in attention, and the people who came to witness the trial rose and bowed ceremoniously to the Emir whose eyes emanated a power that revealed horror to their spirits and fear to their hearts. As the court came to order and the hour of judgment approached, the Emir raised his hand and shouted saying, "Bring forth the criminals singly and tell me what crimes they have committed." The prison door opened like the mouth of a ferocious yawning beast. In the obscure corners of the dungeon one could hear the echo of shackles rattling in unison with the moaning and lamentations of the prisoners. The spectators were eager to see the prey of Death emerging from the depths of that inferno. A few moments later, two soldiers came out leading a young man with his arms pinioned behind his back. His stern face bespoke nobility of spirit and strength of the heart. He was halted in the middle of the court room and the soldiers marched a few steps to the rear. The Emir stared at him steadily and said, "What crime has this man, who is proudly and triumphantly standing before me, committed?" One of the courtmen responded, "He is a murderer; yesterday he slew one of the Emir's officers who was on an important mission in the surrounding villages; he was still grasping the bloody sword when he was arrested." The Emir retorted with anger, "Return the man to the dark prison and tie him with heavy chains, and at dawn cut off his head with his own sword and throw his body in the woods so that the beasts may eat the flesh, and the air may carry its remindful odor into the noses of his family and friends." The youth was returned to prison while the people looked upon him with sorrowful eyes, for he was a young man in the spring of life.

The soldiers returned back again from the prison leading a young woman of natural and frail beauty. She looked pale and upon her face appeared the signs of oppression and disappointment. Her eyes were soaked with tears and her head was bent under the burden of grief. After eyeing her thoroughly, the Emir exclaimed, "And this emaciated woman, who is standing before me like the shadow beside a corpse, what has she done?" One of the soldiers answered him, saying, "She is an adulteress; last night her husband discovered her in the arms of another.

After her lover escaped, her husband turned her over to the law." The Emir looked at her while she raised her face without expression, and he ordered, "Take her back to the dark room and stretch her upon a bed of thorns so she may remember the resting place which she polluted with her fault; give her vinegar mixed with gall to drink so she may remember the taste of those sweet kisses. At dawn drag her naked body outside the city and stone her. Let the wolves enjoy the tender meat of her body and the worms pierce her bones." As she walked back to the dark cell, the people looked upon her with sympathy and surprise. They were astonished with the Emir's justice and grieved over her fate. The soldiers reappeared, bringing with them a sad man with shaking knees and trembling like a tender sapling before the north wind. He looked powerless, sickly and frightened, and he was miserable and poor. The Emir stared at him loathfully and inquired, "And this filthy man, who is like dead amongst the living; what has he done?" One of the guards returned, "He is a thief who broke into the monastery and stole the sacred vases which the priests found under his garment when they arrested him."

As a hungry eagle who looks at a bird with broken wings, the Emir looked at him and said, "Take him back to the jail and chain him, and at dawn drag him into a lofty tree and hang him between heaven and earth so his sinful hands may perish and the members of his body may be turned into particles and scattered by the wind." As the thief stumbled back into the depths of the prison, the people commenced whispering one to another saying, "How dare such a weak and heretic man steal the sacred vases of the monastery?"

At this time the court adjourned and the Emir walked out accompanied by all his wise men, guarded by the soldiers, while the audience scattered and the place became empty except of the moaning and wailing of the prisoners. All this happened while I was standing there like a mirror before passing ghosts. I was meditating the laws, made by man for man, contemplating what the people call "justice," and engrossing myself with deep thoughts of the secrets of life. I tried to understand the meaning of the universe. I was dumbfounded in finding myself lost like a horizon that disappears beyond the cloud. As I left the place I said to myself, "The vegetable feeds upon the elements of the earth, the sheep eats the vegetable, the wolf preys upon the sheep, and the bull kills the wolf while the lion devours the bull; yet Death claims the lion. Is there any power that will overcome Death and make these brutalities an eternal justice? Is there a force that can convert all the ugly things into beautiful objects? Is there any might that can clutch with its hands all the elements of life and embrace them with joy as the sea joyfully engulfs all the brooks into its depths? Is there any power that can arrest the murdered and the murderer, the adulteress and the adulterer, the robber and the robbed, and bring them to a court loftier and more supreme than the court of the Emir?"

PART TWO

The next day I left the city for the fields where silence reveals to the soul that which the spirit desires, and where the pure sky kills the germs of despair, nursed in the city by the narrow streets and obscured places. When I reached the valley, I saw a flock of crows and vultures soaring and descending, filling the sky with cawing, whistling and rustling of the wings. As I proceeded I saw before me a corpse of a man hanged high in a tree, the body of a dead naked woman in the midst of a heap of stones, and a carcass of a youth with his head cut off and soaked with blood mixed with earth. It was a horrible sight that blinded my eyes with a thick, dark veil of sorrows. I looked in every direction and saw naught except the spectre of Death standing by those ghastly remains. Nothing could be heard except the wailing of non-existence, mingled with the cawing of crows hovering about the victims of human laws. Three human beings, who yesterday were in the lap of Life, today fell as victims to Death because they broke the rules of human society. When a man kills another man, the people say he is a murderer, but when the Emir kills him, the Emir is just. When a man robs a monastery, they say he is a thief, but when the Emir robs him of his life, the Emir is honourable. When a woman betrays her husband, they say she is an adulteress, but when the Emir makes her walk naked in the streets and stones her later, the Emir is noble. Shedding of blood is forbidden, but who made it lawful for the Emir? Stealing one's money is a crime, but taking away one's life is a noble act. Betrayal of a husband may be an ugly deed, but stoning of living souls is a beautiful sight. Shall we meet evil with evil and say this is the Law? Shall we fight corruption with greater corruption and say this is the Rule? Shall we conquer crimes with more crimes and say this is Justice? Had not the Emir killed an enemy in his past life? Had he not robbed his weak subjects of money and property? Had he not committed adultery? Was he infallible when he killed the murderer and hanged the thief and stoned the adulteress? Who are those who hanged the thief in the tree? Are they angels descended from heaven, or men looting and usurping? Who cut off the murderer's head? Are they divine prophets, or soldiers shedding blood wherever they go? Who stoned that adulteress? Were they virtuous hermits who came from their monasteries, or humans who loved to commit atrocities with glee, under the protection of ignorant Law? What is Law? Who saw it coming with the sun from the depths of heaven? What human saw the heart of God and found its will or purpose? In what century did the angels walk among the people and preach to them, saying, "Forbid the weak from enjoying life, and kill the outlaws with the sharp edge of the sword, and step upon the sinners with iron feet?"

As my mind suffered in this fashion, I heard a rustling of feet in the grass close by. I took heed and say a young woman coming from behind the trees; she looked carefully in every direction before she approached the three carcasses that were there. As she glanced, she saw the youth's head that was cut off. She cried fearfully, knelt, and embraced it with her trembling arms; then she commenced shedding tears and touching the blood-matted, curly hair with her soft fingers, crying in a voice that came from the remnants of a shattered heart. She could bear the sight no longer. She dragged the body to a ditch and placed the head gently between the shoulders, covered the entire body with earth, and upon the grave she planted the sword with which the head of the young man had been cut off.

As she started to leave, I walked toward her. She trembled when she saw me, and her eyes were heavy with tears. She sighed and said, "Turn me over to the Emir if you wish. It is better for me to die and follow the one who saved my life from the grip of disgrace than to leave his corpse as food for the ferocious beasts." Then I responded, "Fear me not, poor girl, I have lamented the young man before you did. But tell me, how did he save you from the grip of disgrace?" She replied with a choking and fainting voice, "One of the Emir's officers came to our farm to collect the tax; when he saw me, he looked upon me as a wolf looks upon a lamb. He imposed on my father a heavy tax that even a rich man could not pay. He arrested me as a token to take to the Emir in ransom for the gold which my father was unable to give. I begged him to spare me, but he took no heed, for he had no mercy. Then I cried for help, and this young man, who is dead now, came to my help and saved me from a living death. The officer attempted to kill him, but this man took an old sword that was hanging on the wall of our home and stabbed him. He did not run away like a criminal, but stood by the dead officer until the law came and took him into custody." Having uttered these words which would make any human heart bleed with sorrow, she turned her face and walked away.

In a few moments I saw a youth coming and hiding his face with a cloak. As he approached the corpse of the adulteress, he took off the garment and placed it upon her naked body. Then he drew a dagger from under the cloak and dug a pit in which he placed the dead girl with tenderness and care, and covered her with earth upon which he poured his tears. When he finished his task, he plucked some flowers and placed them reverently upon the grave. As he started to leave, I halted him saying, "What kin are you to this adulteress? And what prompted you to endanger your life by coming here to protect her naked body from the ferocious beasts?" When he stared at me, his sorrowful eyes bespoke his misery, and he said, "I am the unfortunate man for whose love she was stoned; I loved her and she loved me since childhood; we grew together; Love, whom we served and revered, was the lord of our hearts. Love joined both of us and embraced our souls. One day I absented myself from the city, and upon my return I discovered that her father obliged her to marry a man she did not love. My life became a perpetual struggle, and all my days were converted into one long and dark night. I tried to be at peace with my heart, but my heart would not be still. Finally I went to see her secretly and my sole purpose was to have a glimpse of her beautiful eyes and hear the sound of her serene voice. When I reached her house I found her lonely, lamenting her unfortunate self. I sat by her; silence was our important conversation and virtue our companion. One hour of understanding quiet passed, when her husband entered. I cautioned him to contain himself but he dragged her with both hands into the street and cried out saying, "Come, come and see the adulteress and her lover!" All the neighbours rushed about and later the law came and took her to the Emir, but I was not touched by the soldiers. The ignorant Law and sodden customs punished the woman for her father's fault and pardoned the man."

Having thus spoken, the man turned toward the city while I remained pondering the corpse of the thief hanging in that lofty tree and moving slightly every time the wind shook the branches, waiting for someone to bring him down and stretch him upon the bosom of the earth beside the Defender of Honour and Martyr of Love. An hour later, a frail and wretched woman appeared, crying. She stood before the hanged man and prayer reverently. Then she struggled up into the tree and gnawed with her teeth on the linen rope until it broke and the dead fell on the ground like a huge wet cloth; whereupon she came down, dug a grave, and buried the thief by the side of the other two victims. After covering him with earth, she took two pieces of wood and fashioned a cross and placed it over the head. When she turned her face to the city and started to depart, I stopped her saying, "What incited you to come and bury this thief?" She looked at me miserably and said, "He is my faithful husband and merciful companion; he is the father of my children—five young ones starving to death; the oldest is eight years of age, and the youngest is still nursing. My husband was not a thief, but a farmer working in the monastery's land, making our living on what little food the priests and monks gave him when he returned home at eventide. He had been farming for them since he was young, and when he became weak, they dismissed him, advising him to go back home and send his children to take his place as soon as they grew older. He begged them in the name of Jesus and the angels of heaven to let him stay, but they took no heed to his plea. They had no mercy on him nor on his starving children who were helplessly crying for food. He went to the city seeking employment, but in vain, for the rich did not employ except the strong and the healthy. Then he sat on the dusty street stretching his hand toward all who passed, begging and repeating the sad song of his defeat in life, while suffering from hunger and humiliation, but the people refused to help him, saying that lazy people did not deserve alms. One night, hunger gnawed painfully at our children, especially the youngest, who tried hopelessly to nurse on my dry breast. My husband's expression changed and he left the house under the cover of night. He entered the monastery's bin and carried out a bushel of wheat. As he emerged, the monks woke up from their slumber and arrested him after beating him mercilessly. At dawn they brought him to the Emir and complained that he came to the monastery to steal the golden vases of the altar. He was placed in prison and hanged the second day. He was trying to fill the stomachs of his little hungry one with the wheat he had raised by his own labour, but the Emir killed him and used his flesh as food to fill the stomachs of the birds and the beasts." Having spoken in this manner, she left me alone in a sorrowful plight and departed.

I stood there before the graves like a speaker suffering wordlessness while trying to recite a eulogy. I was speechless, but my falling tears substituted for my words and spoke for my soul. My spirit rebelled when I attempted to meditate a while, because the soul is like a flower that folds its petals when dark comes, and breathes not its fragrance into the phantoms of the night. I felt as if the earth that enfolded the victims of oppression in that lonely place were filling my ears with sorrowful tunes of suffering souls, and inspiring me to talk. I resorted to silence, but if the people understood what silence reveals to them, they would have been as close to God as the flowers of the valleys. If the flames of my sighing soul had touched the trees, they would have moved from their places and marched like a strong army to fight the Emir with their branches and tear down the monastery upon the heads of those priests and monks. I stood there watching, and felt that the sweet feeling of mercy and the bitterness of sorrow were pouring from my heart upon the newly dug graves—a grave of a young man who sacrificed his life in defending a weak maiden, whose life and honour he had saved from between the paws and teeth of a savage human; a youth whose head was cut off in reward for his bravery; and his sword was planted upon his grave by the one he saved, as a symbol of heroism before the face of the sun that shines upon an empire laden with stupidity and corruption. A grave of a young woman whose heart was inflamed with love before her body was taken by greed, usurped by lust, and stoned by tyranny. . . . She kept her faith until death; her lover placed flowers upon her grave to speak through their withering hours of those souls whom Love had selected and blessed among a people blinded by earthly substance and muted by ignorance. A grave of a miserable man, weakened by hard labour in the monastery's land, who asked for bread to feed his hungry little ones, and was refused. He resorted to begging, but the people took no heed. When his soul led him to restore a small part of the crop which he had raised and gathered, he was arrested and beaten to death. His poor widow erected a cross upon his head as a witness in the silence of the night before the stars of heaven to testify against those priests who converted the kind teaching of Christ into sharp swords by which they cut the people's necks and tore the bodies of the weak.

The sun disappeared behind the horizon as if tiring of the world's troubles and loathing the people's submission. At that moment the evening began to weave a delicate veil from the sinews of silence and spread it upon Nature's body. I stretched my hand toward the graves, pointing at their symbols, lifted my eyes toward heaven and cried out, "Oh, Bravery, this is your sword, buried now in the earth! Oh, Love, these are your flowers, scorched by fire! Oh, Lord Jesus, this is Thy Cross, submerged in the obscurity of the night!"

A LOVER'S CALL

Where are you, my beloved? Are you in that little
Paradise, watering the flowers who look upon you
As infants look upon the breast of their mothers?

Or are you in your chamber where the shrine of
Virtue has been placed in your honour, and upon
Which you offer my heart and soul as sacrifice?

Or amongst the books, seeking human knowledge,
While you are replete with heavenly wisdom?

Oh companion of my soul, where are you? Are you
Praying in the temple? Or calling Nature in the
Field, haven of your dreams?

Are you in the huts of the poor, consoling the
Broken-hearted with the sweetness of your soul, and
Filling their hands with your bounty?

You are God's spirit everywhere;
You are stronger than the ages.

Do you have memory of the day we met, when the
halo of
Your spirit surrounded us, and the Angels of Love
Floated about, singing the praise of the soul's deeds?

Do you recollect our sitting in the shade of the
Branches, sheltering ourselves from Humanity, as
the ribs
Protect the divine secret of the heart from injury?

Remember you the trails and forest we walked, with
hands
Joined, and our heads leaning against each other,
as if
We were hiding ourselves within ourselves?

Recall you the hour I bade you farewell,
And the Miriamite kiss you placed on my lips?
That kiss taught me that joining of lips in Love
Reveals heavenly secrets which the tongue cannot
utter!

That kiss was introduction to a great sigh,
Like the Almighty's breath that turned earth into
man.

That sigh led my way into the spiritual world,
Announcing the glory of my soul; and there
It shall perpetuate until again we meet.

I remember when you kissed me and kissed me,
With tears coursing your cheeks, and you said,

"Earthly bodies must often separate for earthly purpose,
And must live apart impelled by worldly intent.

"But the spirit remains joined safely in the hands of
Love, until death arrives and takes joined souls to God.

"Go, my beloved; Love has chosen you her delegate;
Obey her, for she is Beauty who offers to her follower
The cup of the sweetness of life.
As for my own empty arms, your love shall remain my
Comforting groom; your memory, my Eternal wedding."

Where are you now, my other self? Are you awake in
The silence of the night? Let the clean breeze convey
To you my heart's every beat and affection.

Are you fondling my face in your memory? That image
Is no longer my own, for Sorrow has dropped his
Shadow on my happy countenance of the past.

Sobs have withered my eyes which reflected your beauty
And dried my lips which you sweetened with kisses.

A LOVER'S CALL

Where are you, my beloved? Do you hear my weeping
From beyond the ocean? Do you understand my need?
Do you know the greatness of my patience?

Is there any spirit in the air capable of conveying
To you the breath of this dying youth? Is there any
Secret communication between angels that will carry to
You my complaint?

Where are you, my beautiful star? The obscurity of life
Has cast me upon its bosom; sorrow has conquered me.
Sail your smile into the air; it will reach and enliven me!
Breathe your fragrance into the air; it will sustain me!

Where are you, my beloved?
Oh, how great is Love!
And how little am I!

THE PALACE AND THE HUT

PART ONE

As night fell and the light glittered in the great house, the servants stood at the massive door awaiting the coming of the guests; and upon their velvet garments shone golden buttons.

The magnificent carriages drew into the palace park and the nobles entered, dressed in gorgeous raiment and decorated with jewels. The instruments filled the air with pleasant melodies while the dignitaries danced to the soothing music.

At midnight the finest and most palatable foods were served on a beautiful table embellished with all kinds of the rarest flowers. The feasters dined and drank abundantly, until the sequence of the wine began to play its part. At dawn the throng dispersed boisterously, after spending a long night of intoxication and gluttony which hurried their worn bodies into their deep beds with unnatural sleep.

PART TWO

At eventide, a man attired in the dress of heavy work stood before the door of his small house and knocked at the door. As it opened, he entered and greeted the occupants in a cheerful manner, and then sat between his children who were playing at the fireplace. In a short time, his wife had the meal prepared and they sat at a wooden table consuming their food. After eating they gathered around the oil lamp and talked of the day's events. When early night had lapsed, all stood silently and surrendered themselves to the King of Slumber with a song of praise and a prayer of gratitude upon their lips.

THE LONELY POET

I AM A STRANGER in this world, and there is a severe solitude and painful lonesomeness in my exile. I am alone, but in my aloneness I contemplate an unknown and enchanting country, and this meditation fills my dreams with spectres of a great and distant land which my eyes have never seen.

I am a stranger among my people and I have no friends. When I see a person I say within myself, "Who is he, and in what manner do I know him, and why is he here, and what law has joined me with him?"

I am a stranger to myself, and when I hear my tongue speak, my ears wonder over my voice; I see my inner self smiling, crying, braving, and fearing; and my existence wonders over my substance while my soul interrogates my heart; but I remain unknown, engulfed by tremendous silence.

My thoughts are strangers to my body, and as I stand before the mirror, I see something in my face which my soul does not see, and I find in my eyes what my inner self does not find.

When I walk vacant-eyed through the streets of the clamourous city, the children follow me, shouting, "Here is a blind man! Let us give him a walking cane to feel his way." When I run from them, I meet with a group of maidens, and they grasp the edges of my garment, saying, "He is deaf like the rock; let us fill his ears with the music of love." And when I flee from them, a throng of aged people point at me with trembling fingers and say, "He is a madman who lost his mind in the world of genii and ghouls."

I am a stranger in this world; I roamed the Universe from end to end, but could not find a place to rest my head; nor did I know any human I confronted, neither an individual who would hearken to my mind.

When I open my sleepless eyes at dawn, I find myself imprisoned in a dark cave from whose ceiling hang the insects and upon whose floor crawl the vipers.

When I go out to meet the light, the shadow of my body follows me, but the shadow of my spirit precedes me and leads the way to an unknown place seeking things beyond my understanding, and grasping objects that are meaningless to me.

At eventide I return and lie upon my bed, made of soft feathers and lined with thorns, and I contemplate and feel the troublesome and happy desires, and sense the painful and joyous hopes.

At midnight the ghosts of the past ages and the

spirits of the forgotten civilization enter through the crevices of the cave to visit me . . . I stare at them and they gaze upon me; I talk to them and they answer me smilingly. Then I endeavour to clutch them, but they sift through my fingers and vanish like the mist which rests on the lake.

I am a stranger in this world, and there is no one in the Universe who understands the language I speak. Patterns of bizarre remembrance form suddenly in my mind, and my eyes bring forth queer images and sad ghosts. I walk in the deserted prairies, watching the streamlets running fast, up and up from the depths of the valley to the top of the mountain; I watch the naked trees blooming and bearing fruit, and shedding their leaves in one instant, and then I see the branches fall and turn into speckled snakes. I see the birds hovering above, singing and wailing; then they stop and open their wings and turn into undraped maidens with long hair, looking at me from behind kohled and infatuated eyes, and smiling at me with full lips soaked with honey, stretching their scented hands toward me. Then they ascend and disappear from my sight like phantoms, leaving in the firmament the resounding echo of their taunts and mocking laughter.

I am a stranger in this world . . . I am a poet who composes what life proses, and who proses what life composes.

For this reason I am a stranger, and I shall remain

a stranger until the white and friendly wings of Death carry me home into my beautiful country. There, where light and peace and understanding abide, I will await the other strangers who will be rescued by the friendly trap of time from this narrow, dark world.

SECRETS OF THE HEART

A MAJESTIC mansion stood under the wings of the silent night, as Life stands under the cover of Death. In it sat a maiden at an ivory desk, leaning her beautiful head on her soft hand, as a withering lily leans upon its petals. She looked around, feeling like a miserable prisoner, struggling to penetrate the walls of the dungeon with her eyes in order to witness Life walking in the procession of Freedom.

The hours passed like the ghosts of the night, as a procession chanting the dirge of her sorrow, and the maiden felt seçure with the shedding of her tears in anguished solitude. When she could not resist the pressure of her suffering any longer, and as she felt that she was in full possession of the treasured secrets of her heart, she took the quill and commenced mingling her tears with ink upon parchment, and she inscribed:

"My Beloved Sister,

"When the heart becomes congested with secrets,

and the eyes begin to burn from the searing tears, and the ribs are about to burst with the growing of the heart's confinement, one cannot find expression for such a labyrinth except by a surge of release.

"Sorrowful persons find joy in lamentation, and lovers encounter comfort and condolence in dreams, and the oppressed delight in receiving sympathy. I am writing to you now because I feel like a poet who fancies the beauty of objects whose impression he composes in verse while being ruled by a divine power. . . . I am like a child of the starving poor who cries for food, instigated by bitterness of hunger, disregarding the plight of his poor and merciful mother and her defeat in life.

"Listen to my painful story, my dear sister, and weep with me, for sobbing is like a prayer, and the tears of mercy are like a charity because they come forth from a living and sensitive and good soul and they are not shed in vain. It was the will of my father when I married a noble and rich man. My father was like most of the rich, whose only joy in life is to improve their wealth by adding more gold to their coffers in fear of poverty, and curry nobility with grandeur in anticipation of the attacks of the black days. . . . I find myself now, with all my love and dreams, a victim upon a golden altar which I hate, and an inherited honour which I despise.

"I respect my husband because he is generous and kind to all; he endeavours to bring happiness to me, and spends his gold to please my heart, but I have found that the impression of all these things is not worth one moment of a true and divine love. Do not ridicule me, my sister, for I am now a most enlightened person regarding the needs of a woman's heart—that throbbing heart which is like a bird flying in the spacious sky of love. . . . It is like a vase replenished with the wine of the ages that has been pressed for the sipping souls. . . . It is like a book in whose pages one reads the chapters of happiness and misery, joy and pain, laughter and sorrow. No one can read this book except the true companion who is the other half of the woman, created for her since the beginning of the world.

"Yes, I became most knowing amongst all women as to the purpose of the soul and meaning of the heart, for I have found that my magnificent horses and beautiful carriages and glittering coffers of gold and sublime nobility are not worth one glance from the eyes of that poor young man who is patiently waiting and suffering the pangs of bitterness and misery. . . . That youth who is oppressed by the cruelty and will of my father, and imprisoned in the narrow and melancholy jail of Life. . . .

"Please, my dear, do not contrive to console me, for the calamity through which I have realized the power of my love is my great consoler. Now I am looking forward from behind my tears and awaiting the coming of Death to lead me to where I will meet the companion of my soul and embrace him as I did before we entered this strange world.

"Do not think evil of me, for I am doing my duty as a faithful wife, and complying calmly and patiently with the laws and rules of man. I honour my husband with my sense, and respect him with my heart, and revere him with my soul, but there is a withholding, for God gave part of me to my beloved before I knew him.

"Heaven willed that I spend my life with a man not meant for me, and I am wasting my days silently according to the will of Heaven; but if the gates of Eternity do not open, I will remain with the beautiful half of my soul and look back to the Past, and that Past is this Present. . . . I shall look at life as Spring looks at Winter, and contemplate the obstacles of Life as one who has climbed the rough trail and reached the mountain top."

At that moment the maiden ceased writing and hid her face with her cupped hands and wept bitterly. Her heart declined to entrust to the pen its most sacred secrets, but resorted to the pouring of dry tears that dispersed quickly and mingled with the gentle ether, the haven of the lovers' souls and the flowers' spirits. After a moment she took the quill and added, "Do you remember that youth? Do you recollect the rays which emanated from his eyes, and the sorrowful signs upon his face? Do you recall that laughter which bespoke the tears of a mother, torn from her only child? Can you retrace his serene voice speaking the echo of a distant valley? Do you remember him meditating and staring longingly and calmly at objects and speaking of them in strange words, and then bending his head and sighing as if fearing to reveal the secrets of his great heart? Do you recall his dreams and beliefs? Do you recollect all these things in a youth whom humanity counts as one of her children and upon whom my father looked with eyes of superiority because he is higher than earthly greed and nobler than inherited grandeur?

"You know, my dear sister, that I am a martyr in this belittling world, and a victim of ignorance. Will you sympathize with a sister who sits in the silence of the horrible night pouring down the contents of her inner self and revealing to you her heart's secrets? I am sure that you will sympathize with me, for I know that Love has visited your heart."

Dawn came, and the maiden surrendered herself to Slumber, hoping to find sweeter and more gentle dreams than those she had encountered in her awakeness. . . .

DEAD ARE MY PEOPLE

(*Written in exile during the famine in Syria*)

WORLD WAR I

GONE are my people, but I exist yet,
Lamenting them in my solitude. . . .
Dead are my friends, and in their
Death my life is naught but great
Disaster.

The knolls of my country are submerged
By tears and blood, for my people and
My beloved are gone, and I am here
Living as I did when my people and my
Beloved were enjoying life and the
Bounty of life, and when the hills of
My country were blessed and engulfed
By the light of the sun.

My people died from hunger, and he who
Did not perish from starvation was
Butchered with the sword; and I am
Here in this distant land, roaming
Amongst a joyful people who sleep

Upon soft beds, and smile at the days
While the days smile upon them.

My people died a painful and shameful
Death, and here am I living in plenty
And in peace. . . . This is deep tragedy
Ever-enacted upon the stage of my
Heart; few would care to witness this
Drama, for my people are as birds with
Broken wings, left behind by the flock.

If I were hungry and living amid my
Famished people, and persecuted among
My oppressed countrymen, the burden
Of the black days would be lighter
Upon my restless dreams, and the
Obscurity of the night would be less
Dark before my hollow eyes and my
Crying heart and my wounded soul.
For he who shares with his people
Their sorrow and agony will feel a
Supreme comfort created only by
Suffering in sacrifice. And he will
Be at peace with himself when he dies
Innocent with his fellow innocents.

But I am not living with my hungry
And persecuted people who are walking
In the procession of death toward
Martyrdom. . . . I am here beyond the
Broad seas living in the shadow of

Tranquility, and in the sunshine of
Peace. . . . I am afar from the pitiful
Arena and the distressed, and cannot
Be proud of aught, not even of my own
Tears.

What can an exiled son do for his
Starving people, and of what value
Unto them is the lamentation of an
Absent poet?

Were I an ear of corn grown in the earth
Of my country, the hungry child would
Pluck me and remove with my kernels
The hand of Death from his soul. Were
I a ripe fruit in the gardens of my
Country, the starving woman would
Gather me and sustain life. Were I
A bird flying in the sky of my country,
My hungry brother would hunt me and
Remove with the flesh of my body the
Shadow of the grave from his body.
But alas! I am not an ear of corn
Grown in the plains of Syria, nor a
Ripe fruit in the valleys of Lebanon;
This is my disaster, and this is my
Mute calamity which brings humiliation
Before my soul and before the phantoms
Of the night. . . . This is the painful
Tragedy which tightens my tongue and
Pinions my arms and arrests me usurped

Of power and of will and of action.
This is the curse burned upon my
Forehead before God and man.

And oftentime they say unto me,
"The disaster of your country is
But naught to the calamity of the
World, and the tears and blood shed
By your people are as nothing to
The rivers of blood and tears
Pouring each day and night in the
Valleys and plains of the earth. . . ."

Yes, but the death of my people is
A silent accusation; it is a crime
Conceived by the heads of the unseen
Serpents. . . . It is a songless and
Sceneless tragedy. . . . And if my
People had attacked the despots
And oppressors and died as rebels,
I would have said, "Dying for
Freedom is nobler than living in
The shadow of weak submission, for
He who embraces death with the sword
Of Truth in his hand will eternalize
With the Eternity of Truth, for Life
Is weaker than Death and Death is
Weaker than Truth.

If my nation had partaken in the war
Of all nations and had died in the

Field of battle, I would say that
The raging tempest had broken with
Its might the green branches; and
Strong death under the canopy of
The tempest is nobler than slow
Perishment in the arms of senility.
But there was no rescue from the
Closing jaws. . . . My people dropped
And wept with the crying angels.

If an earthquake had torn my
Country asunder and the earth had
Engulfed my people into its bosom,
I would have said, "A great and
Mysterious law has been moved by
The will of divine force, and it
Would be pure madness if we frail
Mortals endeavoured to probe its
Deep secrets. . . ."
But my people did not die as rebels;
They were not killed in the field
Of battle; nor did the earthquake
Shatter my country and subdue them.
Death was their only rescuer, and
Starvation their only spoils.

My people died on the cross. . . .
They died while their hands
Stretched toward the East and West,
While the remnants of their eyes

Stared at the blackness of the
Firmament. . . . They died silently,
For humanity had closed its ears
To their cry. They died because
They did not befriend their enemy.
They died because they loved their
Neighbours. They died because
They placed trust in all humanity.
They died because they did not
Oppress the oppressors. They died
Because they were the crushed
Flowers, and not the crushing feet.
They died because they were peace
Makers. They perished from hunger
In a land rich with milk and honey.
They died because the monsters of
Hell arose and destroyed all that
Their fields grew, and devoured the
Last provisions in their bins. . . .
They died because the vipers and
Sons of vipers spat out poison into
The space where the Holy Cedars and
The roses and the jasmine breathe
Their fragrance.

My people and your people, my Syrian
Brother, are dead. . . . What can be
Done for those who are dying? Our
Lamentations will not satisfy their
Hunger, and our tears will not quench

Their thirst; what can we do to save
Them from between the iron paws of
Hunger? My brother, the kindness
Which compels you to give a part of
Your life to any human who is in the
Shadow of losing his life is the only
Virtue which makes you worthy of the
Light of day and the peace of the
Night. . . . Remember, my brother,
That the coin which you drop into
The withered hand stretching toward
You is the only golden chain that
Binds your rich heart to the
Loving heart of God. . . .

THE BRIDE'S BED*

The bride and bridegroom, preceded by candle carriers and followed by priests and friends, left the temple accompanied by young men and women who walked by their sides singing and filling the firmament with beautiful and happy melodies.

As the procession reached the bridegroom's residence, the newly wed couple took high seats in the spacious room, and the celebrants seated themselves upon the silken cushions and velvet divans until the place became crowded with multitudes of well wishers. The servants set the tables, and the feasters commenced drinking to the health of the bride and bridegroom, while the musicians were soothing the spirits with their stringed instruments. One could hear the ringing and rattling of the drinking cups in unison with the sound of tambourines. The maidens began to dance gracefully and twist their

* This incident occurred in North Lebanon in the latter part of the nineteenth century and it was conveyed to me by a person who was related to one of the principals in this story, and who attended the function described. (*Kahlil Gibran.*)

flexible bodies to the melodies of the music, while the onlookers watched cheerfully and drank more and more wine.

In a few hours the scene was converted from a gay and pleasant wedding celebration into a coarse and profane orgy of drunkenness. Here is a young man pouring out all of his heart's sentiment and revealing his momentary, questionable love to an attractive maiden. And there is another youth endeavouring to converse with a woman, and having difficulty in bringing to his wine-drugged tongue the beautiful expressions he sought. Now and then you hear an elderly man urging the musicians to repeat a certain song that reminded him of his youthful days. In this group a woman is flirting with a man who, in turn, is looking passionately at her rival. In that corner, a grey-haired woman is watching the maidens smilingly, trying to select a wife for her only son. By the window stands a married woman who affords herself this opportunity to make plans with her lover while her husband is occupied with wine. It seemed that all were reaping the fruits of the present and forgetting the past and the future.

All this was taking place while the beautiful bride watched them with sorrowful eyes. She felt like a miserable prisoner behind the iron bars of a prison, and frequently she glanced across the room toward a young man who was sitting alone and quietly, like a wounded bird left behind by the flock. His arms were folded across his bosom as if he were trying to keep his heart from bursting. He was gazing at something invisible in the sky of the room and seemed to be completely lost in a world of darkness.

Midnight came, and the exultation of the throng mounted higher until it assumed the aspects of unleashed madness, for the minds were free and the tongues were uncontrolled.

The bridegroom, who was an elderly man, already drunk, left the bride to herself and circulated amidst the guests, drinking with the feasters and adding fuel to the flames of his intoxication.

Responding to the bride's signal, a maiden came and sat close by her side, whereupon the bride turned around and looked in every direction before she whispered with a trembling voice, "I beg you, my companion, and appeal to you in the name of our friendship and everything that is dear to you in this world, to go now and tell Saleem to join me in the garden under the willow tree. Please, Susan, beg him for me and ask him to grant my request; remind him of our past and tell him that I will die if I do not see him. Tell him that I must confess my sins to him and ask him to forgive me; tell him that I want to pour out all my heart's secrets before him. Hurry, and do not fear."

Susan dispatched the bride's message with sincerity; Saleem looked at her as a thirsty man looks at a brook far off and he quietly said, "I will wait for her in the garden under the willow tree." He left the house, and a few minutes passed before the bride followed him, stealing her way between the drunken revelers. As she reached the garden, she looked to the rear like a gazelle who is fleeing a wolf, and sped toward the willow tree where the youth awaited her. When she found herself by his side, she threw her arms about him and said tearfully, "My beloved, listen to me; I am sorry for having been hasty and thoughtless. I repented until my heart is crushed with sorrow; I love you and do not love any other; I shall continue to love you to the end of my life. They lied to me and told me that you loved another and Najeebee deceived me when she told me that you had fallen in love with her, and did so in order to induce me to accept her cousin as my bridegroom, as the family had long planned. I am married now but you are the only one I love and you are my bridegroom. Now that the veil has been removed from my eyes and truth is near, I came here to follow you to the end of life, and I will never go back to the man whom falsehood and narrow custom have selected for me as a husband. Let us hurry, my beloved, and leave this place under the protection of night. Let us go to the seacoast and embark upon a ship that will take us to a distant land where we will live together unmolested. Let us start now so when dawn comes we will be safe from the grip of the enemy; I have enough jewelry to take care of us for the rest of our lives . . . Why do you not talk, Saleem? Why do you not look at me? Why do you not kiss me? Are you listening to the wailing of my soul and the crying of my heart? Speak, and let us make haste to leave this place! The minutes we are losing are more precious than diamonds, and dearer than the crowns of the kings."

Her voice was more soothing than Life's whispering, and more anguished than the moaning call of Death, and softer than the rustling of wings, and deeper than the message of the waves . . . it was a voice that vibrated with hope and despair, with pleasure and pain, with happiness and misery, with need for life and desire for death. The youth was listening, but within him Love and Honour fought each other . . . Honour that confronts the spirit, and Love that God places in the human heart . . . After a long silence, the youth raised his head and turned his eyes away from the bride who was quivering with anxiety and he quietly protested, "Return to your destiny, for it is now too late. Sobriety has effaced what intoxication had painted. Go back before the guests see you here and say that you betrayed your husband on the wedding night just as you betrayed me during my absence." When she heard these words, she trembled like a withering flower before a tempest and she said painfully, "I shall never go back to that house which I have left forever. I feel now like a prisoner who leaves his exile . . . do not cast me from you, saying that I betrayed you. The hands that joined your heart and mine are stronger than the Emir's and the priest's hands which committed my body to my revolting bridegroom. There is no power that can take you from me . . . not even Death can separate our souls, for as Heaven has willed it, only Heaven can alter it."

Feigning disinterest and trying to free himself from the grip of her arms around him, Saleem retorted, "Depart from me! I love another with an intensity that causes me to forget you exist in this world. Najeebee was right when she told you that I loved her. Go back to your husband and be a faithful wife to him as the law commands."

The bride desperately protested, "No, no! I do not believe you, Saleem! I know that you love me, and I can read it in your eyes; I sense your love when I am close to you; I shall never leave you for my husband's home as long as my heart beats; I came here to follow you to the end of the world. Lead the way, Saleem, or shed my blood and take my life now." With a voice no stronger than before, Saleem returned, "Leave me, or I will shout and gather the people in this garden and disgrace you before God and man and let my beloved Najeebee laugh at you and be proud of her triumph."

As Saleem was endeavouring to unclasp her arms, she turned from a hopeful, kind, and pleading woman into a furious lioness who had lost her cubs, and she cried out saying, "No one shall ever triumph over me and take my love from me!" Having uttered these words, she drew a dagger from beneath her wedding gown, and swift as lightning, she sheathed it in the youth's heart. He fell upon the ground like a tender branch broken by the storms and she bent over him, holding the blood-stained dagger in her hand. He opened his eyes and his lips vibrated when he faltered, "Come now, my beloved; come, Lyla, and do not leave me. Life is weaker than Death, and Death is weaker than Love. Listen to the cruel laughter of the feasters inside the house, and hear the tinkling and breaking of the drinking cups, my beloved. Lyla, you have rescued me from Life's suffering. Let me kiss the hand that broke the chains and let me free. Kiss me and forgive me, for I have not been truthful.

"Place your blood-cleansed hands upon my withering heart, and when my soul ascends into the spacious sky, place the dagger in my right hand and say that I took my own life." He choked for breath and whispered, "I love you, Lyla, and never loved another. Self-sacrifice is nobler than fleeing with you. Kiss me, oh beloved sweetheart of my soul. Kiss me, oh Lyla . . ." And he placed his hand upon his wounded heart and breathed his last. The bride looked toward the house and cried in piercing agony, "Emerge from your stupor, for here is the wedding! The bride and the bridegroom are awaiting you! Come and see our soft bed! Wake up, you madmen and drunkards; hurry to this place so we can reveal to you the truth of Love, Death and Life!" Her hysterical voice rang through every corner of the house, echoing into the guests' ears. As if in a trance, they were drawn to the door and they walked out, looking in every direction. As they approached the scene of tragic beauty, and saw the bride weeping over Saleem, they retreated in fright and none dared come close by. It seemed that the stream of blood from the youth's heart, and the dagger in the bride's hand, had fascinated them and frozen the blood in their bodies. The bride looked at him and moaned bitterly, "Come, you cowards! Fear not the spectre of Death whose greatness will refuse to approach your littleness, and dread not this dagger, for it is a divine instrument which declines to touch your filthy bodies and empty hearts. Look at this handsome youth . . . he is my beloved, and I killed him because I loved him . . . he is my bridegroom and I am his bride. We sought a bed worthy of our love in this world which you have made so small with your ignorance and traditions. But we chose this bed. Where is that wicked woman who slandered my beloved and said that he loved her? Where is the one who believed she triumphed over me? Where is Najeebee, that hell-viper who deceived me? Where is the woman who gathered you here to celebrate my beloved's departure and not the wedding of the man she had chosen for me? My words are vague to you, for the abyss cannot understand the song of the stars. You shall tell your children that I killed my beloved on the wedding night. My name shall be upon your dirty lips uttered with blasphemy, but your grandchildren shall bless me, for Tomorrow shall be for the freedom of truth and the spirit. And you, my ignorant husband, who bought my body but not my love, and who owns me but will never possess me, you are the symbol of this miserable nation, seeking light in darkness, and awaiting the coming of water from the rock; you symbolize a country ruled by blindness and stupidity; you represent a false humanity which cuts throats and arms in order to reach for a necklace or bracelet. I forgive you now, for the happy, departing soul forgives the sins of all the people."

Then the bride lifted her dagger toward the sky, and like a thirsty person who brings the edge of a drinking glass to his lips, she brought it down and planted it in her bosom. She fell by the side of her beloved like a lily whose flower was cut off by a sharp scythe. The women gazed upon the horrible scene and cried frightfully; some of them fell into a swoon, and the uproar of the men filled the sky. As they shamefully and reverently approached the victims, the dying bride looked at them, and with blood streaming from her stricken body, she said, "Stay away from us and separate not our bodies, for if you commit such a sin, the spirit that hovers over your heads will grasp you and take your lives. Let this hungry earth swallow our bodies and hide us in its bosom. Let it protect us as it protects the seeds from the snow until Spring comes, and restores pure life and awakening."

She came close to her beloved, placed her lips

upon his cold lips, and uttered her last words, "Look, my forever . . . look at our friends. How the jealous are gathering about our bed! Hear the grating of their teeth and the crushing of their fingers! You have waited for me a long time, Saleem, and here I am, for I have broken the chains and shackles. Let us go toward the sun, for we have been waiting too long in this confining, dark world. All objects are disappearing from my sight and I can see naught but you, my beloved. These are my lips, my greatest earthly possession . . . accept my last human breath. Come, Saleem, let us leave now. Love has lifted his wings and ascended into the great light." She dropped her head upon his bosom and her unseeing eyes were still open and gazing upon him.

Silence prevailed, as if the dignity of death had stolen the people's strength and prevented them from moving. Whereupon the priest who had performed the wedding ceremony came forth and pointed with his forefinger at the death-bound couple shouting, "Cursed are the hands that touch these blood-spattered carcasses that are soaked with sin. And cursed are the eyes that shed tears of sorrow upon these two evil souls. Let the corpse of the son of Sodom and that of the daughter of Gomorrah remain lying in this diseased spot until the beasts devour their flesh and the wind scatters their bones. Go back to your homes and flee from the pollution of these sinners! Disperse now, before the flames of hell sting you, and he who remains here shall be cursed and excommunicated from the Church and shall never again enter the temple and join the Christians in offering prayers to God!"

Susan, who acted as the last messenger between the bride and her beloved, walked forth bravely and stood before the priest. She looked at him with tearful eyes and said, "I shall remain here, you merciless heretic, and I shall guard them until dawn comes. I shall dig a grave for them under these hanging branches and bury them in the garden of their last earthly kiss. Leave this place immediately, for the swine detest the aromatic scent of incense, and the thieves fear the lord of the house and dread the coming of the brilliant sunrise. Hurry to your obscured beds, for the hymns of the angels will not enter your ears, blocked with the hardened cement of cruel and stupid rules."

The throng departed slowly with the stern-faced priest, and Susan remained watching over Lyla and Saleem as a loving mother guards her children in the silence of the night. And when the multitude was gone, she dropped down and wept with the crying angels.

BOOK 8

THE PROCESSION

INTRODUCTION

THE MOTIVE of Gibran in writing this work probably finds its basis in his never-ending efforts to analyze human society, its laws, rules and customs. In society Gibran perceives a general falsehood of living that leads the people from the truth, elating some persons, humiliating others. He admonishes that no individual can experience fullness of life and enjoy the bounty of Nature while his fellowman is pursuing greed in order to attain his goal.

To illustrate his precepts, Gibran chooses two metaphorical characters. The first is *Age,* represented by a bent old man who lives in the city and suffers through its man-made laws, traditions, inheritances and corruptions. He wearies of the stifling clamour, and departs for the field in order to relax his trembling hands and meditate. In the field he meets *Youth,* symbolized by a handsome, robust young man whose eyes have seen only the trees, mountains and brooks, whose body has inhaled only the pure air, and whose ears have listened only to the singing of the streams and birds, and the whistling of the wind through the autumn leaves.

At this meeting, *Youth* is carrying a flute in his hand, preparing to greet Nature with his eternal melody of the open field. *Youth* and *Age* discuss freely their respective conceptions of life, *Age* commenting that naught but evil and misery are created in the city by human society, while *Youth* insists that only by leading a life close to the heart of Nature can one's heart find true pleasure and contentment, filling the heart's domain to its fullest with simple, God-given joy.

From this debate between *Age* and *Youth,* Kahlil Gibran's approaches to life, death, and religion are revealed. He does not propose that all persons abandon urbanity for life on the mountainside, but he endeavours to focus attention upon a simple formula for better life, and urges the people to unchain themselves from the rattling shackles of society and avail themselves, to as great a degree as possible, of the natural freedom and tranquility of rural existence. The field which Gibran describes is symbolic of the life of rich wholesomeness accruing to the heart of the person who abides close by the earth.

By reason of the nebulous, untranslatable character of the Arabic language, this play-poem is variously called *The Procession* and *The Cortège.* Despite Gibran's sadness as reflected herein, the translator determined that *The Procession* was best suited, as a title, to the author's intention. This same indefiniteness, inherent in the Arabic, required occasional departure from strict translation in order that Gibran's mighty message be captured intact.

Age: True, good deed by man is ever done,
But when man is gone, evil does not
Perish with him. Like turning wheels
We are controlled by the hands of
Time where e'er man resides. Say not
"This man is famed and learned, or
Master of knowledge from the angels
Sent," for in the city the best of
Man is but one of a flock, led by
The shepherd in strong voice. And he
Who follows not the command must soon
Stand before his killers.

Youth: There is no shepherd over man in
The beautiful field, nor sheep to
Graze nor hearts to bleed. Winter
Departs with her garment and Spring
Must come, but only by God's great
Command. Your people are born as
Slaves, and by your tyrants their
Souls are torn. Where e'er goes the
Leader, so go they, and woe unto
Him who would refuse!
Give me the flute and let me sing,
And through my soul let music ring;

The song of the flute is more sublime
Than all glory of kings in all of time.

Age: Life amid the throngs is but brief
And drug-laden slumber, mixed with
Mad dreams and spectres and fears.
The secret of the heart is encased
In sorrow, and only in sorrow is
Found our joy, while happiness serves
But to conceal the deep mystery of life,
And if sorrow I were to abandon for
The calm of the field, naught but
Emptiness would be my lot.

Youth: The joy of one is the sorrow of the
Other, and there is no sorrow in the
Beautiful field, or sadness brought
By scornful deed. The frolicsome
Breeze brings joy to sad hearts, and
Your sorrow of heart is but a dream of
Fancy, passing swiftly, like the quick
Brook. Your sorrow would in the field
Vanish, as the autumn leaf is sped off
On the forehead of the brook, and your
Heart would be calm, as the broad lake
Is calm under the great lights of God.
Give me the flute and let me sing,
And through my soul let music ring;
Heaven's melody alone will ever remain,
All of earth's objects are but vain.

Age: Few are those content with life and far
From care. The river of the field is
But a carrier of emptiness; the river
Of human life has been diverted into old
Cups of knowledge and presented to man
Who drinks of life's richness but heeds
Not its warnings. He is joyous when the
Cups are of happiness, but he grumbles
When he prays to God and asks for the
Wealth he scarce merits. And when he
Attains his goal of iron riches his
Dreams of fear enslave him forever.
This world is but a wine shop whose
Owner is Time, and the drunkards
Demand much for little offering.

Youth: There is no wine in the beautiful
Field, for glorious intoxication of
The soul is the reward of all who
Seek it in the bosom of Nature. The
Cloud which shelters the moon must
Be pierced with ardour if one needs
Behold the moon's light. The people
Of the city abuse the wine of Time,
For they think upon it as a temple,
And they drink of it with ease and
With unthinking, and they flee,
Scurrying into old age with deep
But unknowing sorrow.
Give me the flute and let me sing,
And through my soul let music ring;

The song of God must ever stay,
All other things must pass away.

Age: Religion to man is like your field,
For it is planted with hope and
Tilled by the faithful; or it is
Tended by the shivering ignorant,
Fearing the fire of hell; or it is
Sowed by the strong in wealth of
Empty gold who look upon religion
As a kind of barter, ever seeking
Profit in earthly reward. But
Their hearts are lost despite
Their throbbing, and the product
Of their spiritual farming is but
The unwanted weed of the valley.

Youth: There is no religion in the Godly
And beautiful field, nor any heretic
Nor color nor creed, for when the
Nightingale sings, all is beauty and
Joy and religion, and the spirit is
Soothed and the reward is peace.
Give me the flute and let me sing,
Prayer is my music, love is my string;
The moaning flute will surely sound
The misery of those in the city bound.

Age: What of justice and earthly rule
That makes us laugh and weep? For the
Criminal who is weak and poor the

Narrow cell or death awaits; but
Honour and glory await the rich who
Conceal their crimes behind their
Gold and silver and inherited glory.

Youth: All is justice in Nature's field; to
None does Nature grant neglect or
Favor. The trees are grown in each
Other's way, but when the breeze is
Scampering all will sway. Justice in
The field is like the snow, for it
Blankets all things, and when the sun
Appears, all things must emerge in
Strength and in beauty and in fragrance.
Give me the flute and let me sing
For the song of God is everything;
The truth of the flute will e'er remain,
While crimes and men are but disdain.

Age: The people of the city are enmeshed
In the web of the tyrant who rages
In fury when he grows old. In the
Lion's den there is a scent, and be
The lion there or not, the fox will
Not approach. The starling is timid
When he soars the infinite, but the
Eagle is proud, even when he dies.
The strength of the spirit alone is
The power of powers, and must in time
Crumble to powder all things opposing
It. Do not condemn, but pity the

Faithless and their weakness and their
Ignorance and their nothingness.

Youth: The field sees not the weak nor the
Strong, for to Nature, all are one
And all are strong. When the lion
Roars, the field does not say, "He is
A terrible beast . . . let us flee!" Man's
Shadow passes in speed through his
Brief and sorrowful visit to earth,
And rests in the vast firmament of
Thought, which is heaven's field; and
Like leaves of autumn that fall to the
Heart of earth, all must again appear in
The great springtime of colourful youth,
Beautiful in their re-birth. And the leaf
Of the tree will thrive in hearty life
After man's objects of substance perish
Into vapour and forgottenness.
Give me the flute and let me sing,
For strength of soul my song will bring;
The heavenly flute will long be cherished
But man and his greed will soon be perished.

Age: Man is weak by his own hand, for he
Has refashioned God's law into his own
Confining manner of life, chaining
Himself with the coarse irons of the
Rules of society which he desired; and
He is steadfast in refusing to be aware
Of the great tragedy he has cast upon

Himself and his children and their sons.
Man has erected on this earth a prison
Of quarrels from which he cannot now
Escape, and misery is his voluntary lot.

Youth: To Nature all are alive and all are
Free. The earthly glory of man is an
Empty dream, vanishing with the bubbles
In the rocky stream. When the almond
Tree spreads her blossoms on the small
Plants growing below, she does not say,
"How rich am I! How poor are they!"
Give me the flute and let me sing,
And through my soul let music ring;
The melody of God will never wane,
While all on earth is naught but vain.

Age: The kindness of the people is but an
Empty shell containing no gem or
Precious pearl. With two hearts do
People live; a small one of deep
Softness, the other of steel. And
Kindness is too often a shield,
And generosity too often a sword.

Youth: The field has but one great heart;
The willow lives by the oak, and
Has no fear of its strength or
Its size. And the peacock's garb
Is magnificent to behold, but the
Peacock knows not whether it be a

Thing of beauty or of ugliness.
Give me the flute and let me sing,
And through my soul let music ring;
For music is the hymn of the meek,
Mightier than the strong and the weak.

Age: The people of the city feign great
Wisdom and knowledge, but their
Fancy remains false forever, for
They are but experts of imitation.
It gives them pride to calculate
That a barter will bring no loss
Or gain. The idiot imagines himself
A king and no power can alter his
Great thoughts and dreams. The
Proud fool mistakes his mirror for
The sky, and his shadow for a
Moon that gleams high from the
Heavens.

Youth: No clever or handsome inhabit
The field, for Nature is not in
Need of beauty or sweetness. The
Running stream is sweet nectar,
And as it broadens and stills,
It reflects only the truth of
Its neighbours and self.
Give me the flute and let me sing,
And through my soul let music ring;
The moaning flute is more divine
Than the golden cup of deep, red wine.

Age: The kind of love for which man
Struggles and dies is like the
Bush that bears no fruit. Only
The wholesome love, like the
Enormous sorrow of soul, will
Enliven and lift the heart into
Understanding. When abused, it
Is the purveyor of misery and the
Omen of danger and the dark cloud
Of blackness. If humanity were to
Lead love's cavalcade to a bed of
Faithless motive, then love there
Would decline to abide. Love is a
Beautiful bird, begging capture,
But refusing injury.

Youth: The field fights not to acquire
The throne of love, for love and
Beauty abide forever and in peace
And in bounty in the field. Love,
When sought out, is an ailment
Between the flesh and the bone,
And only when youth has passed
Does the pain bring rich and
Sorrowful knowledge.
Give me the flute and let me sing,
And through my soul let music ring;
For song is the arm of love
Descending in beauty from God above.

Age: The youth who is visited by a great
Love through the truth of the light
Of heaven, and in whom thirst and
Hunger rage to protect that love,
Is the true child of God. And yet
The people say, "He is insane! He
Profits not from love, and the one
He loves is far from beauty, and
His pain and woe avail him naught!"
Pity those ignorants! Their spirits
Were dead before they were born on
Labour's bed!

Youth: No sentry or blamer abides in the
Field, and no secret is withheld
By Nature. The gazelle capers in
Merriment at eventide and the
Eagle never utters smile or frown,
But all things in the field are
Heard and known and seen.
Give me the flute and let me sing,
And through my soul let music ring;
For music is the heart's great bliss,
From heaven a joy, from God a kiss.

Age: We forget the greatness of the
Invader but remember e'er his rage
And madness. From the heart of
Alexander lust grew strong, and
Through the soul of Kais ignorance
Was defeated. The triumph of

Alexander was naught but defeat;
The torture of Kais was triumph
And glory. Through the spirit,
Not the body, love must be shown,
As it is to enliven, not to deaden,
That the wine is pressed.

Youth: The memories of the lover hover
In the field, but the deeds of
A tyrant ne'er bring a thought,
For his crime is recorded in
History's book. For love, all of
Existence is an eternal shrine.
Give me the flute and let me sing,
And through my soul let music ring:
Forget the cruelty of the strong,
To Nature alone all things belong;
The lilies were made as cups for dew
Not for blood or potions new.

Age: Happiness on earth is but a fleet,
Passing ghost, which man craves
At any cost in gold or time. And
When the phantom becomes the
Reality, man soon wearies of it.
The river runs like the racing
Stallion, swirling on the plain,
Turning it to dust. Man endeavours
That his body provide the things
Prohibited; and when gotten, the
Desire then subsides. When you

Behold a man turning aside from
Things forbidden that bring
Abysmal crime to self, look
Upon him with eyes of love, for
He is a preserver of God in him.

Youth: Empty and barren of hope and care
Is the beautiful field; it gives
No heed to desire, and craves not
For part of any thing, for God
Almighty has provided her with all.
Give me the flute and let me sing,
And through my soul let music ring;
Singing is love and hope and desire,
The moaning flute is the light and fire.

Age: The purpose of the spirit in the
Heart is concealed, and by outer
Appearance cannot be judged. One
Often says, "When the soul has
Reached perfection, then from
Life it is released, for if the
Soul were fruit, then when ripe
It would fall from the tree by
The strength of God's wind." And
Another adds, "When the body rests
In death the soul will depart it,
As the shadow on the lake vanishes
As the searing heat dries its bed."
But the spirit is not born to
Perish, but ever will thrive and

Flourish. For even as the north
Wind blows and folds the flower
To earth, so comes the south wind
To restore its beauty.

Youth: The field distinguishes not the
Body from the soul. The sea and
The fog and the dew and the mist
Are all but one, whether clouded
Or clear.
Give me the flute and let me sing,
And through my soul let music ring;
For song is all of body and soul,
From the rich depth of the golden bowl.

Age: The body is the womb for the
Soul's tranquility, and there it
Rests until light is born. The
Soul is an embryo in the body of
Man, and the day of death is the
Day of awakening, for it is the
Great era of labour and the rich
Hour of creation. But cruelty's
Barrenness accompanies man, and
Intrudes upon the fertility of
The soul's mind. How many flowers
Possess no fragrance from the day
Of their birth! How many clouds
Gather in the sky, barren of rain,
Dropping no pearls!

Youth: No soul is barren in the good
Field, and intruders cannot
Invade our peace. The seed which
The ripe date contains in its
Heart is the secret of the palm
Tree from the beginning of all
Creation.
Give me the flute and let me sing,
And through my soul let music ring;
For music is a heart that grows
With love, and like the spring it flows.

Age: Death is an ending to the son of
The earth, but to the soul it is
The start, the triumph of life.
He who embraces the dawn of truth
With his inner eyes will ever be
Ecstatic, like the murmuring brook,
But he who slumbers through the
Light of heaven's day must perish
In the eternal darkness he loves.
If to earth one clings when awake,
And if he caresses Nature who is
Close to God, then this child of
God will cross the valley of death
As though crossing but a narrow
Stream.

Youth: There is no death in the good
Field, or graves for burial or
Prayers to read. When Nisan
Departs, the joy continues to

Live, for death removes but the
Touch, and not the awareness of
All good. And he who has lived
One spring or more possesses the
Spiritual life of one who has
Lived a score of springs.
Give me the flute and let me sing,
And through my soul let music ring;
For music opens the secret of life,
Bringing peace, abolishing strife.

Age: The field has much, man has but
Little. Man is the spirit of his
Creator on earth, and all of the
Field is made for man, but man by
His own choice flees from the nearby
Love and Beauty of God which is the
Beautiful field.

Youth: Give me the flute and let me sing;
Forget what we said about everything.
Talk is dust, speckling the
Ether and losing itself in the vast
Firmament. What have you done that
Is good? Why do you not adopt the
Field as your heavenly shelter? Why
Do you not desert the palace of the
Noisome city and climb the knolls and
Pursue the stream, and breathe of the
Fragrance, and revel with the sun?
Why do you not drink dawn's wine from
Her great cup of wisdom, and ponder

The clusters of fine fruit of the
Vine, hanging like golden chandeliers?
Why do you not fashion a blanket of
The endless sky, and a bed of the
Flowers from which to view the land
Of God? Why do you not renounce the
Future and forget the past? Have you
No desire to live as you were born
To live?

Banish your misery and leave all
Things of substance, for society
Is of naught but clamour and woe
And strife. She is but the web of
The spider, the tunnel of the mole.
Nature will greet you as one of
Her own, and all that is good will
Exist for you. The child of the
Field is the child of God.

Age: To abide in the field is my hope
And my longing and my desire, and
For such life of beauty and peace
I beg. But the iron will of fate
Has placed me in the lap of the
City, and man possesses a destiny
Which impels his thoughts and
Actions and words, and that not
Sufficing, directs his footsteps to
A place of unwilling abode.

THE MERMAIDS

IN THE depths of the sea, surrounding the nearby islands where the sun rises, there is a profoundness. And there, where the pearl exists in abundance, lay a corpse of a youth encircled by sea maidens of long golden hair; they stared upon him with their deep blue eyes, conversing among themselves with musical voices. And the conversation, heard by the depths and conveyed to the shore by the waves, was brought to me by the frolicsome breeze.

One of them said, "This is a human who entered into our world yesterday, while our sea was raging."

And the second one said, "The sea was not raging. Man, who claims that he is a descendant of the Gods, was making iron war, and his blood is being shed until the colour of the water is now crimson; this human is a victim of war."

The third one ventured, "I do not know what war is, but I do know that man, after having subdued the land, became aggressive and resolved to subdue the sea. He devised a strange object which carried him upon the seas, whereupon our severe Neptune became enraged over his greed. In order to please Neptune, man commenced offering gifts and sacrifices, and the still body before us is the most recent gift of man to our great and terrible Neptune."

The fourth one asserted, "How great is Neptune, and how cruel is his heart! If I were the Sultan of the sea I would refuse to accept such payment. . . . Come now, and let us examine this ransom. Perhaps we may enlighten ourselves as to the human clan."

The mermaids approached the youth, probed the pockets, and found a message close to his heart; one of them read it aloud to the others:

"My Beloved:

"Midnight has again come, and I have no consolation except my pouring tears, and naught to comfort me save my hope in your return to me from between the bloody paws of war. I cannot forget your words when you took departure: 'Every man has a trust of tears which must be returned some day.'

"I know not what to say, My Beloved, but my soul will pour itself into parchment . . . my soul that suffers through separation, but is consoled by Love that renders pain a joy, and sorrow a happiness. When Love unified our hearts, and we looked to the day when our two hearts would be joined by the mighty breath of God. War shouted her horrible call and you followed her, prompted by your duty to the leaders.

"What is this duty that separates the lovers, and causes the women to become widows, and the children to become orphans? What is this patriotism which provokes wars and destroys kingdoms through trifles? And what cause can be more than trifling when compared to but one life? What is this duty which invites poor villagers, who are looked upon as nothing by the strong and by the sons of the inherited nobility, to die for the glory of their oppressors? If duty destroys peace among nations, and patriotism disturbs the tranquility of man's life, then let us say, 'Peace be with duty and patriotism.'

"No, no, My Beloved! Heed not my words! Be courageous and faithful to your country. . . . Hearken not unto the talk of a damsel, blinded by Love, and lost through farewell and aloneness. . . . If Love will not restore you to me in this life, then Love will surely join us in the coming life.

Your Forever"

The mermaids replaced the note under the youth's raiment and swam silently and sorrowfully away. As they gathered together at a distance from the body of the dead soldier, one of them said, "The human heart is more severe than the cruel heart of Neptune."

THE AMBITIOUS VIOLET

There was a beautiful and fragrant violet who lived placidly amongst her friends, and swayed happily amidst the other flowers in a solitary garden. One morning, as her crown was embellished with beads of dew, she lifted her head and looked about; she saw a tall and handsome rose standing proudly and reaching high into space, like a burning torch upon an emerald lamp.

The violet opened her blue lips and said, "What an unfortunate am I among these flowers, and how humble is the position I occupy in their presence! Nature has fashioned me to be short and poor. . . . I live very close to the earth and I cannot raise my head toward the blue sky, or turn my face to the sun, as the roses do."

And the rose heard her neighbour's words; she laughed and commented, "How strange is your talk! You are fortunate, and yet you cannot understand your fortune. Nature has bestowed upon you fragrance and beauty which she did not grant to any other. . . . Cast aside your thoughts and be contented, and remember that he who humbles himself will be exalted, and he who exalts himself will be crushed."

The violet answered, "You are consoling me because you have that which I crave. . . . You seek to embitter me with the meaning that you are great. . . . How painful is the preaching of the fortunate to the heart of the miserable! And how severe is the strong when he stands as advisor among the weak!"

And Nature heard the conversation of the violet and the rose; she approached and said, "What has happened to you, my daughter violet? You have been humble and sweet in all your deeds and words. Has greed entered your heart and numbed your senses?" In a pleading voice, the violet answered her, saying, "Oh great and merciful mother, full of love and sympathy, I beg you, with all my heart and soul, to grant my request and allow me to be a rose for one day."

And Nature responded, "You know not what you are seeking; you are unaware of the concealed disaster behind your blind ambition. If you were a rose you would be sorry, and repentance would avail you but naught." The violet insisted, "Change me into a tall rose, for I wish to lift my head high with pride; and regardless of my fate, it will be my own doing." Nature yielded, saying, "Oh ignorant and rebellious violet, I will grant your request. But if calamity befalls you, your complaint must be to yourself."

And Nature stretched forth her mysterious and magic fingers and touched the roots of the violet, who immediately turned into a tall rose, rising above all other flowers in the garden.

At eventide the sky became thick with black clouds, and the raging elements disturbed the silence of existence with thunder, and commenced to attack the garden, sending forth a great rain and strong winds. The tempest tore the branches and uprooted the plants and broke the stems of the tall flowers, sparing only the little ones who grew close to the friendly earth. That solitary garden suffered greatly from the belligerent skies, and when the storm calmed and the sky cleared, all the flowers were laid waste and none of them had escaped the wrath of Nature except the clan of small violets, hiding by the wall of the garden.

Having lifted her head and viewed the tragedy of the flowers and trees, one of the violet maidens smiled happily and called to her companions, saying, "See what the tempest has done to the haughty flowers!" Another violet said, "We are small, and live close to the earth, but we are safe from the wrath of the skies." And a third one added, "Because we are poor in height the tempest is unable to subdue us."

At that moment the queen of violets saw by her

side the converted violet, hurled to earth by the storm and distorted upon the wet grass like a limp soldier in a battle field. The queen of the violets lifted her head and called to her family, saying, "Look, my daughters, and meditate upon that which Greed has done to the violet who became a proud rose for one hour. Let the memory of this scene be a reminder of your good fortune."

And the dying rose moved and gathered the remnants of her strength, and quietly said, "You are contented and meek dullards; I have never feared the tempest. Yesterday I, too, was satisfied and contented with Life, but Contentment has acted as a barrier between my existence and the tempest of Life, confining me to a sickly and sluggish peace and tranquility of mind. I could have lived the same life you are living now by clinging with fear to the earth. . . . I could have waited for winter to shroud me with snow and deliver me to Death, who will surely claim all violets. . . . I am happy now because I have probed outside my little world into the mystery of the Universe . . . something which you have not yet done. I could have overlooked Greed, whose nature is higher than mine, but as I hearkened to the silence of the night, I heard the heavenly world talking to this earthly world, saying, 'Ambition beyond existence is the essential purpose of our being.' At that moment my spirit revolted and my heart longed for a position higher than my limited existence. I realized that the abyss cannot hear the song of the stars, and at that moment I commenced fighting against my smallness and craving for that which did not belong to me, until my rebelliousness turned into a great power, and my longing into a creating will. . . . Nature, who is the great object of our deeper dreams, granted my request and changed me into a rose with her magic fingers."

The rose became silent for a moment, and in a weakening voice, mingled with pride and achievement, she said, "I have lived one hour as a proud rose; I have existed for a time like a queen; I have looked at the Universe from behind the eyes of the rose; I have heard the whisper of the firmament through the ears of the rose and touched the folds of Light's garment with rose petals. Is there any here who can claim such honour?" Having thus spoken, she lowered her head, and with a choking voice she gasped, "I shall die now, for my soul has attained its goal. I have finally extended my knowledge to a world beyond the narrow cavern of my birth. This is the design of Life. . . . This is the secret of Existence." Then the rose quivered, slowly folded her petals, and breathed her last with a heavenly smile upon her lips . . . a smile of fulfillment of hope and purpose in Life . . . a smile of victory . . . a God's smile.

Then you captured my fancy, and since
That hypnotic moment I felt like a
Prisoner dragging his shackles and
Impelled into an unknown place. . . .
I became intoxicated with your sweet
Wine that has stolen my will, and I
Now find my lips kissing the hand
That strikes me sharply. Can you
Not see with your soul's eye the
Crushing of my heart? Halt for a
Moment; I am regaining my strength
And untying my weary feet from the
Heavy chains. I have crushed the
Cup from which I have drunk your
Tasty venom. . . . But now I am in
A strange land, and bewildered;
Which road shall I follow?

My freedom has been restored; will
You now accept me as a willing
Companion, who looks at the Sun
With glazed eyes and grasps the
Fire with untrembling fingers?

I have unbound my wings and I am
Ready to ascend; will you accompany
A youth who spends his days roaming
The mountains like the lone eagle, and
Wastes his nights wandering in the
Deserts like the restless lion?

Will you content yourself with the
Affection of one who looks upon Love
As but an entertainer, and declines
To accept her as his master?

Will you accept a heart that loves,
But never yields? And burns, but
Never melts? Will you be at ease
With a soul that quivers before the
Tempest, but never surrenders to it?
Will you accept one as a companion
Who makes not slaves, nor will become
One? Will you own me but not possess
Me, by taking my body and not my heart?

Then here is my hand—grasp it with
Your beautiful hand; and here is my
Body—embrace it with your loving
Arms; and here are my lips—bestow
Upon them a deep and dizzying kiss.

THE GRAVE DIGGER

In the terrible silence of the night, as all heavenly things disappeared behind the grasping veil of thick clouds, I walked lonely and afraid in the Valley of the Phantoms of Death.

As midnight came, and the spectres leaped about me with their horrible, ribbed wings, I observed a giant ghost standing before me, fascinating me with his hypnotic ghastliness. In a thundering voice he said, "Your fear is two-fold! You fear being in fear of me! You cannot conceal it, for you are weaker than the thin thread of the spider. What is your earthly name?"

I leaned against a great rock, gathered myself from this sudden shock, and in a sickly, trembling voice replied, "My name is Abdallah, which means 'slave of God.'" For a few moments he remained silent with a frightening silence. I grew accustomed to his appearance, but was again shaken by his weird thoughts and words, his strange beliefs and con templations.

He rumbled, "Numerous are the slaves of God,

and great are God's woes with His slaves. Why did not your father call you 'Master of Demons' instead, adding one more disaster to the huge calamity of earth? You cling with terror to the small circle of gifts from your ancestors, and your affliction is caused by your parents' bequest, and you will remain a slave of death until you become one of the dead.

"Your vocations are wasteful and deserted, and your lives are hollow. Real life has never visited you, nor will it; neither will your deceitful self realize your living death. Your illusioned eyes see the people quivering before the tempest of life and you believe them to be alive, while in truth they have been dead since they were born. There were none who would bury them, and the one good career for you is that of grave digger, and as such you may rid the few living of the corpses heaped about the homes, the paths, and the churches."

I protested, "I cannot pursue such a vocation. My wife and children require my support and companionship."

He leaned toward me, showing his braided muscles that seemed as the roots of a strong oak tree, abounding with life and energy, and he bellowed, "Give to each a spade and teach them to dig graves; your life is naught but black misery hidden behind walls of white plaster. Join us, for we genii are the only possessors of reality! The digging of graves brings a slow but positive benefit which causes the vanishing of the dead creatures who tremble with the storm and never walk with it." He mused and then inquired, "What is your religion?"

Bravely I stated, "I believe in God and I honour His prophets; I love virtue and I have faith in eternity."

With remarkable wisdom and conviction he responded, "These empty words were placed on human lips by past ages and not by knowledge, and you actually believe in yourself only; and you honour none but yourself, and you have faith only in the eternity of your desires. Man has worshipped his own self since the beginning, calling that self by appropriate titles, until now, when he employs the word 'God' to mean that same self." Then the giant roared with laughter, the echoes reverberating through the hollows of the caverns, and he taunted, "How strange are those who worship their own selves, their real existence being naught but earthly carcasses!"

He paused, and I contemplated his sayings and meditated their meanings. He possessed a knowledge stranger than life and more terrible than death, and deeper than truth. Timidly, I ventured, "Do you have a religion or a God?"

"My name is The Mad God," he offered, "and I was born at all times, and I am the god of my own self. I am not wise, for wisdom is a quality of the weak. I am strong, and the earth moves under the steps of my feet, and when I stop, the procession of stars stops with me. I mock at the people. . . . I accompany the giants of night. . . . I mingle with the great kings of the genii. . . . I am in possession of the secrets of existence and non-existence.

"In the morning I blaspheme the sun . . . at noontide I curse humanity . . . at eventide I submerge nature . . . at night I kneel and worship myself. I never sleep, for I am time, the sea, and myself. . . . I eat human bodies for food, drink their blood to quench my thirst, and use their dying gasps to draw my breath. Although you deceive yourself, you are my brother and you live as I do. Begone . . . hypocrite! Crawl back to earth and continue to worship your own self amid the living dead!"

I staggered from the rocky, cavernous valley in narcotic bewilderment, scarcely believing what my ears had heard and my eyes had seen! I was torn in pain by some of the truths he had spoken, and wandered trough the fields all that night in melancholy contemplation.

I procured a spade and said within myself, "Dig deeply the graves. . . . Go, now, and wherever you find one of the living dead, bury him in the earth."

Since that day I have been digging graves and burying the living dead. But the living dead are numerous and I am alone, having none to aid me. . . .

THE BEAUTY OF DEATH

Dedicated to M. E. H.

PART ONE—THE CALLING

LET ME sleep, for my soul is intoxicated with
love, and
Let me rest, for my spirit has had its bounty of days
and nights;
Light the candles and burn the incense around my
bed, and
Scatter leaves of jasmine and roses over my body;
Embalm my hair with frankincense and sprinkle my
feet with perfume,
And read what the hand of Death has written on
my forehead.

Let me rest in the arms of Slumber, for my open
eyes are tired;
Let the silver-stringed lyre quiver and soothe my
spirit;
Weave from the harp and lute a veil around my
withering heart.

Sing of the past as you behold the dawn of hope in
  my eyes, for
Its magic meaning is a soft bed upon which my
  heart rests.

Dry your tears, my friends, and raise your heads as
  the flowers
Raise their crowns to greet the dawn.
Look at the bride of Death standing like a column
  of light
Between my bed and the infinite;
Hold your breath and listen with me to the beckon-
  ing rustle of
Her white wings.

Come close and bid me farewell; touch my eyes
  with smiling lips.
Let the children grasp my hands with soft and rosy
  fingers;
Let the aged place their veined hands upon my head
  and bless me;
Let the virgins come close and see the shadow of
  God in my eyes,
And hear the echo of His will racing with my breath.

PART TWO—THE ASCENDING

I have passed a mountain peak and my soul is soaring in the
Firmament of complete and unbound freedom;
I am far, far away, my companions, and the clouds
  are

Hiding the hills from my eyes.
The valleys are becoming flooded with an ocean of silence, and the
Hands of oblivion are engulfing the roads and the houses;
The prairies and fields are disappearing behind a white spectre
That looks like the spring cloud, yellow as the candlelight
And red as the twilight.

The songs of the waves and the hymns of the streams
Are scattered, and the voices of the throngs reduced to silence;
And I can hear naught but the music of Eternity
In exact harmony with the spirit's desires.
I am cloaked in full whiteness;
I am in comfort; I am in peace.

PART THREE—THE REMAINS

Unwrap me from this white linen shroud and clothe me
With leaves of jasmine and lilies;
Take my body from the ivory casket and let it rest
Upon pillows of orange blossoms.
Lament me not, but sing songs of youth and joy;
Shed not tears upon me, but sing of harvest and the winepress;
Utter no sigh of agony, but draw upon my face with your

Finger the symbol of Love and Joy.
Disturb not the air's tranquility with chanting and requiems,
But let your hearts sing with me the song of Eternal Life;
Mourn me not with apparel of black,
But dress in colour and rejoice with me;
Talk not of my departure with sighs in your hearts; close
Your eyes and you will see me with you forevermore.

Place me upon clusters of leaves and
Carry me upon your friendly shoulders and
Walk slowly to the deserted forest.
Take me not to the crowded burying ground lest my slumber
Be disrupted by the rattling of bones and skulls.
Carry me to the cypress woods and dig my grave where violets
And poppies grow not in the other's shadow;
Let my grave be deep so that the flood will not
Carry my bones to the open valley;
Let my grave be wide, so that the twilight shadows
Will come and sit by me.

Take from me all earthly raiment and place me deep in my
Mother Earth; and place me with care upon my mother's breast.

Cover me with soft earth, and let each handful be mixed
With seeds of jasmine, lilies, and myrtle; and when they
Grow above me and thrive on my body's element they will
Breathe the fragrance of my heart into space;
And reveal even to the sun the secret of my peace;
And sail with the breeze and comfort the wayfarer.

Leave me then, friends—leave me and depart on mute feet,
As the silence walks in the deserted valley;
Leave me to God and disperse yourselves slowly, as the almond
And apple blossoms disperse under the vibration of Nisan's breeze.

Go back to the joy of your dwellings and you will find there
That which Death cannot remove from you and me.
Leave this place, for what you see here is far away in meaning
From the earthly world. Leave me.

BOOK 9

YESTERDAY AND TODAY

THE GOLD-HOARDER WALKED in his palace park and with him walked his troubles. And over his head hovered worries as a vulture hovers over a carcass, until he reached a beautiful lake surrounded by magnificent marble statuary.

He sat there pondering the water which poured from the mouths of the statues like thoughts flowing freely from a lover's imagination, and contemplating heavily his palace which stood upon a knoll like a birth-mark upon the cheek of a maiden. His fancy revealed to him the pages of his life's drama which he read with falling tears that veiled his eyes and prevented him from viewing man's feeble additions to Nature.

He looked back with piercing regret to the images of his early life, woven into pattern by the gods, until he could no longer control his anguish. He said aloud, "Yesterday I was grazing my sheep in the green valley, enjoying my existence, sounding my flute, and holding my head high. Today I am a prisoner of greed. Gold leads into gold, then into restlessness, and finally into crushing misery.

"Yesterday I was like a singing bird, soaring freely here and there in the fields. Today I am a slave to fickle wealth, society's rules, the city's customs, and purchased friends, pleasing the people by conforming to the strange and narrow laws of man. I was born to be free and enjoy the bounty of life, but I find myself like a beast of burden so heavily laden with gold that his back is breaking.

"Where are the spacious plains, the singing brooks, the pure breeze, the closeness of Nature? Where is my deity? I have lost all! Naught remains save loneliness that saddens me, gold that ridicules me, slaves who curse to my back, and a palace that I have erected as a tomb for my happiness, and in whose greatness I have lost my heart.

"Yesterday I roamed the prairies and the hills together with the Bedouin's daughter; Virtue was our companion, Love our delight, and the moon our guardian. Today I am among women with shallow beauty who sell themselves for gold and diamonds.

"Yesterday I was carefree, sharing with the shepherds all the joy of life; eating, playing, working, singing, and dancing together to the music of the heart's truth. Today I find myself among the people like a frightened lamb among the wolves. As I walk in the roads, they gaze at me with hateful eyes and point at me with scorn and jealousy, and as I steal through the park I see frowning faces all about me.

"Yesterday I was rich in happiness and today I am poor in gold.

"Yesterday I was a happy shepherd looking up my herd as a merciful king looks with pleasure upon his contented subjects. Today I am a slave standing before my wealth, my wealth which robbed me of the beauty of life I once knew.

"Forgive me, my Judge! I did not know that riches would put my life in fragments and lead me into the dungeons of harshness and stupidity. What I thought was glory is naught but an eternal inferno."

He gathered himself wearily and walked slowly toward the palace, sighing and repeating, "Is this what people call wealth? Is this the god I am serving and worshipping? Is this what I seek of the earth? Why can I not trade it for one particle of contentment? Who would sell me one beautiful thought for a ton of gold? Who would give me one moment of love for a handful of gems? Who would grant me an eye that can see others' hearts, and take all my coffers in barter?"

As he reached the palace gates he turned and looked toward the city as Jeremiah gazed toward Jerusalem. He raised his arms in woeful lament and shouted, "Oh people of the noisome city, who are living in darkness, hastening toward misery, preaching falsehood, and speaking with stupidity . . . until when shall you remain ignorant? Until when shall you abide in the filth of life and continue to desert its gardens? Why wear you tattered robes of narrowness while the silk raiment of Nature's beauty is fashioned for you? The lamp of wisdom is dimming;

it is time to furnish it with oil. The house of true fortune is being destroyed; it is time to rebuild it and guard it. The thieves of ignorance have stolen the treasure of your peace; it is time to retake it!"

At that moment a poor man stood before him and stretched forth his hand for alms. As he looked at the beggar, his lips parted, his eyes brightened with a softness, and his face radiated kindness. It was as if the yesterday he had lamented by the lake had come to greet him. He embraced the pauper with affection and filled his hand with gold, and with a voice sincere with the sweetness of love he said, "Come back tomorrow and bring with you your fellow sufferers. All your possessions will be restored."

He entered his palace saying, "Everything in life is good; even gold, for it teaches a lesson. Money is like a stringed instrument; he who does not know how to use it properly will hear only discordant music. Money is like love; it kills slowly and painfully the one who withholds it, and it enlivens the other who turns it upon his fellow men."

BEFORE THE THRONE OF BEAUTY

ONE HEAVY day I ran away from the grim face of society and the dizzying clamour of the city and directed my weary steps to the spacious valley. I pursued the beckoning course of the rivulet and the musical sounds of the birds until I reached a lonely spot where the flowing branches of the trees prevented the sun from touching the earth.

I stood there, and it was entertaining to my soul—my thirsty soul who had seen naught but the mirage of life instead of its sweetness.

I was engrossed deeply in thought and my spirits were sailing the firmament when a Houri, wearing a sprig of grapevine that covered part of her naked body, and a wreath of poppies about her golden hair, suddenly appeared to me. As she realized my astonishment, she greeted me saying, "Fear me not; I am the Nymph of the Jungle."

"How can beauty like yours be committed to live in this place? Please tell me who you are and whence you come?" I asked. She sat gracefully on the green grass and responded, "I am the symbol of Nature! I am the Ever-Virgin your forefathers worshipped, and to my honour they erected shrines and temples at Baalbek and Djabeil." And I dared say, "But those temples and shrines were laid waste and the bones of my adoring ancestors became a part of the earth; nothing was left to commemorate their goddess save a pitiful few and forgotten pages in the book of history."

She replied, "Some goddesses live in the lives of their worshippers and die in their death, while some live an eternal and infinite life. My life is sustained by the world of Beauty which you will see wherever you rest your eyes, and this Beauty is Nature itself; it is the beginning of the shepherd's joy among the hills, and a villager's happiness in the fields, and the pleasure of the awe-filled tribes between the mountains and the plains. This Beauty promotes the wise into the throne of Truth."

Then I said, "Beauty is a terrible power!" And she retorted, "Human beings fear all things, even yourselves. You fear heaven, the source of spiritual peace; you fear Nature, the haven of rest and tranquility; you fear the God of goodness and accuse him of anger, while he is full of love and mercy."

After a deep silence, mingled with sweet dreams, I asked, "Speak to me of that Beauty which the people interpret and define, each one according to his own conception; I have seen her honoured and worshipped in different ways and manners."

She answered, "Beauty is that which attracts your soul, and that which loves to give and not to receive. When you meet Beauty, you feel that the hands deep within your inner self are stretched forth to bring her into the domain of your heart. It is a magnificence combined of sorrow and joy; it is the Unseen which you see, and the Vague which you understand, and the Mute which you hear—it is the Holy of Holies that begins in yourself and ends vastly beyond your earthly imagination."

Then the Nymph of the Jungle approached me and laid her scented hand upon my eyes. And as she withdrew, I found me alone in the valley. When I returned to the city, whose turbulence no longer vexed me, I repeated her words:

"Beauty is that which attracts your soul,
And that which loves to give and not to receive."

TWO WISHES

In the silence of the night Death descended from God toward the earth. He hovered above a city and pierced the dwellings with his eyes. He saw the spirits floating on wings of dreams, and the people who were surrendered to the mercy of Slumber.

When the moon fell below the horizon and the city became black, Death walked silently among the houses—careful to touch nothing—until he reached a palace. He entered through the bolted gates undisturbed, and stood by the rich man's bed; and as Death touched his forehead, the sleeper's eyes opened, showing great fright.

When he saw the spectre, he summoned a voice mingled with fear and anger, and said, "Go away, oh horrible dream; leave me, you dreadful ghost. Who are you? How did you enter this place? What do you want? Leave this place at once, for I am the lord of the house and will call my slaves and guards, and order them to kill you!"

Then Death spoke, softly but with smouldering thunder, "I am Death. Stand and bow!"

The man responded, "What do you want? Why have you come here when I have not yet finished my affairs? What seek you from strength such as mine? Go to the weak man, and take him away!

"I loathe the sight of your bloody paws and hollow face, and my eyes take sick at your horrible ribbed wings and cadaverous body."

After a quiet moment of fearful realization he added, "No, no, oh merciful Death! Mind not my talk, for fear reveals what the heart forbids.

"Take a bushelful of my gold, or a handful of my slaves' souls, but leave me. I have accounts with Life requiring settling; I have due from the people much gold; my ships have not reached the harbour; my wheat has not been harvested. Take anything you demand, but spare my life. Death, I own harems of supernatural beauty; your choice is my gift to you. Give heed, Death—I have but one child, and I love him dearly for he is my only joy in this life. I offer supreme sacrifice—take him, but spare me!"

Death murmured, "You are not rich, but pitifully poor." Then Death took the hand of that earthly slave, removed his reality, and gave to the angels the heavy task of correction.

And Death walked slowly amidst the dwellings of the poor until he reached the most miserable he could find. He entered and approached a bed upon which a youth slept fitfully. Death touched his eyes;

the lad sprang up as he saw Death standing by, and, with a voice full of love and hope he said, "Here I am, my beautiful Death. Accept my soul, for you are the hope of my dreams. Be their accomplishment! Embrace me, oh beloved Death! You are merciful; do not leave me. You are God's messenger; deliver me to Him. You are the right hand of Truth and the heart of Kindness; do not neglect me.

"I have begged for you many times, but you did not come; I have sought you, but you avoided me; I called out to you, but you listened not. You hear me now—embrace my soul, beloved Death!"

Death placed his softened hand upon the trembling lips, removed all reality, and enfolded it beneath his wings for secure conduct. And returning to the sky, Death looked back and whispered his warning:

> "Only those return to Eternity
> Who on earth seek out Eternity."

THE PLAYGROUND OF LIFE

ONE HOUR devoted to the pursuit of Beauty
And Love is worth a full century of glory
Given by the frightened weak to the strong.

From that hour comes man's Truth; and
During that century Truth sleeps between
The restless arms of disturbing dreams.

In that hour the soul sees for herself
The Natural Law, and for that century she
Imprisons herself behind the law of man;
And she is shackled with irons of oppression.

That hour was the inspiration of the Songs
Of Solomon, and that century was the blind
Power which destroyed the temple of Baalbek.

That hour was the birth of the Sermon on the
Mount, and that century wrecked the castles of
Palmyra and the tower of Babylon.

That hour was the Hegira of Mohammed, and that
Century forgot Allah, Golgotha, and Sinai.

One hour devoted to mourning and lamenting the
Stolen equality of the weak is nobler than a
Century filled with greed and usurpation.

It is at that hour when the heart is
Purified by flaming sorrow, and
Illuminated by the torch of Love.
And in the century, desires for Truth
Are buried in the bosom of the earth.
That hour is the root which must flourish.
That hour is the hour of contemplation,
The hour of meditation, the hour of
Prayer, and the hour of a new era of good.

And that century is a life of Nero spent
On self-investment taken solely from
Earthly substance.

This is life.
Portrayed on the stage for ages;
Recorded earthily for centuries;
Lived in strangeness for years;
Sung as a hymn for days;
Exalted for but an hour, but the
Hour is treasured by Eternity as a jewel.

JOY AND SORROW

I WOULD not exchange the laughter of my heart for the fortunes of the multitudes; nor would I be content with converting my tears, invited by my agonized self, into calm. It is my fervent hope that my whole life on this earth will ever be tears and laughter.

Tears that purify my heart and reveal to me the secret of life and its mystery,
Laughter that brings me closer to my fellowmen!
Tears with which I join the broken-hearted,
Laughter that symbolizes joy over my very existence.

I prefer death through happiness a thousandfold to life in vain and in despair.

An eternal hunger for love and beauty is my desire; I know now that those who possess bounty alone are naught but miserable, but to my spirit the sighs of lovers are more soothing than music of the lyre.

When night comes, the flower folds its petals and slumbers with Love, and at dawn, it opens its lips to receive the Sun's kisses, bespeckled by quick dartings of clouds which come, but surely go.

The life of flowers is hope and fulfillment and peace; tears and laughter.

The water disappears and ascends until it turns into clouds that gather upon the hills and valleys; and when it meets the breeze, it falls down upon the fields and joins the brook that sings its way toward the sea.

The life of clouds is a life of farewell and a life of reunion; tears and laughter.

Thus the spirit separates itself from the body and walks into the world of substance, passing like clouds over the valleys of sorrow and mountains of happiness until it meets the breeze of death and returns to its starting place, the endless ocean of love and beauty which is God.

A POET'S DEATH IS HIS LIFE

THE DARK WINGS of night enfolded the city upon which Nature had spread a pure and white garment of snow; and men deserted the streets for their houses in search of warmth, while the north wind probed in contemplation of laying waste the gardens. There in the suburb stood an old hut heavily laden with snow and on the verge of falling. In a dark recess of that hovel was a poor bed in which a dying youth was lying, staring at the dim light of his oil lamp, made to flicker by the entering winds. He was a man in the spring of life who foresaw fully that the peaceful hour of freeing himself from the clutches of life was fast nearing. He was awaiting Death's visit gratefully, and upon his pale face appeared the dawn of hope; and on his lips a sorrowful smile; and in his eyes forgiveness.

He was a poet perishing from hunger in the city of living rich. He was placed in the earthly world to enliven the heart of man with his beautiful and profound sayings. He was a noble soul, sent by the Goddess of Understanding to soothe and make gentle the human spirit. But alas! He gladly bade the cold earth farewell without receiving a smile from its strange occupants.

He was breathing his last and had no one at his bedside save the oil lamp, his only companion, and some parchments upon which he had inscribed his heart's feeling. As he salvaged the remnants of his withering strength he lifted his hands heavenward; he moved his eyes hopelessly, as if wanting to penetrate the ceiling in order to see the stars from behind the veil of clouds.

And he said, "Come, oh beautiful Death; my soul is longing for you. Come close to me and unfasten the irons of life, for I am weary of dragging them. Come, oh sweet Death, and deliver me from my neighbours who looked upon me as a stranger because I interpret to them the language of the angels. Hurry, oh peaceful Death, and carry me from these multitudes who left me in the dark corner of oblivion because I do not bleed the weak as they do. Come, oh gentle Death, and enfold me under your white wings, for my fellowmen are not in want of me. Embrace me, oh Death, full of love and mercy; let your lips touch my lips which never tasted a mother's kiss, nor touched a sister's cheeks, nor caressed a sweetheart's fingertips. Come and take me, my beloved Death."

Then, at the bedside of the dying poet appeared an angel who possessed a supernatural and divine beauty, holding in her hand a wreath of lilies. She embraced him and closed his eyes so he could see no more, except with the eye of his spirit. She impressed a deep and long and gently withdrawn kiss that left an eternal smile of fulfillment upon his lips. Then the hovel became empty and nothing was left save parchments and papers which the poet had strewn about with bitter futility.

Hundreds of years later, when the people of the city arose from the diseased slumber of ignorance and saw the dawn of knowledge, they erected a monument in the most beautiful garden of the city and celebrated a feast every year in honour of that poet, whose writings had freed them. Oh, how cruel is man's ignorance!